PRENTICE HALL MATHEMATICS

ALGEBRA 1

ALL-IN-ONE
Student Workbook
VERSION B

PEARSON

Prentice
Hall

Boston, Massachusetts
Upper Saddle River, New Jersey

ISBN 0-13-165722-4

2 3 4 5 6 7 8 9 10   10 09 08 07 06

Daily Notetaking Guide

Practice, Guided Problem Solving, Vocabulary

Chapter 1 Variables, Function Patterns, and Graphs

Chapter 2 Rational Numbers

Chapter 3 Solving Equations

Chapter 4 Solving Inequalities

Chapter 5 Graphs and Functions

Chapter 6 Linear Equations and Their Graphs

Chapter 7 Systems of Equations and Inequalities

Chapter 8 Exponents and Exponential Functions

Chapter 9 Polynomials and Factoring

Chapter 10 Quadratic Equations and Functions

Chapter 11 Radical Expressions and Equations

Chapter 12 Rational Expressions and Functions

A Note to the Student:

This section of your workbook contains notetaking pages for each lesson in your student edition. They are structured to help you take effective notes in class. They will also serve as a study guide as you prepare for tests and quizzes.

Lesson 1-1

Using Variables

Lesson Objectives	NAEP 2005 Strand: Algebra
▼ 1 Model relationships with variables	**Topic:** Variables, Expressions, and Operations
▼ 2 Model relationships with equations	**Local Standards:** _____

Vocabulary

A _____ is a symbol, usually a letter, that represents one or more numbers.

An algebraic expression is _____

_____

An _____ is a mathematical sentence that uses an equal sign.

An open sentence is _____

_____

Examples

1 Writing an Algebraic Expression Write an algebraic expression for "the sum of n and 8."

"Sum" indicates addition. Add the first number, ☐, and the second number, ☐.

n ☐ 8

2 Writing an Algebraic Expression Define a variable and write an algebraic expression for "ten more than twice a number."

Relate | ten more than | twice | a number |

Define Let y = the number.

Write ☐ ☐ ☐

☐ + ☐

3 Writing an Equation Write an equation to show the total income from selling tickets to a school play for $5 each.

Relate The | total income | is | 5 | times | the number of tickets sold |.

Define Let t = the number of tickets sold.

Let i = the total income.

Write ☐ = ☐ · ☐

☐ = ☐

Name_____ Class_____ Date _____

Quick Check

1. Write an algebraic expression for each phrase.

a. the quotient of 4.2 and c

b. t minus 15

2. Define a variable and write an algebraic expression for each phrase.

a. 9 less than a number

b. the sum of twice a number and 31

3. Suppose the price of a CD is $15. Write an equation to find the cost of n CDs.

Lesson 1-2

Exponents and Order of Operations

Lesson Objectives	NAEP 2005 Strand: Algebra
▼ Simplify and evaluate expressions and formulas	Topic: Variables, Expressions, and Operations
▼ Simplify and evaluate expressions containing grouping symbols	Local Standards: _____

Vocabulary and Key Concepts

Order of Operations

1. Perform any operation(s) ⬚ .

2. Simplify ⬚ .

3. ⬚ in order from left to right.

4. ⬚ in order from left to right.

Examples

❶ Simplifying a Numerical Expression Simplify $32 + 6^2 - 14 \cdot 3$.

$32 + 6^2 - 14 \cdot 3 = 32 + \boxed{} - 14 \cdot 3$ **Simplify the power:** $6^2 = 6 \cdot \boxed{} = \boxed{}$.

$\qquad = 32 + \boxed{} - \boxed{}$ **Multiply 14 and 3.**

$\qquad = \boxed{} - 42$ **Add and subtract in order from left to right.**

$\qquad = \boxed{}$ **Subtract.**

❷ Evaluating Expressions with Exponents Evaluate each expression for $x = 11$ and $z = 16$.

a. $(xz)^2$

$(xz)^2 = \left(\boxed{} \cdot \boxed{} \right)^2$ **Substitute** $\boxed{}$ **for** x **and** $\boxed{}$ **for** z.

$\qquad = \left(\boxed{} \right)^2$ **Simplify within parentheses.**

$\qquad = \boxed{}$ **Simplify the power.**

b. xz^2

$xz^2 = \boxed{} \cdot \boxed{}^2$ **Substitute** $\boxed{}$ **for** x **and** $\boxed{}$ **for** z.

$\qquad = 11 \cdot \boxed{}$ **Simplify the power.**

$\qquad = \boxed{}$ **Multiply.**

❸ **Simplifying an Expression** Simplify $4[(2 \cdot 9) + (15 \div 3)^2]$.

$4[(2 \cdot 9) + (15 \div 3)^2] = 4\left[\boxed{} + \left(\boxed{}\right)^2\right]$ **First simplify $(2 \cdot 9)$ and $(15 \div 3)$.**

$= 4\left[18 + \boxed{}\right]$ **Simplify the power.**

$= 4\left[\boxed{}\right]$ **Add within brackets.**

$= \boxed{}$ **Multiply.**

❹ **Carpentry** A carpenter wants to build three decks in the shape of regular hexagons. The perimeter p of each deck will be 60 ft. The perpendicular distance a from the center of each deck to one of the sides will be 8.7 ft. Use the formula $A = 3\left(\dfrac{pa}{2}\right)$ to find the total area of all three decks.

$A = 3\left(\dfrac{pa}{2}\right)$

$= 3\left(\dfrac{\boxed{} \cdot \boxed{}}{2}\right)$ **Substitute** $\boxed{}$ **for p and** $\boxed{}$ **for a.**

$= 3\left(\dfrac{\boxed{}}{2}\right)$ **Simplify the numerator.**

$= 3\left(\boxed{}\right)$ **Simplify the fraction.**

$= \boxed{}$ **Multiply.**

The total area of all three decks is $\boxed{}$ ft^2.

Quick Check

1. Simplify each expression.

a. $6 - 10 \div 5$

b. $3 \cdot 6 - 4^2 \div 2$

c. $4 \cdot 7 + 4 \div 2^2$

2. Evaluate each expression for $c = 2$ and $d = 5$.

a. $4c - 2d \div c$

b. $d + 6c \div 4$

c. $c^4 - d \cdot 2$

3. Simplify each expression.

a. $(5 + 3) \div 2 + (5^2 - 3)$

b. $8 \div (9 - 7) + (13 \div 2)$

4. The area of a trapezoid can be found using the formula $\frac{1}{2}h(b_1 + b_2)$. Find the area of a trapezoid with height $h = 300$ ft and bases $b_1 = 250$ ft and $b_2 = 170$ ft.

Lesson 1-3

Exploring Real Numbers

Lesson Objectives	NAEP 2005 Strand: Number Properties and Operations
▼ Classify numbers ▼ Compare numbers	**Topic:** Number Sense **Local Standards:** _____

Vocabulary and Key Concepts

Real Numbers

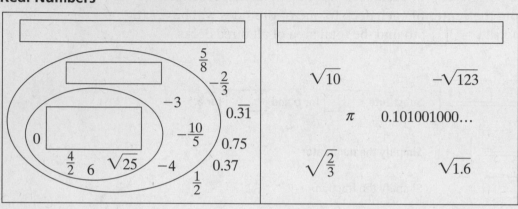

Examples

❶ Classifying Numbers Name the set(s) of numbers to which each number belongs.

a. −13

b. 3.28

❷ Using Counterexamples Determine whether the statement is true or false. If it is false, give a counterexample.

All negative numbers are integers.

A negative number can be a [   ], such as $-\frac{2}{3}$. This is not an integer. The statement is [   ].

❸ Ordering Fractions Write $-\frac{3}{4}$, $-\frac{7}{12}$, and $-\frac{5}{8}$ in order from least to greatest.

$-\frac{3}{4} =$ [   ]

$-\frac{7}{12} =$ [   ]   **Write each fraction as a decimal.**

$-\frac{5}{8} =$ [   ]

[   ] < [   ] < [   ]   **Order the decimals from least to greatest.**

From least to greatest, the fractions are [   ], [   ], and [   ].

Name_____ Class_____ Date _____

④ Finding Absolute Value Find each absolute value.

a. $|-2.5|$ -2.5 is ☐ units from 0 on a number line. $|-2.5| =$ ☐

b. $|7|$ 7 is ☐ units from 0 on a number line. $|7| =$ ☐

Quick Check

1. Name the set(s) of numbers to which each number belongs.

a. -12

b. $\frac{5}{12}$

2. Is each statement true or false? If it is false, give a counterexample.

a. All whole numbers are integers.

b. No fractions are whole numbers.

3. Write $\frac{1}{12}$, $-\frac{2}{3}$, and $-\frac{5}{8}$ in order from least to greatest.

4. Find each absolute value.

a. $|5|$

b. $|-4|$

c. $|-3.7|$

Lesson 1-4

Patterns and Functions

Lesson Objectives	NAEP 2005 Strand: Algebra
▼ Write a function rule ② Understand relationships of quantities in a function	**Topic:** Patterns, Relations, and Functions **Local Standards:** _____

Vocabulary

A _____ is a relationship that assigns exactly one output value for each input value.

A function rule _____

The value of the dependent variable [_____] the value of the independent variable.

The possible values for the input, or independent variable, of a function are the

[_____] of the function. The possible values of the output, or the dependent

variable, are the [_____] of the function.

Examples

① **Writing a Function Rule** Suppose you are making batches of muffins for a bake sale. The relationship between the number of batches (input) and the number of muffins (output) is a function. Use the table to write a function rule.

Number of Batches	1	2	3	4
Number of Muffins	12	24	36	48

Relate   Total number of muffins is [_____]

Define   Let $n =$ [_____]   The number of batches is the input.

Let $m =$ [_____]   The total number of muffins is the output.

Write $m = \boxed{}n$

The function rule is [_____].

② **Identifying Independent and Dependent Quantities** The table and graph model a function relating time of day and temperature. Identify the independent and dependent quantities.

Time of Day	Temperature (°F)
10:00 AM	66
2:00 PM	71
6:00 PM	63
10:00 PM	54

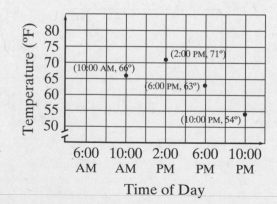

The [_____] is the dependent quantity because it depends on the [_____].

[_____] is the independent quantity.

Name_____ Class_____ Date _____

Example

❸ Reasonable Domain and Range Mateen has 3 hours a night for homework and fun. He never has more than 2 hours of homework each night.

a. Identify the independent and dependent quantities for this situation. The amount of time for [   ] depends on the amount of time for [   ].
So the amount of time for fun is the [   ] variable. The amount of time for homework is the [   ] variable.

b. Find reasonable domain and range values for this situation. A reasonable domain is from [   ] to [   ] hours. If Mateen has no homework, he has [   ] for fun. If he has [   ] of homework, he has [   ] for fun.

Quick Check

1. Write a function rule for the relationship between the number of hours (input) and the number of miles (output).

Hours	1	2	3	4
Total Miles	60	120	180	240

2. The cooking time for an unstuffed turkey is about 20 minutes per pound. What are the independent quantity and dependent quantity for this situation?

3. Charlie downloads songs for $.75 each. He has between $3.00 and $6.00 to spend on songs. Identify the independent and dependent quantities for this situation and find reasonable domain and range values.

Lesson 1-5

Lesson Objectives	NAEP 2005 Strand: Algebra; Data Analysis and Probability
▼ Analyze data using scatter plots	Topics: Algebraic Representations; Data Representation (Histograms, Line Graphs, Scatter Plots, Box Plots, Circle Graphs, Stem and Leaf Plots, Frequency Distributions, and Tables); Characteristics of Data Sets
	Local Standards: _____

Vocabulary

A scatter plot is _____

_____

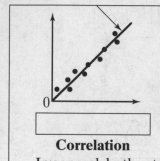   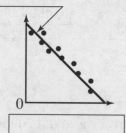   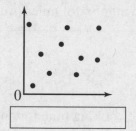

Correlation
In general, both sets of data increase together.

Correlation
In general, one set of data decreases as the other set increases.

Correlation
Sometimes data sets are not related.

A ⬚ on a scatter plot shows a correlation more clearly.

Examples

❶ **Making a Scatter Plot** The table shows the number of hours worked and the amount of money each person earned. Make a scatter plot of the data.

Name	Hours Worked	Amount Earned
Janel	6	$25.50
Roscoe	12	$51.00
Victoria	11	$46.75
Alex	9	$38.25
Jordan	15	$63.75
Jennifer	10	$42.50

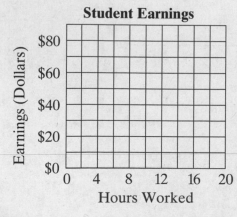

The greatest amount earned is ⬚ . A reasonable scale on the vertical axis is from 0 to 70 with every $10 labeled.

For 6 hours worked and earnings of $25.50, plot (⬚ , ⬚).

Name_____ Class_____ Date_____

❷ Identifying a Correlation from a Scatter Plot Use the scatter plot in
Example 1 to answer the following question: Is there a positive correlation,
negative correlation, or no correlation between the number of hours worked
and the amount earned? Explain.

As the number of hours worked increases, the earnings [   ].

There is a [   ] correlation between hours worked and earnings.

Quick Check

1. Use the data in the table. Make a scatter plot of the data.

Year	Daily Newspaper Circulation (millions)	Households With Television (millions)
1950	54	4
1960	59	46
1970	62	59
1980	62	76
1990	62	92
2000	55	101

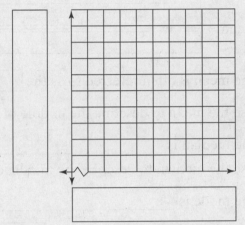

2. Use the scatter plot from Example 1.

a. Critical Thinking What does the data point at (11, 46.75) represent?

b. Use the graph to predict how much Conrad would earn if he worked 2 hours.

Name_____ Class_____ Date_____

Lesson 1-6

Mean, Median, Mode, and Range

Lesson Objectives	NAEP 2005 Strand: Data Analysis and Probability
1 Find mean, median, and mode **2** Make and use stem-and-leaf plots	**Topics:** Data Representation; Characteristics of Data Sets **Local Standards:** _____

Vocabulary and Key Concepts

Mean, Median, Mode

$$\text{Mean} = \frac{\boxed{}}{\boxed{}}$$

The mean is often referred to as the $\boxed{}$.

Use the mean to describe the middle of a set of data that $\boxed{}$ have an outlier.

The median is _____

Use the median to describe the middle of a set of data that $\boxed{}$ have an outlier.

The mode is _____

Use the mode when the data are $\boxed{}$ or when choosing

the $\boxed{}$ item.

Examples

1 **Applying Measures of Central Tendency** Find the mean, median, and mode of the data below. Which measure of central tendency best describes the data?

    14   10   2   13   16   3   12   11

Mean: $\dfrac{14 + 10 + 2 + 13 + 16 + 3 + 12 + 11}{\boxed{}} = \boxed{}$

            ↖ **total number of data items**

Median: 2   3   10   <u>11</u>   <u>12</u>   13   14   16   **List the data in order.**

$$\frac{11 + 12}{2} = \boxed{}$$ **For an even number of data items, find the mean of the two middle terms.**

Mode: $\boxed{}$ **the data item that occurs most often**

The mean is $\boxed{}$, the median is $\boxed{}$, and there is

$\boxed{}$ mode. The mean is less than $\boxed{}$ of the 8 data items because of

the outliers 2 and $\boxed{}$. The $\boxed{}$ best describes the data.

❷ Making a Stem-and-Leaf Plot Make a stem-and-leaf plot for the data.

56	44	63	58	51	59	47
51	67	50	65	49	66	63

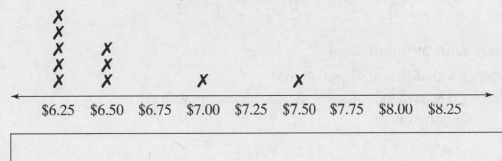

5|1 means ⬜ .

Quick Check

1. a. The hourly wages of employees at a local restaurant are listed in the line plot below. Find the mean, median, and mode of the data.

Wages of Employees per Hour

$6.25 $6.50 $6.75 $7.00 $7.25 $7.50 $7.75 $8.00 $8.25

b. Critical Thinking Which measure best describes the data? Explain why.

2. Make a stem-and-leaf plot for the data below.

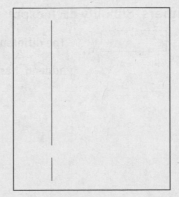

4.5	4.3	0.8	3.5	2.6
1.4	0.2	0.8	4.3	6.0

Name_____ Class_____ Date_____

Lesson 2-1

Adding Rational Numbers

Lesson Objectives	NAEP 2005 Strand: Number Properties and Operations
▼ Add real numbers using models and rules	**Topic:** Number Operations
▼ Apply addition	**Local Standards:** _____

Vocabulary and Key Concepts

Adding Numbers With the Same Sign

To add two numbers with the same sign, [ ] their absolute values.

The sum has the [ ] sign as the addends.

Examples $2 + 6 =$ [ ] $-2 + (-6) =$ [ ]

Adding Numbers With Different Signs

To add two numbers with different signs, find the [ ] of their absolute values. The sum has the same sign as the addend with the [ ] absolute value.

Examples $-2 + 6 =$ [ ] $2 + (-6) =$ [ ]

An _____ is the opposite of a number.

The sum of additive inverses is _____

Examples

❶ **Using a Number Line Model** Use a number line to simplify the expression.

$3 + (-5)$

$3 + (-5) =$ [ ]

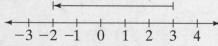

Start at [ ].

Move left [ ] units.

❷ **Adding Numbers** Simplify each expression.

$12 + (-23) =$ [ ]   The difference of the absolute values is [ ]. The [ ]

addend has the greater absolute value, so the sum is [ ].

❸ Evaluating Expressions A scuba diver who is 88 ft below sea level begins to ascend to the surface.

   a. Write an expression to represent the diver's depth below sea level after rising any number of feet.

   Relate | 88 ft below sea level | plus | feet diver rises |

   Define   Let | r | = the number of feet diver rises.

   Write   [   ]   +   [   ]

   b. Find the new depth of the scuba diver after rising 37 ft.

   $-88 + r = -88 +$ [   ]   **Substitute** [   ] **for r.**

   $ =$ [   ]   **Simplify.**

   The scuba diver is [   ] ft below sea level.

Quick Check

1. Use the number line to find each sum.

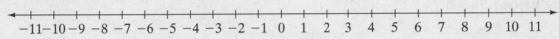

   a. $-6 + 4$ **b.** $4 + (-6)$ **c.** $-3 + (-8)$

   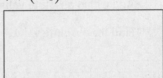   

2. Find each sum.

   a. $-7 + (-4)$ **b.** $-26.3 + 8.9$ **c.** $-\frac{3}{4} + \left(-\frac{1}{2}\right)$

3. The temperature falls 15 degrees and then rises 18 degrees. Use addition to find the change in temperature.

Lesson 2-2

Subtracting Rational Numbers

Lesson Objectives	NAEP 2005 Strand: Number Properties and Operations
▼ Subtract rational numbers	**Topic:** Number Operations
▼ Apply subtraction	**Local Standards:** _____

Key Concepts

Subtracting Numbers

To subtract a number, add [   ].

Examples $3 - 5 = 3 + $ [   ] $= -2$ $3 - (-5) = 3 + $ [   ] $= 8$

Examples

❶ **Absolute Values** Simplify $|-13 - (-21)|$.

$|-13 - (-21)| = \left|-13 + \boxed{}\right|$ The opposite of -21 is $\boxed{}$.

$ = \left|\boxed{}\right|$ Add within absolute value symbols.

$ = \boxed{}$ Find the absolute value.

❷ **Evaluating Expressions** Evaluate $x - (-y)$ for $x = -3$ and $y = -6$.

$x - (-y) = \boxed{} - \left[-\left(\boxed{}\right)\right]$ Substitute $\boxed{}$ for x and $\boxed{}$ for y.

$ = \boxed{} - \boxed{}$ The opposite of -6 is $\boxed{}$.

$ = \boxed{}$ Subtract.

❸ **Temperature** The temperature in Montreal, Canada, at 6:00 P.M. was $-8°C$. Find the temperature at 10:00 P.M. if it fell 7°C.

Find the temperature at 10:00 P.M. by subtracting $\boxed{}$ from the temperature at 6:00 P.M.

$-8 - 7 = \boxed{} + \left(\boxed{}\right)$ Add the opposite.

$ = \boxed{}$ Simplify.

The temperature at 10:00 P.M. was $\boxed{}°C$.

Name_____ Class_____ Date _____

Quick Check

1. Simplify each expression.

    a. $|8 - 7|$

    b. $|7 - 8|$

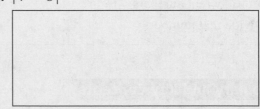

    c. $|-10 - (-4)|$

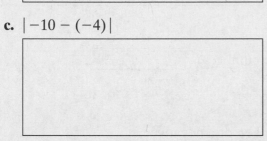

    d. $|-4 - (-10)|$

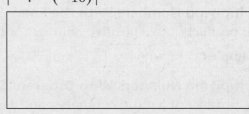

2. Evaluate each expression for $t = -2$ and $r = -7$.

    a. $r - t$

    b. $t - r$

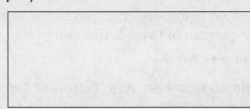

    c. $-t - r$

    d. $-r - (-t)$

3. The temperature in Minneapolis, Minnesota, at 4:00 p.m. was $-5°$F. Find the temperature at 11:00 p.m. if it fell 8°F.

Lesson 2-3

Multiplying and Dividing Rational Numbers

Lesson Objectives	NAEP 2005 Strand: Number Properties and Operations
▼1 Multiply real numbers	**Topic:** Number Operations
▼2 Divide real numbers	**Local Standards:** _____

Vocabulary and Key Concepts

Multiplying Numbers With the Same Sign

The product of two positive numbers or two negative numbers is [ ].

Examples $5 \cdot 2 =$ [ ] $-5(-2) =$ [ ]

Multiplying Numbers With Different Signs

The product of a positive number and a negative number, or a negative

number and a positive number, is [ ].

Examples $3(-6) =$ [ ] $-3 \cdot 6 =$ [ ]

Dividing Numbers With the Same Sign

The quotient of two positive numbers or two negative numbers is [ ].

Examples $6 \div 3 =$ [ ] $-6 \div (-3) =$ [ ]

Dividing Numbers With Different Signs

The quotient of a positive number and a negative number, or a negative

number and a positive number, is [ ].

Examples $-6 \div 3 =$ [ ] $6 \div (-3) =$ [ ]

The _____ of a nonzero rational number $\frac{a}{b}$ is $\frac{b}{a}$.

A reciprocal is _____

Examples

❶ Multiplying Numbers Simplify the expression $-6(5)$.

$-6(5) =$ [ ]   **The product of a positive number and
a negative number is** [ ].

Name_____ Class_____ Date_____

② Simplifying Exponential Expressions Use the order of operations to simplify each expression.

a. $-0.2^4 = -\left(\boxed{} \cdot \boxed{} \cdot \boxed{} \cdot \boxed{}\right)$ **Write as repeated multiplication.**

$ = -\boxed{}$ **Simplify.**

b. $(-0.2)^4 = \left(\boxed{}\right) \cdot \left(\boxed{}\right) \cdot \left(\boxed{}\right) \cdot \left(\boxed{}\right)$ **Write as repeated multiplication.**

$ = \boxed{}$ **Simplify.**

③ Dividing Numbers Simplify the expression $-54 \div (-9)$.

$-54 \div (-9) = \boxed{}$ **The quotient of a negative number and a negative number is** $\boxed{}$.

④ Evaluating Expressions Evaluate $-\frac{x}{y} - 4z^2$ for $x = 4, y = -2,$ and $z = -4$.

$-\dfrac{x}{y} - 4z^2 = -\left(\dfrac{\boxed{}}{\boxed{}}\right) - 4\left(\boxed{}\right)^2$ **Substitute** $\boxed{}$ **for x,** $\boxed{}$ **for y, and** $\boxed{}$ **for z.**

$\phantom{-\dfrac{x}{y} - 4z^2} = -\left(\dfrac{\boxed{}}{\boxed{}}\right) - 4\left(\boxed{}\right)$ **Simplify the power.**

$\phantom{-\dfrac{x}{y} - 4z^2} = \left(\boxed{}\right) - \boxed{}$ **Divide and multiply.**

$\phantom{-\dfrac{x}{y} - 4z^2} = \boxed{}$ **Subtract.**

Quick Check

Simplify each expression.

1. a. $4(-6)$

$\boxed{}$

b. $-10(-5)$

$\boxed{}$

c. $-4.9(-8)$

$\boxed{}$

2. a. -4^3

$\boxed{}$

b. $(-2)^4$

$\boxed{}$

c. $(-0.3)^2$

$\boxed{}$

3. a. $-18 \div 3$

$\boxed{}$

b. $-72 \div (-8)$

$\boxed{}$

c. $56 \div (-7)$

$\boxed{}$

4. Evaluate each expresssion for $x = 8, y = -5,$ and $z = -3$.

a. $3x \div 2z + y \div 10$

b. $\dfrac{2z + x}{2y}$

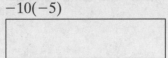

c. $3z^2 - 4y \div x$

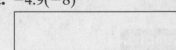

Lesson 2-4

Lesson Objectives	**NAEP 2005 Strand:** Algebra
▼ Use the Distributive Property	**Topic:** Variables, Expressions, and Operations
▼ Simplify algebraic expressions	**Local Standards:** _____

Vocabulary and Key Concepts

Distributive Property

For every real number a, b, and c,

$a(b + c) =$ ⬚ $(b + c)a =$ ⬚

$a(b - c) =$ ⬚ $(b - c)a =$ ⬚

Examples

$5(20 + 6) =$ ⬚ + ⬚

$(20 + 6)5 =$ ⬚ + ⬚

$9(30 - 2) =$ ⬚ − ⬚

$(30 - 2)9 =$ ⬚ − ⬚

A _____ is a number, variable, or the product of a number and one or more variables.

A _____ is a term that has no variable.

A _____ is the numerical factor when a term has a variable.

Like _____ are terms with exactly the same variable factors in a variable expression.

Examples

❶ Simplifying an Expression Simplify $3(4m - 7)$.

$3(4m - 7) =$ ⬚(⬚) − ⬚(⬚)   **Use the Distributive Property.**

$=$ ⬚$m -$ ⬚   **Simplify.**

❷ Using the Multiplication Property of −1 Simplify $-(5q - 6)$.

$-(5q - 6) =$ ⬚$(5q - 6)$ **Rewrite the expression using −1.**

$=$ ⬚(⬚) − ⬚(⬚)   **Use the Distributive Property.**

$=$ ⬚$q +$ ⬚   **Simplify.**

Examples

❸ **Combining Like Terms** Simplify $-2w^2 + w^2$.

$-2w^2 + w^2 = \left(\boxed{} + \boxed{}\right)w^2$ **Use the Distributive Property.**

$= \boxed{}$ **Simplify.**

❹ **Writing an Expression** Write an expression for the product of -6 and the quantity 7 minus m.

Relate $\boxed{-6}$ times $\boxed{\text{the quantity 7 minus } m}$

Write $\boxed{}$ · $\boxed{}$

$-6(7 - \boxed{}\,)$

Quick Check

1. Simplify each expression.

   a. $2(3 - 7t)$ **b.** $(0.4 + 1.1c)(3)$

2. Simplify each expression.

   a. $-(2x + 1)$ **b.** $(3 - 8a)(-1)$

3. Simplify each expression.

   a. $7y + 6y$ **b.** $3t - t$

4. Write an expression for the phrase -2 times the quantity t plus 7.

Lesson 2-5

Properties of Numbers

Lesson Objectives	NAEP 2005 Strand: Geometry
① Identify properties ② Use deductive reasoning	Topic: Mathematical Reasoning Local Standards: _____

Vocabulary and Key Concepts

Properties of Real Numbers
For every real number a, b, and c,

Commutative Property of Addition

[ ]

Example $3 + 7 = $ [ ] $+$ [ ]

Commutative Property of Multiplication

[ ]

Example $3 \cdot 7 = $ [ ] $\cdot$ [ ]

Associative Property of Addition

[ ]

Example $(6 + 4) + 5 = $ [ ] $+ ($[ ] $+$ [ ]$)$

Associative Property of Multiplication

[ ]

Example $(6 \cdot 4) \cdot 5 = $ [ ] $\cdot ($[ ] $\cdot$ [ ]$)$

Identity Property of Addition

[ ]

Example $9 + 0 = $ [ ]

Identity Property of Multiplication

[ ]

Example $6 \cdot 1 = $ [ ]

Inverse Property of Addition
For every a, there is an additive inverse [ ] such that [ ].
Example $5 + (-5) = $ [ ]

Inverse Property of Multiplication
For every a ($a \neq 0$), there is a multiplicative inverse $\frac{1}{a}$ such that [ ].

Example $5 \cdot $ [ ] $= 1$

_____ is the process of reasoning logically from given facts to a conclusion.

Examples

❶ **Identifying Properties** Name the property each equation illustrates. Explain.

a. $3 \cdot a = a \cdot 3$ illustrates [   ],

because _____

b. $p \cdot 0 = 0$ illustrates [   ],

because _____

❷ **Justifying Steps** Simplify $3x - 4(x - 8)$. Justify each step.

$3x - 4(x - 8) = 3x -$ ☐ $+$ ☐   ☐ **Property**

$= ($ ☐ $)x + 32$ ☐ **Property**

$=$ ☐ $x + 32$ **Subtract.**

$=$ ☐ $+ 32$ ☐ **of Multiplication**

Quick Check

1. Name the property that each equation illustrates. Explain.

a. $(-3 + 4) + 5 = -3 + (4 + 5)$

☐

b. $3(8 \cdot 0) = (3 \cdot 8)0$

☐

c. $np = pn$

☐

2. Simplify the expression. Justify each step.

$5a + 6 + a$

☐

Lesson 2-6

Theoretical and Experimental Probability

Lesson Objectives	NAEP 2005 Strand: Data Analysis and Probability
▼ 1 Find theoretical probability ▼ 2 Find experimental probability	Topic: Probability Local Standards: _____

Vocabulary

The _____ of an event, or P(event), is how likely it is that something will occur.

An outcome is _____

An _____ is any outcome or group of outcomes.

A _____ is all possible outcomes.

event	sample space	favorable outcome
↓	↓	↓
rolling an even number on a number cube	☐	☐

Theoretical probability is _____

_____

The _____ of an event is all possible outcomes that are not in the event.

possible outcomes for rolling a number cube	outcomes for rolling an even number	complement of rolling an even number
↓	↓	↓
☐	☐	☐

Experimental probability is _____

_____

_____ describes the likelihood of an event by comparing favorable and unfavorable outcomes.

Examples

1 Finding Theoretical Probability A bowl contains 12 slips of paper, each with a different name of a month on it. Find the theoretical probability that a slip selected at random from the bowl has the name of a month that ends with "ber."

$P(\text{event}) = \dfrac{\text{number of favorable outcomes}}{\text{number of possible outcomes}}$

$= \dfrac{\boxed{}}{12}$ **There are** ☐ **months out of 12 that end with "ber":**
September, October, November, and December.

$= \dfrac{\boxed{}}{\boxed{}}$ **Simplify.**

The probability of picking a month that ends with "ber" is ☐ .

Name_____ Class_____ Date_____

❷ Finding the Complement of an Event For a number cube, find the probability of *not* rolling a number evenly divisible by 3.

$$P(\div 3) = \frac{\text{number of favorable outcomes}}{\text{number of possible outcomes}} = \frac{\boxed{}}{6} \text{ or } \frac{\boxed{}}{\boxed{}}$$

$$P(not \div 3) = \boxed{} - P(\div 3) \qquad \textbf{Use the complement formula.}$$

$$= 1 - \frac{\boxed{}}{\boxed{}} = \frac{\boxed{}}{\boxed{}} \qquad \textbf{Simplify.}$$

The probability of *not* rolling a number evenly divisible by 3 is $\boxed{}$.

❸ Finding Experimental Probability Quality control inspected 500 belts at random. They found no defects in 485 belts. What is the probability that a belt selected at random will pass quality control? Express your answer as a percent.

$$P(\text{no defects}) = \frac{\text{number of times an event occurs}}{\text{number of time the experiment is done}}$$

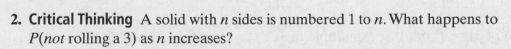

$$= \frac{\boxed{}}{500} \qquad \textbf{Substitute.}$$

$$= \boxed{} = \boxed{}\% \qquad \textbf{Simplify. Write as a percent.}$$

The probability that a belt has no defects is $\boxed{}$ %.

Quick Check

1. Suppose you write the names of days of the week on identical pieces of paper. Find the theoretical probability of picking a piece of paper at random that has the name of a day that starts with the letter T.

2. **Critical Thinking** A solid with *n* sides is numbered 1 to *n*. What happens to $P(not$ rolling a 3) as *n* increases?

3. A manufacturer decides to inspect 2,500 skateboards. There are 2,450 skateboards that have no defects. Find the probability that a skateboard selected at random has no defects.

Name_____ Class_____ Date_____

Lesson 2-7

Probability of Compound Events

Lesson Objectives	NAEP 2005 Strand: Data Analysis and Probability
1 Find the probability of independent events	**Topic:** Probability
2 Find the probability of dependent events	**Local Standards:** _____

Vocabulary and Key Concepts

> **Probability of Two Independent Events**
> If A and B are independent events,
> $P(A \text{ and } B) = P(A) \cdot P(B)$
>
> **Probability of Two Dependent Events**
> If A and B are dependent events,
> $P(A \text{ then } B) = P(A) \cdot P(B \text{ after } A)$

_____ events are events that do not influence one another.

Dependent events are _____

_____

Examples

1 **Independent Events** Suppose you roll two number cubes. What is the probability that you will roll an odd number on the first cube and a multiple of 3 on the second cube?

$$P(\text{odd}) = \frac{\boxed{}}{6} = \frac{\boxed{}}{\boxed{}} \qquad \text{There are } \boxed{} \text{ odd numbers out of six numbers.}$$

$$P(\text{multiple of 3}) = \frac{\boxed{}}{6} = \frac{\boxed{}}{\boxed{}} \qquad \text{There are } \boxed{} \text{ multiples of 3 out of six numbers.}$$

$$P(\text{odd and multiple of 3}) = P(\text{odd}) \cdot P(\text{multiple of 3})$$

$$= \frac{\boxed{}}{\boxed{}} \cdot \frac{\boxed{}}{\boxed{}} \qquad \textbf{Substitute.}$$

$$= \frac{\boxed{}}{\boxed{}} \qquad \textbf{Simplify.}$$

The probability that you will roll an odd number on the first cube and a multiple

of 3 on the second cube is  .

❷ **Selecting Without Replacement** Suppose you have 3 quarters and 5 dimes in your pocket. You take out one coin, but you do not put it back. Then you take out another coin. What is the probability of first taking out a dime and then a quarter?

Since you do not replace the first coin, the events are ▭.

$P(\text{dime}) = \dfrac{\Box}{\Box}$ **There are** ▭ **out of** ▭ **coins that are dimes.**

$P(\text{quarter after dime}) = \dfrac{\Box}{\Box}$ **There are** ▭ **out of the** ▭ **remaining coins that are quarters.**

$P(\text{dime then quarter}) = P(\text{dime}) \cdot P(\text{quarter after dime})$

$= \dfrac{\Box}{\Box} \cdot \dfrac{\Box}{\Box}$ **Multiply.**

$= \dfrac{\Box}{\Box}$

The probability that you will take out a dime and then a quarter is ▭.

Quick Check

1. Suppose you roll a red number cube and a blue number cube. What is the probability that you will roll a 5 on the red cube and a 1 or 2 on the blue cube?

2. Looking at the letter tiles, find the probability of picking a *U* and then an *I* after replacing the first tile.

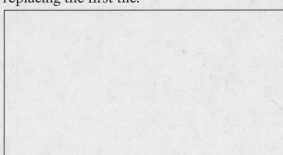

Lesson 3-1

Solving Two-Step Equations

Lesson Objectives	NAEP 2005 Strand: Algebra; Geometry
1 Solve two-step equations	**Topics:** Equations and Inequalities; Mathematical Reasoning
2 Use deductive reasoning	**Local Standards:** _____

Key Concepts

Solving Two-Step Equations

Step 1 Use the Addition or Subtraction Property of Equality to get the term with a variable alone on one side of the equation.

Step 2 Use the Multiplication or Division Property of Equality to write an equivalent equation in which the variable has a coefficient of [ ].

Examples

1 **Solving Two-Step Equations** Solve $20 = \frac{x}{4} - 13$.

$20 + \boxed{} = \frac{x}{4} - 13 + \boxed{}$ **Add** $\boxed{}$ **to each side.**

$\boxed{} = \boxed{}$ **Simplify.**

$\boxed{} \cdot 33 = \frac{x}{4} \cdot \boxed{}$ **Multiply each side by 4.**

$132 = x$ $\boxed{}$

2 **Using Deductive Reasoning** Solve $3 - 5z = 18$. Justify each step.

$3 - 5z \,\boxed{}\boxed{} = 18 \,\boxed{}\boxed{}$ **Subtraction Property of Equality**

$-5z = \boxed{}$ **Simplify.**

$\dfrac{-5z}{\boxed{}} = \dfrac{15}{\boxed{}}$ $\boxed{}$ **Property of Equality**

$z = \boxed{}$ **Simplify.**

Quick Check

1. Solve each equation. Check your answer.

a. $7 = 2y - 3$

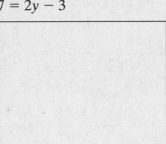

b. $\dfrac{x}{9} - 15 = 12$

c. $-x + 15 = 12$

2. Solve $-9 - 4m = 3$. Justify each step.

Lesson 3-2

Solving Multi-Step Equations

Lesson Objectives	NAEP 2005 Strand: Algebra
▼ 1 Use the Distributive Property when combining like terms	**Topics:** Variables, Expressions, and Operations; Equations and Inequalities
▼ 2 Use the Distributive Property when solving equations	**Local Standards:** _____

Key Concepts

Steps for Solving a Multi-Step Equation

Step 1 Clear the equation of fractions and decimals.

Step 2 Use the Distributive Property to remove parentheses on each side.

Step 3 Combine like terms on each side.

Step 4 Undo addition or [ ].

Step 5 Undo multiplication or [ ].

Example

❶ Combining Like Terms Solve $3a + 6 + a = 90$.

$4a + 6 = 90$ **Combine like terms.**

$4a + 6 - \boxed{} = 90 - \boxed{}$ **Subtract** $\boxed{}$ **from each side.**

$4a = \boxed{}$ **Simplify.**

$\dfrac{\boxed{4a}}{\boxed{}} = \dfrac{\boxed{}}{\boxed{}}$ **Divide each side by** $\boxed{}$ **.**

$a = \boxed{}$ **Simplify.**

Quick Check

1. Solve each equation.

a. $3x - 4x + 6 = -2$

b. $7 = 4m - 2m + 1$

Example

② Solving an Equation With Grouping Symbols Solve $2(x - 3) = 8$.

$$\boxed{} - \boxed{} = 8 \qquad \text{Use the } \boxed{} \text{ Property.}$$

$$\boxed{} - \boxed{} + \boxed{} = 8 + \boxed{} \qquad \text{Add } \boxed{} \text{ to each side.}$$

$$2x = \boxed{} \qquad \text{Simplify.}$$

$$\frac{2x}{\boxed{}} = \frac{\boxed{}}{\boxed{}} \qquad \text{Divide each side by } \boxed{}.$$

$$x = \boxed{} \qquad \text{Simplify.}$$

Check $\quad 2(x - 3) = 8$

$$2\left(\boxed{} - 3\right) \stackrel{?}{=} 8 \qquad \text{Substitute } \boxed{} \text{ for } x.$$

$$2\left(\boxed{}\right) \stackrel{?}{=} 8$$

$$\boxed{} = 8 \checkmark$$

Quick Check

2. Solve each equation. Check your answers.

a. $3(k + 8) = 21$

b. $15 = -3(x - 1) + 9$

Lesson 3-3   Equations With Variables on Both Sides

Lesson Objectives	NAEP 2005 Strand: Algebra
▼ Solve equations with variables on both sides	**Topics:** Variables, Expressions, and Operations; Equations and Inequalities
▼ Identify equations that are identities or have no solution	**Local Standards:** _____

Vocabulary

An identity is _____

Example

1 **Variables on Both Sides** You can buy a skateboard for $60 from a friend and rent the safety equipment for $1.50 per hour. Or you can rent all items you need for $5.50 per hour. How many hours must you use the skateboard to justify buying your friend's skateboard?

Relate | cost of friend's skateboard | plus | equipment rental | equals | skateboard and equipment rental |

Define Let $\boxed{h}$ = the number of hours you must skateboard.

Write $\boxed{}$ $+$ $\boxed{}$ $=$ $\boxed{}$

$60 + \boxed{}\,h = \boxed{}\,h$

$60 + 1.5h - \boxed{}\,h = 5.5h - \boxed{}\,h$ **Subtract** $\boxed{}\,h$ **from each side.**

$60 = \boxed{}\,h$ **Combine like terms.**

$\dfrac{60}{\boxed{}} = \dfrac{4h}{\boxed{}}$ **Divide each side by** $\boxed{}$.

$\boxed{} = h$ **Simplify.**

Quick Check

1. Solve each equation.

a. $-6d = d + 4$

b. $7k - 4 = 5k + 16$

Name_____ Class_____ Date _____

Example

② **Identities and Equations With No Solutions** Solve each equation.

a. $-6z + 8 = z + 10 - 7z$

$-6z + 8 = -\boxed{}z + 10$ **Combine like terms.**

$-6z + 8 + \boxed{} = -6z + 10 + \boxed{}$ **Add** $\boxed{}$ **to each side.**

$\boxed{} = \boxed{}$ $\boxed{}$ **true for any value of z!**

The equation has $\boxed{}$ solution.

b. $4 - 4y = -2(2y - 2)$

$4 - 4y = -\boxed{}y + \boxed{}$ **Use the Distributive Property.**

$4 - 4y + \boxed{} = -4y + 4 + \boxed{}$ **Add** $\boxed{}$ **to each side.**

$\boxed{} = \boxed{}$ $\boxed{}$ **true!**

The equation is true for every value of y, so the equation is an _____

Quick Check

2. Determine whether each equation is an *identity* or whether it has *no solution*.

a. $9 + 5n = 5n - 1$ **b.** $9 + 5x = 7x + 9 - 2x$

Lesson 3-4

Lesson Objectives	**NAEP 2005 Strand:** Number Properties and Operations; Measurement
▼ Find ratios and rates	**Topics:** Ratios and Proportional Reasoning; Measuring Physical Attributes
▼ Solve proportions	**Local Standards:** _____

Vocabulary and Key Concepts

Cross Products of a Proportion

If $\frac{a}{b} = \frac{c}{d}$ then $ad = \boxed{}$.

Example $\frac{2}{3} = \frac{8}{12}$, so $2 \cdot 12 = 3 \cdot 8$

A _____ is a comparison of two numbers by division.

A rate is _____

_____

A _____ is a rate with a denominator of 1.

Unit analysis is _____

_____

A _____ is an equation that states that two ratios are equal.

In the proportion $\frac{a}{b} = \frac{c}{d}$, the extremes of proportion are _____

In the proportion $\frac{a}{b} = \frac{c}{d}$, the _____ of a proportion are b and c.

In the proportion $\frac{a}{b} = \frac{c}{d}$, the cross products are _____

Examples

❶ Converting Rates The fastest recorded speed for an eastern gray kangaroo is 40 mi per hour. What is the kangaroo's speed in feet per second?

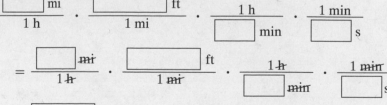

$\dfrac{\boxed{}\ \text{mi}}{1\ \text{h}} \cdot \dfrac{\boxed{}\ \text{ft}}{1\ \text{mi}} \cdot \dfrac{1\ \text{h}}{\boxed{}\ \text{min}} \cdot \dfrac{1\ \text{min}}{\boxed{}\ \text{s}}$ **Use appropriate conversion factors.**

$= \dfrac{\boxed{}\ \text{mi}}{1\ \text{h}} \cdot \dfrac{\boxed{}\ \text{ft}}{1\ \text{mi}} \cdot \dfrac{1\ \text{h}}{\boxed{}\ \text{min}} \cdot \dfrac{1\ \text{min}}{\boxed{}\ \text{s}}$ **Divide the common units.**

$= \boxed{}\ \text{ft/s}$ **Simplify.**

The kangaroo's speed is about $\boxed{}$ ft/s.

❷ Solving Multi-Step Proportions Solve the proportion.

$$\frac{z + 3}{4} = \frac{z - 4}{6}$$

$(z + 3)\left(\boxed{}\right) = 4\left(\boxed{}\right)$ **Write cross products.**

$6z + \boxed{} = \boxed{} - 16$ **Use the Distributive Property.**

$\boxed{} + 18 = -16$ **Subtract** $\boxed{}$ **from each side.**

$2z = -\boxed{}$ **Subtract** $\boxed{}$ **from each side.**

$\dfrac{2z}{\boxed{}} = -\dfrac{\boxed{}}{\boxed{}}$ **Divide each side by** $\boxed{}$.

$z = \boxed{}$ **Simplify.**

Quick Check

1. A sloth travels 0.15 miles per hour. Convert this speed to feet per minute.

2. Solve each proportion.

a. $\dfrac{x + 2}{14} = \dfrac{x}{10}$

b. $\dfrac{y - 15}{y + 4} = \dfrac{35}{7}$

c. $\dfrac{3}{w + 6} = \dfrac{5}{w - 4}$

Name_____ Class_____ Date_____

Lesson 3-5

Proportions and Similar Figures

<table>
<tr><td>

Lesson Objectives

▼ 1 Find missing measures of similar figures

▼ 2 Use similar figures when measuring indirectly

</td><td>

NAEP 2005 Strand: Number Properties and Operations; Geometry; Measurement

Topics: Ratios and Proportional Reasoning; Transformation of Shapes and Preservation of Properties; Measuring Physical Attributes

Local Standards: _____

</td></tr>
</table>

Vocabulary

Similar (~) figures are _____

A _____ is an enlarged or reduced drawing that is similar to an actual object or plane.

A scale is _____

The _____ is the ratio of the dimensions of the new image to the dimensions of the original figure.

A dilation is _____

Example

1 **Finding the Length of a Side** In the figure at the right, $\triangle ABC \sim \triangle DEF$. Find AB.

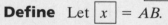

Relate $\dfrac{\boxed{}}{BC} = \dfrac{DE}{\boxed{}}$ Write a proportion comparing the lengths of the corresponding sides.

Define Let $\boxed{x}$ = AB.

Write $\dfrac{\boxed{}}{\boxed{}} = \dfrac{\boxed{}}{\boxed{}}$ Substitute $\boxed{}$ for EF, $\boxed{}$ for BC, $\boxed{}$ for DE, and $\boxed{}$ for AB.

$\boxed{}\boxed{} = 9\left(\boxed{}\right)$ Write cross products.

$\dfrac{\boxed{}}{\boxed{}} = \dfrac{\boxed{}}{\boxed{}}$ Divide each side by $\boxed{}$.

$x = \boxed{}$ Simplify.

AB is $\boxed{}$ mm.

Quick Check

1. In the figure, $\triangle FGH \sim \triangle KLM$. Find LM.

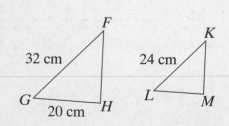

Examples

❷ Applying Similarity A flagpole casts a shadow 102 feet long. A 6-ft tall man casts a shadow 17 ft long. How tall is the flagpole?

$$\frac{\boxed{}}{17} = \frac{x}{\boxed{}}$$ **Write a proportion.**

$\boxed{}\, x = \boxed{} \cdot \boxed{}$ **Write cross products.**

$\boxed{}\, x = \boxed{}$ **Simplify.**

$\dfrac{\boxed{}\, x}{\boxed{}} = \dfrac{\boxed{}}{\boxed{}}$ **Divide each side by** $\boxed{}$.

$x = \boxed{}$ **Simplify.**

The flagpole is $\boxed{}$ ft tall.

❸ Finding Distances on Maps The scale of the map is 1 inch : 10 miles. The map distance from Valkaria to Gifford is 2.375 inches. How far is the actual distance?

map⟶ $\dfrac{1}{\boxed{}}$ = $\dfrac{\boxed{}}{x}$ ⟵map
actual⟶   ⟵actual   **Write a proportion.**

$1 \cdot x = \boxed{} \cdot \boxed{}$ **Write cross products.**

$x = \boxed{}$ **Simplify.**

The actual distance from Valkaria to Gifford is $\boxed{}$ mi.

Quick Check

2. A tree casts a 26-ft shadow. A boy standing nearby casts a 12-ft shadow. His height is 4.5 ft. How tall is the tree?

3. a. On the map in Example 3, measure the map distance from Grant to Gifford. Find the actual distance.

b. Critical Thinking If another map showed the distance from Valkaria to Wabasso but had a scale of 1 inch : 5 miles, what would the map distance be between the two locations?

Lesson 3-6

Equations and Problem Solving

Lesson Objectives	**NAEP 2005 Strand:** Algebra; Measurement
▼ Define a variable in terms of another variable	**Topics:** Equations and Inequalities; Measuring Physical Attributes
▼ Model distance-rate-time problems	**Local Standards:** _____

Vocabulary

Consecutive integers are _____

_____

An object in _____ is an object that moves at a constant rate.

Examples

❶ Consecutive Integer Problem The sum of three consecutive integers is 72. Find the integers.

Relate $\boxed{\text{first integer}}$ plus $\boxed{\text{second integer}}$ plus $\boxed{\text{third integer}}$ is $\boxed{72}$

Define Let $\boxed{x}$ = the first integer.

Then $\boxed{x + 1}$ = the second integer,

and $\boxed{}$ = the third integer.

Write $\boxed{}$ + $\boxed{}$ + $\boxed{}$ = $\boxed{}$

$x + \boxed{} + \boxed{} = 72$

$\boxed{}x + \boxed{} = 72$ **Combine like terms.**

$3x + 3 - \boxed{} = 72 - \boxed{}$ **Subtract** $\boxed{}$ **from each side.**

$3x = \boxed{}$ **Simplify.**

$\dfrac{3x}{\boxed{}} = \dfrac{\boxed{}}{\boxed{}}$ **Divide each side by** $\boxed{}$ **.**

$x = \boxed{}$ **Simplify.**

If $x = 23$, then $x + 1 = \boxed{}$, and $x + 2 = \boxed{}$. The three integers are $\boxed{}$, $\boxed{}$, and $\boxed{}$.

❷ Opposite-Direction Travel Two jets leave Dallas at the same time and fly in opposite directions. One is flying west 50 mi/h faster than the other. After 2 hours, they are 2500 miles apart. Find the speed of each jet.

Define Let $\boxed{x}$ = the speed of the jet flying east.

Then $\boxed{}$ = the speed of the jet flying west.

Relate

Jet	Rate	Time	Distance Traveled
Eastbound	x		$2x$
Westbound		2	$2(x + 50)$

Write

$2x + 2(\boxed{}) = 2500$

$2x + 2x + \boxed{} = 2500$ **Use the Distributive Property.**

$\boxed{} + 100 = 2500$ **Combine like terms.**

$4x + 100 - \boxed{} = 2500 - \boxed{}$ **Subtract $\boxed{}$ from each side.**

$4x = 2400$ **Simplify.**

$\dfrac{4x}{\boxed{}} = \dfrac{2400}{\boxed{}}$ **Divide each side by $\boxed{}$.**

$x = \boxed{}$

$x + 50 = \boxed{}$

The jet flying east is flying at $\boxed{}$ mi/h. The jet flying west is flying at $\boxed{}$ mi/h.

Quick Check

1. The sum of three consecutive integers is 48. Write and solve an equation to find the three integers.

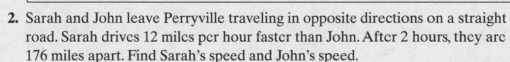

2. Sarah and John leave Perryville traveling in opposite directions on a straight road. Sarah drives 12 miles per hour faster than John. After 2 hours, they are 176 miles apart. Find Sarah's speed and John's speed.

Name_____ Class_____ Date_____

Lesson 3-7

Percent of Change

Lesson Objectives	NAEP 2005 Strand: Number Properties and Operations
Find percent of change Find percent error	Topics: Ratios and Proportional Reasoning Local Standards: _____

Vocabulary

Percent of change is the ratio $\dfrac{\boxed{}}{\boxed{}}$ expressed as a $\boxed{}$.

Percent of increase is _____

_____

Percent of _____ is the percent of change found when a value decreases from its

original amount.

The greatest possible error in a measurement is _____

_____

Percent _____ is the ratio of the greatest possible error and the measurement.

Examples

❶ **Finding Percent of Change** The price of a skirt decreased from $32.95 to $28.95. Find the percent of decrease.

percent of decrease $= \dfrac{\text{amount of change}}{\text{original amount}}$

$= \dfrac{32.95 - \boxed{}}{32.95}$ **Subtract to find the amount of change.**
     Substitute the original amount.

$= \dfrac{\boxed{}}{32.95}$ **Simplify the numerator.**

$\approx \boxed{}$ or $\boxed{}$%   **Write as a decimal and then as a percent.**

The price of the skirt decreased by about $\boxed{}$.

Daily Notetaking Guide   L1

❷ Finding the Greatest Possible Error You read the bathroom scale as 122 lb. What is your greatest possible error?

The scale is read to the nearest [ ] lb, so the greatest possible error is

one half of 1 lb, or [ ] lb.

Quick Check

1. a. Find the percent of change if the price of a CD increases from $12.99 to $13.99. Round to the nearest percent.

b. Find the percent of change if the CD is on sale, and its price decreases from $13.99 to $12.99. Round to the nearest percent.

2. You measure a picture for the yearbook and record its height as 9 cm. What is your greatest possible error?

Lesson 3-8

Finding and Estimating Square Roots

Lesson Objectives	NAEP 2005 Strand: Number Properties and Operations
▼ 1 Find square roots ▼ 2 Estimate and use square roots	**Topics:** Number Sense; Estimation **Local Standards:** _____

Vocabulary and Key Concepts

Square Root

The number a is a square root of b if $a^2 = \boxed{}$.

Example $4^2 = \boxed{}$ and $(-4)^2 = \boxed{}$, so 4 and -4 are square roots of $\boxed{}$.

The principal square root is _____

The _____ square root of b is $-\sqrt{b}$.

The radicand is _____

_____ are squares of integers.

Examples

1 Simplifying Square Root Expressions Simplify each expression.

a. $\sqrt{25}$ = [   ]   positive square root

b. $\pm\sqrt{\dfrac{9}{25}}$ = $\pm$ [   ]   The square roots are [   ] and [   ].

c. $-\sqrt{64}$ = [   ]   Negative square root

d. $\sqrt{-49}$ = [   ]   For real numbers, the square root of a negative number is [   ].

e. $\pm\sqrt{0}$ = [   ]   There is only one square root of 0.

2 Rational and Irrational Square Roots Tell whether each expression is *rational* or *irrational*.

a. $\pm\sqrt{144}$ = [   ]   [   ]

b. $\sqrt{\dfrac{1}{5}}$ = 0.44721359…   [   ]

c. $-\sqrt{6.25}$ = [   ]   [   ]

d. $\sqrt{\dfrac{1}{9}} = 0.\overline{3}$ [   ]

e. $\sqrt{7}$ = [   ]   [   ]

❸ Estimating Square Roots Between what two consecutive integers is $\sqrt{28.34}$?

$\sqrt{\boxed{}} < \sqrt{28.34} < \sqrt{\boxed{}}$ **28.34 is between the two consecutive perfect squares** $\boxed{}$ **and** $\boxed{}$ **.**

$\boxed{} < \sqrt{28.34} < \boxed{}$ **The square roots of 25 and 36 are** $\boxed{}$ **and** $\boxed{}$ **, respectively.**

$\sqrt{28.34}$ is between $\boxed{}$ and $\boxed{}$.

❹ Applying Square Roots Suppose a rectangular field has a length y three times its width x. The formula $d = \sqrt{x^2 + y^2}$ gives the length of the diagonal of a rectangle. Find the distance of the diagonal across the field if $x = 8$ ft.

$d = \sqrt{x^2 + (3x)^2}$ **Substitute 3x for** $\boxed{}$ **.**

$d = \sqrt{\boxed{}^2 + \left(3 \cdot \boxed{}\right)^2}$ **Substitute** $\boxed{}$ **for x.**

$d = \sqrt{\boxed{} + \boxed{}}$ **Simplify.**

$d = \sqrt{\boxed{}}$

$d \approx \boxed{}$ **Use a calculator. Round to the nearest tenth.**

The diagonal is about $\boxed{}$ ft long.

Quick Check

1. Simplify each expression.

a. $\sqrt{49}$ $\boxed{}$ **b.** $\pm\sqrt{36}$ $\boxed{}$ **c.** $-\sqrt{121}$ $\boxed{}$ **d.** $\sqrt{\frac{1}{25}}$ $\boxed{}$

2. Tell whether each expression is rational or irrational.

a. $\sqrt{8}$ **b.** $\pm\sqrt{225}$ **c.** $-\sqrt{75}$ **d.** $\sqrt{\frac{1}{4}}$

3. Between what two consecutive integers is $-\sqrt{105}$?

4. Using the formula from Example 4, suppose $x = 10$ ft. How long is the diagonal across the field? Round to the nearest tenth of a foot.

Lesson 3-9   The Pythagorean Theorem

Lesson Objectives	NAEP 2005 Strand: Geometry
V Solve problems using the Pythagorean Theorem	Topic: Relationships Among Geometric Figures
2 Identify right triangles	Local Standards: _____

Vocabulary and Key Concepts

The Pythagorean Theorem

In any right triangle, the sum of the squares of the lengths of the legs is equal to the square of the length of the hypotenuse.

$$\boxed{}^2 + \boxed{}^2 = \boxed{}^2$$

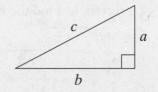

The Converse of the Pythagorean Theorem

If a triangle has sides of lengths a, b, and c, and $a^2 + b^2 = c^2$, then the triangle is

a $\boxed{}$ with hypotenuse of length c.

The hypotenuse is _____

_____

The _____ are the sides that form the right angle of a right triangle.

A conditional is _____

A _____ is the part following *if* in a conditional.

A conclusion is _____

A _____ is a statement obtained by reversing the *if* and *then* parts of an *if-then*

statement.

Examples

1 Using the Pythagorean Theorem What is the length of the hypotenuse of this triangle?

$a^2 + b^2 = c^2$ **Use the Pythagorean Theorem.**

$\boxed{}^2 + \boxed{}^2 = c^2$ **Substitute** $\boxed{}$ **for** *a* **and** $\boxed{}$ **for** *b*.

$\boxed{} + \boxed{} = c^2$ **Simplify.**

$\sqrt{\boxed{}} = \sqrt{c^2}$ **Find the principal square root of each side.**

$\boxed{} = c$ **Simplify.**

The length of the hypotenuse is 17 m.

❷ Using the Converse of the Pythagorean Theorem Determine whether the given lengths are sides of a right triangle.

a. 5 in., 5 in., and 7 in.

$\boxed{}^2 + \boxed{}^2 \overset{?}{=} \boxed{}^2$ Determine whether $a^2 + b^2 = c^2$, where c is the longest side.

$\boxed{} + \boxed{} \overset{?}{=} \boxed{}$ Simplify.

$\boxed{} \neq \boxed{}$

This triangle $\boxed{}$ a right triangle.

b. 10 cm, 24 cm, and 26 cm

$\boxed{}^2 + \boxed{}^2 \overset{?}{=} \boxed{}^2$ Determine whether $a^2 + b^2 = c^2$, where c is the longest side.

$\boxed{} + \boxed{} \overset{?}{=} \boxed{}$ Simplify.

$\boxed{} = \boxed{}$

This triangle $\boxed{}$ a right triangle.

❸ Physics If two forces pull at right angles to each other, the resultant force is represented as the diagonal of a rectangle, as shown in the diagram. The diagonal forms a right triangle with two of the perpendicular sides of the rectangle.

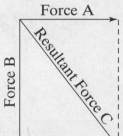

For a 50-lb force and a 120-lb force, the resultant force is 130 lb. Are the forces pulling at right angles to each other?

$\boxed{}^2 + \boxed{}^2 \overset{?}{=} \boxed{}^2$ Determine whether $a^2 + b^2 = c^2$, where c is the greatest force.

$\boxed{} + \boxed{} \overset{?}{=} \boxed{}$

$\boxed{} = \boxed{}$

The forces of 50 lb and 120 lb $\boxed{}$ at right angles to each other.

Quick Check

1. What is the length of the hypotenuse of a right triangle with legs of lengths 7 cm and 24 cm?

$\boxed{}$

2. A triangle has sides of lengths 10 m, 24 m, and 26 m. Is the triangle a right triangle?

$\boxed{}$

3. Physics Consider Example 3. For a 70-lb force and a 60-lb force, the resultant force is 100 lb. Are the forces pulling at right angles to each other?

$\boxed{}$

Lesson 4-1

Inequalities and Their Graphs

Lesson Objectives	NAEP 2005 Strand: Algebra
▼ Identify solutions of inequalities ▼ Graph and write inequalities	**Topics:** Variables, Expressions, and Operations; Equations and Inequalities
	Local Standards: _____

Vocabulary

A _____ of an inequality is any value or values of a variable in the inequality that makes the inequality true.

Example

1 **Identifying Solutions by Evaluating** Is each number a solution of $3 + 2x < 8$?

a. -2

$$3 + 2x < 8$$

$$3 + 2(\boxed{}) < 8 \qquad \leftarrow \text{Substitute for } x. \rightarrow$$

$$3 - \boxed{} < 8 \qquad \leftarrow \text{Simplify.} \rightarrow$$

$$\boxed{} < 8 \qquad \leftarrow \text{Compare.} \rightarrow$$

-2 is a solution.

b. 3

$$3 + 2x < 8$$

$$3 + 2(\boxed{}) < 8$$

$$3 + \boxed{} < 8$$

$$\boxed{} < 8$$

3 is not a solution.

Quick Check

1. Is each number a solution of $x \geq -4.1$?

   a. -5 **b.** -4.1 **c.** 8 **d.** 0

2. Is each number a solution of $6x - 3 > 10$?

   a. 1 **b.** 2 **c.** 3 **d.** 4

  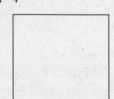

Name_____ Class_____ Date _____

Examples

❷ **Graphing Inequalities**

a. Graph $d < 3$.

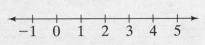

The solutions of $d < 3$ are all the points to the

[   ] of 3.

b. Graph $-3 \geq g$.

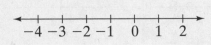

The solutions of $-3 \geq g$ are [   ] and all the

points to the [   ] of -3.

❸ **Writing an Inequality From a Graph** Write an inequality for each graph.

a. 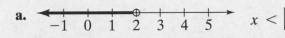 $\quad x < \boxed{}$ Numbers [   ] 2 are graphed.

b. 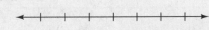 $\quad x \leq \boxed{}$ Numbers [   ] -3 are graphed.

Quick Check

2. Graph each inequality.

a. $a < 1$

b. $n \geq -3$

c. $2 > p$

3. Write an inequality for each graph.

a. 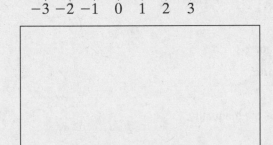

b.

Lesson 4-2

**Solving Inequalities
Using Addition and Subtraction**

Lesson Objectives	NAEP 2005 Strand: Algebra
1 Use addition to solve inequalities	**Topic:** Equations and Inequalities
2 Use subtraction to solve inequalities	**Local Standards:** _____

Vocabulary and Key Concepts

Addition Property of Inequality

For every real number $a, b,$ and $c,$

if $a > b,$ then [ ];   if $a < b,$ then [ ].

Examples

$3 > 1,$ so $3 + 2$ [ ] $1 + 2.$ $-5 < 4,$ so $-5 + 2$ [ ] $4 + 2.$

This property is also true for $\geq$ and $\leq$.

Subtraction Property of Inequality

For every real number $a, b,$ and $c,$

if $a > b,$ then [ ];   if $a < b,$ then [ ].

Examples

$3 > -1,$ so $3 - 2$ [ ] $-1 - 2.$ $-5 < 4,$ so $-5 - 2$ [ ] $4 - 2.$

This property is also true for $\geq$ and $\leq$.

_____ inequalities are inequalities with the same set of solutions.

Examples

1 **Using the Addition Property of Inequality** Solve $8 \geq d - 2.$ Graph and check your solution.

$8 + $ [ ] $\geq d - 2 + $ [ ]   **Add** [ ] **to each side.**

[ ] $\geq d,$ or $d \leq 10$ **Simplify.**

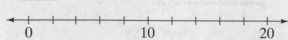

Check $8 = d - 2$ **Check the computation.**

$8 \overset{?}{=} $ [ ] $- 2$ **Substitute** [ ] **for d.**

$8 = 8$ ✓

$8 \geq d - 2$ **Check the direction of the inequality.**

$8 \geq 9 - 2$ **Substitute 9 for d.**

$8 \geq 7$ [ ]

❷ Using the Subtraction Property of Inequality To receive a B in your literature class, you must earn more than 350 points of reading credits. Last week you earned 120 points. This week you earned 90 points. How many more points must you earn to receive a B?

Relate | points earned | plus | points needed | is more than | points required |.

Define Let $\boxed{p}$ = the number of points needed.

Write $\boxed{}$ + $\boxed{}$ $\boxed{}$ $\boxed{}$

$120 + 90 + \boxed{}\boxed{}$

$\boxed{} + p \boxed{} 350$ **Combine like terms.**

$\boxed{} + p - \boxed{} \boxed{} 350 - \boxed{}$ **Subtract** $\boxed{}$ **from each side.**

$p \boxed{} 140$ **Simplify.**

You must earn 141 more points.

Quick Check

1. a. Solve $m - 6 > -4$. Graph your solution.

b. Solve $n - 7 \le -2$. Graph and check your solution.

2. a. Solve $t + 3 \ge 8$. Graph and check your solution.

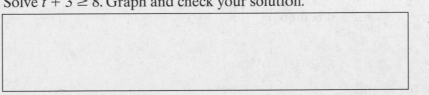

b. Your baseball team has a goal to collect at least 160 blankets for a shelter. Team members brought 42 blankets on Monday and 65 blankets on Wednesday. How many blankets must the team donate on Friday to meet or exceed their goal?

Lesson 4-3

**Solving Inequalities
Using Multiplication and Division**

Lesson Objectives	NAEP 2005 Strand: Algebra
Use multiplication to solve inequalities Use division to solve inequalities	**Topics:** Equations and Inequalities **Local Standards:** _____

Key Concepts

Multiplication Property of Inequality

For every real number a and b, and for $c > 0$,

if $a > b$, then $ac \ \square \ bc$;   if $a < b$, then $ac \ \square \ bc$.

Examples

$4 > -1$, so $4(5) \ \square \ -1(5)$. $-6 < 3$, so $-6(5) \ \square \ 3(5)$.

For every real number a and b, and for $c < 0$,

if $a > b$, then $ac \ \square \ bc$;   if $a < b$, then $ac \ \square \ bc$.

Examples

$4 > -1$, so $4(-2) \ \square \ -1(-2)$. $-6 < 3$, so $-6(-2) \ \square \ 3(-2)$.

This property is also true for $\geq$ and $\leq$.

Division Property of Inequality

For every real number a and b, and for $c > 0$,

if $a > b$, then $\frac{a}{c} \ \square \ \frac{b}{c}$;   if $a < b$, then $\frac{a}{c} \ \square \ \frac{b}{c}$.

Examples

$6 > 4$, so $\frac{6}{2} \ \square \ \frac{4}{2}$. $2 < 8$, so $\frac{2}{2} \ \square \ \frac{8}{2}$.

For every real number a and b, and for $c < 0$,

if $a > b$, then $\frac{a}{c} \ \square \ \frac{b}{c}$;   if $a < b$, then $\frac{a}{c} \ \square \ \frac{b}{c}$.

Examples

$6 > 4$, so $\frac{6}{-2} \ \square \ \frac{4}{-2}$. $2 < 8$, so $\frac{2}{-2} \ \square \ \frac{8}{-2}$.

This property is also true for $\geq$ and $\leq$.

Name_____ Class_____ Date _____

Examples

❶ Multiplying to Solve an Inequality Solve $3 \le -\frac{3}{5}x$. Graph the solutions.

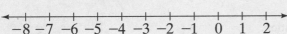 $\left(\square\dfrac{\square}{\square}\right)(3) \ge \left(\square\dfrac{\square}{\square}\right)\left(-\dfrac{3}{5}x\right)$ **Multiply each side by the reciprocal of $-\frac{3}{5}$, which is** $\square$ **, and reverse the inequality symbol.**

$-5 \ge x$, or $x \le -5$ **Simplify.**

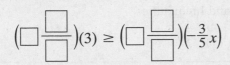

❷ Dividing to Solve an Inequality Solve $-4c < 24$. Graph the solutions.

$\dfrac{-4c}{\square} > \dfrac{24}{\square}$ **Divide each side by** $\square$ **. Reverse the inequality symbol.**

$c < -6$ **Simplify.**

Quick Check

1. Solve each inequality. Graph and check the solution.

a. $\dfrac{-k}{4} > -1$

b. $-t < \dfrac{1}{2}$

c. $6 \le \dfrac{-3}{5}w$

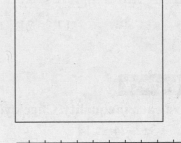

2. Solve the inequality. Graph and check your solution.

a. $-2t < -8$

b. $-3w \ge 12$

c. $0.6 > -0.2n$

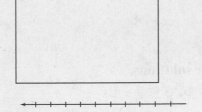

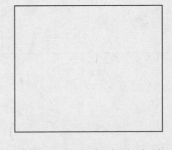

Lesson 4-4

Solving Multi-Step Inequalities

Lesson Objectives	NAEP 2005 Strand: Algebra
▼ Solve multi-step inequalities with variables on one side	**Topics:** Equations and Inequalities
② Solve multi-step inequalities with variables on both sides	**Local Standards:** _____

Example

① Using More Than One Step Solve $5 + 4b < 21$.

$5 + 4b - \boxed{} < 21 - \boxed{}$ **Subtract** $\boxed{}$ **from each side.**

$4b < \boxed{}$ **Simplify.**

$\dfrac{4b}{\boxed{}} < \dfrac{16}{\boxed{}}$ **Divide each side by** $\boxed{}$.

$b < \boxed{}$ **Simplify.**

Check $5 + 4b = 21$ **Check the computation.**

$5 + 4\left(\boxed{}\right) \stackrel{?}{=} 21$ **Substitute** $\boxed{}$ **for** *b*.

$21 = 21$ ✓

$5 + 4b < 21$ **Check the direction of the inequality.**

$5 + 4\left(\boxed{}\right) < 21$ **Substitute 3 for** *b*.

$17 < 21$ $\boxed{}$

Quick Check

1. Solve each inequality. Check your solutions.

   a. $-3x - 4 \leq 14$ **b.** $5 < 7 - 2t$ **c.** $-8 < 5n - 23$

Examples

❷ Using the Distributive Property Solve $3x + 4(6 - x) < 2$.

$3x + \boxed{} - \boxed{} < 2$	Use the Distributive Property.
$\boxed{} + 24 < 2$	Combine like terms.
$-x + 24 - \boxed{} < 2 - \boxed{}$	Subtract $\boxed{}$ from each side.
$-x < \boxed{}$	Simplify.
$\dfrac{-x}{\boxed{}} > \dfrac{-22}{\boxed{}}$	Divide each side by $\boxed{}$. Reverse the inequality symbol.
$x\ \boxed{}\ \boxed{}$	Simplify.

❸ Multi-Step Inequalities Solve $5(-3 + d) \le 3(3d - 2)$.

$\boxed{} + \boxed{}d \le \boxed{}d - \boxed{}$	Use the Distributive Property.
$-15 + 5d - \boxed{} \le 9d - 6 - \boxed{}$	Subtract $\boxed{}$ from each side.
$-15 - \boxed{} \le -6$	Combine like terms.
$-15 - 4d + \boxed{} \le -6 + \boxed{}$	Add $\boxed{}$ to each side.
$-4d \le \boxed{}$	Simplify.
$\dfrac{-4d}{\boxed{}} \ge \dfrac{9}{\boxed{}}$	Divide each side by $\boxed{}$. Reverse the inequality symbol.
$d\ \boxed{}\ \boxed{}$	Simplify.

Quick Check

2. Solve each inequality. Check your solutions.

  a. $4p + 2(p + 7) < 8$

  b. $15 \le 5 - 2(4m + 7)$

3. Solve $-6(x - 4) \ge 7(2x - 3)$. Check your solution.

Lesson 4-5

Compound Equalities

Lesson Objectives	NAEP 2005 Strand: Algebra
▼ Solve and graph inequalities containing *and* ▼ Solve and graph inequalities containing *or*	**Topics:** Variables, Expressions, and Operations; Equations and Inequalities **Local Standards:** _____

Vocabulary

A _____ inequality is two inequalities that are joined by the word *and* or the word *or*.

Examples

1 Writing a Compound Inequality Write two compound inequalities that represent each situation. Graph the solutions.

a. all real numbers that are at least −1 and at most 3

$b \geq -1$ and $b \leq \boxed{}$

$-1 \leq b \leq 3$

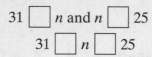

b. all real numbers that are less than 31 but greater than 25

$31 \boxed{} n$ and $n \boxed{} 25$

$31 \boxed{} n \boxed{} 25$

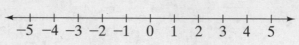

2 Solving a Compound Inequality Containing And Solve $5 > 5 - f > 2$. Graph the solutions.

Write the compound inequality as two inequalities joined by $\boxed{}$.

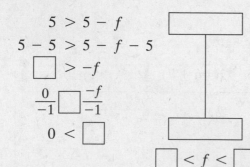

$5 > 5 - f$

$5 - 5 > 5 - f - 5$

$\boxed{} > -f$

$\dfrac{0}{-1} \boxed{} \dfrac{-f}{-1}$

$0 < \boxed{}$

$5 - f > 2$

$5 - f - 5 > 2 - 5$

$-f > \boxed{}$

$\dfrac{-f}{-1} \boxed{} \dfrac{-3}{-1}$

$f < \boxed{}$

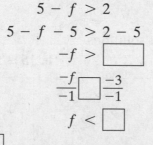

$\boxed{} < f < \boxed{}$

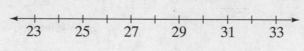

3 Writing Compound Inequalities Write an inequality that represents the situation. Graph the solutions.

all real numbers that are less than 0 or greater than 3

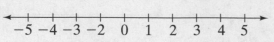

$n < \boxed{}$ or $n > \boxed{}$

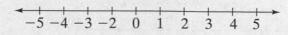

④ Solving a Compound Inequality Containing *Or* Solve the compound inequality $3x + 2 < -7$ or $-4x + 5 < 1$. Graph the solutions.

$$3x + 2 < -7 \qquad \text{or} \qquad -4x + 5 < 1$$

$$3x + 2 - \boxed{} < -7 - \boxed{} \qquad -4x + 5 - \boxed{} < 1 - \boxed{}$$

$$3x < \boxed{} \qquad\qquad -4x < \boxed{}$$

$$\frac{3x}{\boxed{}} < \frac{-9}{\boxed{}} \qquad\qquad \frac{-4x}{\boxed{}} \boxed{} \frac{-4}{\boxed{}}$$

$$x < \boxed{} \qquad \text{or} \qquad x > \boxed{}$$

Quick Check

1. Write a compound inequality that represents each situation. Graph the solutions.

   a. all real numbers greater than −2 but less than 9

   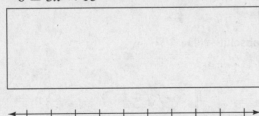

   b. The books were priced between $3.50 and $6.00, inclusive.

   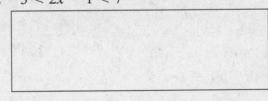

2. Solve each inequality. Graph your solutions.

   a. $-6 \le 3x < 15$

   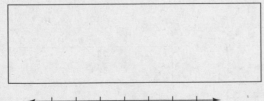

   b. $-3 < 2x - 1 < 7$

   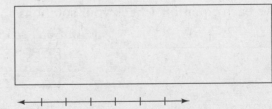

3. Write an inequality that represents all real numbers that are at most −5 or at least 3. Graph the solutions.

4. Solve the compound inequality $-2x + 7 > 3$ or $3x - 4 \ge 5$. Graph the solutions.

Lesson 4-6

Absolute Value Equations and Inequalities

Lesson Objectives	NAEP 2005 Strand: Number Properties and Operations; Algebra
▼ Solve equations that involve absolute value	**Topics:** Number Sense; Equations and Inequalities
② Solve inequalities that involve absolute value	**Local Standards:** _____

Key Concepts

Solving Absolute Value Equations

To solve an equation in the form $|A| = b$, where A represents a variable expression and $b > 0$, solve _____

Solving Absolute Value Inequalities

To solve an inequality in the form $|A| < b$, where A is a variable expression and $b > 0$, solve _____

To solve an inequality in the form $|A| > b$, where A is a variable expression and $b > 0$, solve _____

Similar rules are true for $|A| \le b$ and $|A| \ge b$.

Example

① Solving an Absolute Value Equation Solve and check $|a| - 3 = 5$.

$|a| - 3 + \boxed{} = 5 + \boxed{}$ **Add** $\boxed{}$ **to each side.**

$|a| = \boxed{}$ **Simplify.**

$a = \boxed{}$ or $a = -\boxed{}$ **Definition of absolute value.**

Check $|a| - 3 = 5$

$\left|\boxed{}\right| - 3 \overset{?}{=} 5$ ← **Substitute** $\boxed{}$ **and** $\boxed{}$ **for a.** → $\left|\boxed{}\right| - 3 \overset{?}{=} 5$

$\boxed{} - 3 = 5$ ✓ $\boxed{} - 3 = 5$ ✓

Quick Check

1. Solve each equation. Check your solutions.

a. $|t| - 2 = -1$ **b.** $3|n| = 15$ **c.** $4 = 3|w| - 2$

Examples

❷ **Solving an Absolute Value Equation** Solve $|3c - 6| = 9$.

$$3c - 6 = 9 \quad \leftarrow \text{Write two equations.} \rightarrow \quad 3c - 6 = -9$$

$$3c - 6 + \boxed{} = 9 + \boxed{} \quad \leftarrow \text{Add } \boxed{} \text{ to each side.} \rightarrow \quad 3c - 6 + \boxed{} = -9 + \boxed{}$$

$$3c = \boxed{} \qquad\qquad\qquad 3c = \boxed{}$$

$$\frac{3c}{\boxed{}} = \frac{\boxed{}}{\boxed{}} \quad \leftarrow \text{Divide each side by } \boxed{}. \rightarrow \quad \frac{3c}{\boxed{}} = \frac{\boxed{}}{\boxed{}}$$

$$c = \boxed{} \qquad\qquad\qquad c = \boxed{}$$

The value of c is $\boxed{}$ or $\boxed{}$.

❸ **Solving an Absolute Value Inequality** Solve $|y - 5| \leq 2$. Graph the solutions.

$$y - 5 \geq -2 \qquad \text{and} \quad y - 5 \leq 2 \qquad\qquad \textbf{Write a compound inequality.}$$

$$y - 5 + \boxed{} \geq -2 + \boxed{} \quad \Big| \quad y - 5 + \boxed{} \leq 2 + \boxed{} \qquad \textbf{Add } \boxed{} \textbf{ to each side.}$$

$$y \geq \boxed{} \qquad \text{and} \quad y \leq \boxed{} \qquad\qquad \textbf{Simplify.}$$

$$\boxed{} \leq y \leq \boxed{}$$

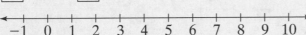

Quick Check

2. Solve each equation. Check your solutions.

a. $|c - 2| = 6$

b. $-5.5 = |t + 2|$

c. $|7d| = 14$

3. Solve and graph $|w + 2| > 5$.

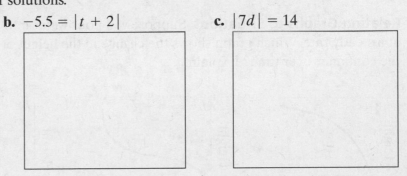

Lesson 5-1

Relating Graphs to Events

Lesson Objective	NAEP 2005 Strand: Algebra
▼ Interpret, sketch, and analyze graphs from situations	**Topic:** Algebraic Representations
	Local Standards: _____

Examples

❶ Interpreting Graphs This graph shows someone taking a walk in the neighborhood. Describe what it shows by labeling each part.

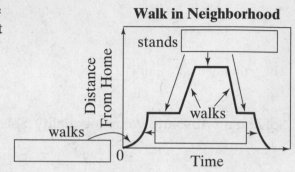

Walk in Neighborhood

❷ Sketching a Graph A pelican flies above the water searching for fish. Sketch a graph of its altitude from takeoff from shore to diving to the water to catch a fish. Label each section.

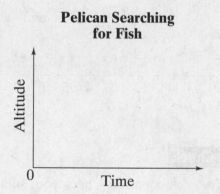

Pelican Searching for Fish

❸ Relating Graphs to Situations Suppose you pour water into the container at a steady rate. Which graph shows the change in the height of the liquid in the container over time? Explain.

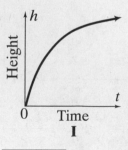
I

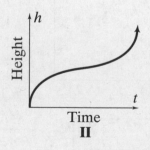
II

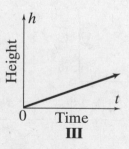
III

 The height of the water will [   ] at a steady rate.

Name_____ Class_____ Date _____

1. The graph shows a trip from home to school and back. The trip involves walking and getting a ride from a neighbor. Label each section of the graph.

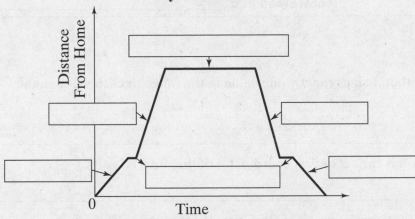

Daily Commute

2. Sketch a graph of the distance from a child's feet to the ground as the child jumps rope. Label each section.

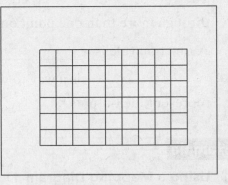

3. The graph at the right shows the time and distance of a moving object. Which of the following situations could be described by the graph?

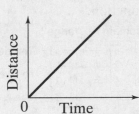

   A. A car travels at a steady speed.
   B. A cyclist slows down as she rides up a hill and speeds up as she peddles over the top.
   C. A train slows down as it arrives at the station.
   D. A plane accelerates steadily down the runway until it takes off.

Lesson 5-2

Relations and Functions

Lesson Objectives	NAEP 2005 Strand: Algebra
▼ Identify relations and functions ▼ Evaluate functions	Topic: Patterns, Relations, and Functions Local Standards: _____

Vocabulary

A _____ is a relation that assigns exactly one value in the range to each value in the domain.

A relation is _____

The _____ of a relation is the set of first coordinates of the ordered pairs.

The range of a relation is _____

The _____ says that, on the graph of a relation, if any vertical line passes through more than one point on the graph, the relation is not a function.

A function rule is _____

_____ is a way to write a function using x to represent the inputs and $f(x)$ to represent the outputs.

Example

❶ Using a Mapping Diagram Determine whether the relation $\{(4, 3), (2, -1), (-3, -3), (2, 4)\}$ is a function.

The domain value 2 corresponds

to two range values, ☐ and ☐.

The relation ☐ a function.

Quick Check

1. Use a mapping diagram to determine whether each relation is a function.

a. $\{(3, -2), (8, 1), (9, 2), (3, 3), (-4, 0)\}$ **b.** $\{(6.5, 0), (7, -1), (6, 2), (2, 6), (5, -1)\}$

Name_____ Class_____ Date _____

Examples

❷ Using the Vertical-Line Test Determine whether the relation
$\{(0, -2), (1, -2), (-3, 1), (-2, 0), (-1, -1), (3, 2), (2, -3)\}$ is a function.

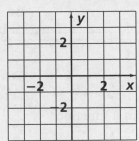

Graph the ordered pairs on a coordinate plane

[ ] vertical line passes through more than one point.
The relation [ ] a function.

❸ Finding the Range Evaluate the function rule $f(g) = -2g + 4$ to find the
range for the domain $\{-1, 3, 5\}$.

$f(g) = -2g + 4$ $f(g) = -2g + 4$ $f(g) = -2g + 4$

$f(\boxed{}) = -2(\boxed{}) + 4$ $f(\boxed{}) = -2(\boxed{}) + 4$ $f(\boxed{}) = -2(\boxed{}) + 4$

$f(\boxed{}) = \boxed{} + 4$ $f(\boxed{}) = \boxed{} + 4$ $f(\boxed{}) = \boxed{} + 4$

$f(\boxed{}) = \boxed{}$ $f(\boxed{}) = \boxed{}$ $f(\boxed{}) = \boxed{}$

The range is $\{\boxed{}\}$.

Quick Check

2. Use the vertical-line test to determine whether the relation
$\{(0, 2), (1, -1), (-1, 4), (0, -3), (2, 1)\}$ is a function.

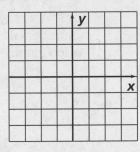
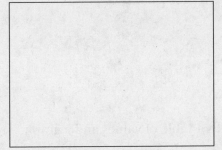

3. Find the range of each function for the domain $\{-2, 0, 5\}$.

a. $f(x) = x - 6$ **b.** $y = -4x$ **c.** $g(t) = t^2 + 1$

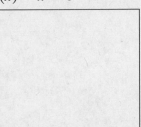

Lesson 5-3

Function Rules, Tables, and Graphs

Lesson Objective	NAEP 2005 Strand: Algebra
▼ Model functions using rules, tables, and graphs	**Topic:** Algebraic Representations
	Local Standards: _____

Vocabulary

An _____ is a variable that provides the input values of a function.

A dependent variable is _____

_____

Example

❶ **Three Views of a Function** At the local video store you can rent a video game for $3. It costs you $5 a month to operate your video game player. The total monthly cost $C(v)$ depends on the number of video games v you rent.

Use the function rule $C(v) = 5 + 3v$ to make a table of values and a graph.

v	$C(v) = 5 + 3v$	$(v, C(v))$
0	$C(\boxed{}) = 5 + 3(\boxed{}) = \boxed{}$	$(\boxed{}, \boxed{})$
1	$C(\boxed{}) = 5 + 3(\boxed{}) = \boxed{}$	$(\boxed{}, \boxed{})$
2	$C(\boxed{}) = 5 + 3(\boxed{}) = \boxed{}$	$(\boxed{}, \boxed{})$

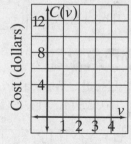

Number of video games

Quick Check

1. Model the rule $f(x) = 3x + 4$ with a table of values and a graph.

x	$f(x)$
0	
1	
−1	
−2	

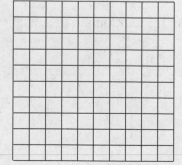

Name_____ Class_____ Date_____

Example

2 **Graphing Functions**

a. Make a table of values and graph the function $y = |x| + 2$.

x	$y = |x| + 2$	(x, y)
−3	$y = \boxed{}\,\Big|\, + 2 = \boxed{}$	$\left(-3,\ \boxed{}\right)$
−1	$y = \boxed{}\,\Big|\, + 2 = \boxed{}$	$\left(-1,\ \boxed{}\right)$
0	$y = \boxed{}\,\Big|\, + 2 = \boxed{}$	$\left(0,\ \boxed{}\right)$
1	$y = \boxed{}\,\Big|\, + 2 = \boxed{}$	$\left(1,\ \boxed{}\right)$
3	$y = \boxed{}\,\Big|\, + 2 = \boxed{}$	$\left(3,\ \boxed{}\right)$

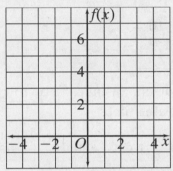

b. Make a table of values and graph the function $f(x) = x^2 + 2$.

x	$f(x) = x^2 + 2$	(x, f(x))
−2	$f\left(\boxed{}\right) = \boxed{} + 2 = \boxed{}$	$\left(-2,\ \boxed{}\right)$
−1	$f\left(\boxed{}\right) = \boxed{} + 2 = \boxed{}$	$\left(-1,\ \boxed{}\right)$
0	$f\left(\boxed{}\right) = \boxed{} + 2 = \boxed{}$	$\left(0,\ \boxed{}\right)$
1	$f\left(\boxed{}\right) = \boxed{} + 2 = \boxed{}$	$\left(1,\ \boxed{}\right)$
2	$f\left(\boxed{}\right) = \boxed{} + 2 = \boxed{}$	$\left(2,\ \boxed{}\right)$

Quick Check

2. Make a table of values and graph each function.

a. $f(x) = |x| - 1$

x	f(x)
−2	
−1	
0	
1	
2	

b. $f(x) = x^2 - 1$

x	f(x)
−2	
−1	
0	
1	
2	

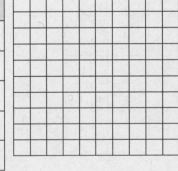

Name_____ Class_____ Date _____

Lesson 5-4

Lesson Objective	NAEP 2005 Strand: Algebra
▼ Write a function rule given a table or a real-world situation	Topics: Patterns, Relations, and Functions; Algebraic Representations; Variables, Expressions, and Operations
	Local Standards: _____

Example

① **Writing a Rule from a Table** Write a function rule for the table.

x	y
1	2
2	5
3	10
4	17

Ask yourself, "What can I do to 1 to get 2, 2 to get 5, . . . ?" You multiply each x-value times [   ] and add [   ] to get the y-value.

Relate   [y]   equals   [x times itself]   plus   [1]

Write   [   ]   =   [   ]   +   [   ]

A rule for the function is [   ].

Quick Check

1. Write a function rule for each table.

a.

x	f(x)
1	−1
2	0
3	1
4	2

b.

x	y
1	2
2	4
3	6
4	8

Daily Notetaking Guide   L1

Example

❷ Writing a Function Rule The journalism class makes $25 per ad sold in the yearbook. If the class sells *n* ads, how much money will it earn?

a. Write a function rule to describe this relationship.

Relate | money earned | is | 25 | times | number of ads sold |

Define Let | *n* | = number of ads sold.

Let | *P(n)* | = money earned.

Write | ⬚ | = | ⬚ | · | ⬚ |

The function rule | ⬚ | = | ⬚ | describes the relationship between the number of ads sold and the money earned.

b. The class sold 6 ads. How much money did the class make?

$P(n) = 25 \cdot \boxed{}$

$P\left(\boxed{}\right) = 25 \cdot \boxed{}$ **Substitute 6 for *n*.**

$P\left(\boxed{}\right) = \boxed{}$ **Simplify.**

The class made $\boxed{}$.

Quick Check

2. a. A carpenter buys finishing nails by the pound. Each pound of nails costs $1.19. Write a function rule to describe this relationship.

b. How much does 12 lb of finishing nails cost?

c. Suppose you buy a word-processing software package for $199. You charge $15 per hour for word processing. Write a rule to describe your profit as a function of the number of hours you work.

Lesson 5-5

Direct Variation

<table>
<tr><td>

Lesson Objectives

▼ Write an equation of a direct variation

❷ Use ratios and proportions with direct variations

</td><td>

NAEP 2005 Strand: Algebra

Topics: Patterns, Relations, and Functions; Algebraic Representations

Local Standards: _____

</td></tr>
</table>

Key Concepts

Direct Variation

A function in the form $y = kx$, where $k \neq 0$, is a [_____].

The constant of variation k is the coefficient of x. The variables y and x are said to vary [_____] with each other.

Example

❶ **Is an Equation a Direct Variation?** Is the equation a direct variation? If it is, find the constant of variation.

$2x - 3y = 0$

$-3y = $ [____]   **Subtract** [____] **from each side.**

$y = $ [____] x **Divide each side by** [____].

The equation [____] have the form $y = kx$, so the equation [____] a direct variation. The constant of variation is [____].

Quick Check

1. Is each equation a direct variation? If it is, find the constant of variation.

  a. $7y = 2x$ **b.** $3y + 4x = 8$

Examples

❷ **Writing an Equation Given a Point** Write an equation for the direct variation that includes the point $(-3, 2)$.

$y = kx$ — **Use the general form of a direct variation.**

$\boxed{} = k\left(\boxed{}\right)$ — **Substitute** $\boxed{}$ **for** x **and** $\boxed{}$ **for** y.

$-\boxed{} = k$ — **Divide each side by** $\boxed{}$ **to solve for** k.

$y = \boxed{} x$ — **Write an equation. Substitute** $\boxed{}$ **for** k **in** $y = kx$.

The equation of the direct variation is $\boxed{}$.

❸ **Direct Variations and Tables** For the data in the table at the right, tell whether y varies directly with x. If it does, write an equation for the direct variation.

The ratio $\frac{y}{x}$ is $\boxed{}$ for each pair of data, so y $\boxed{}$ vary directly with x.

x	y	$\dfrac{y}{x}$
-1	2	$\dfrac{2}{-1} = \boxed{}$
1	2	$\dfrac{\boxed{}}{\boxed{}} = \boxed{}$
2	-4	$\dfrac{\boxed{}}{\boxed{}} = \boxed{}$

Quick Check

2. Write the equation of the direct variation that includes the point $(-3, -6)$.

3. For the equation in each table, tell whether y varies directly with x. If it does, write an equation for the direct variation.

a.

x	y
-2	3.2
1	2.4
4	1.6

b.

x	y
4	6
8	12
10	15

Lesson 5-6

Inverse Variation

Lesson Objectives	NAEP 2005 Strand: Algebra
▼ Solve inverse variations ② Compare direct and inverse variation	**Topic:** Patterns, Relations, and Functions **Local Standards:** _____

Vocabulary and Key Concepts

Direct and Inverse Variation

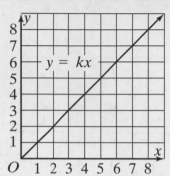

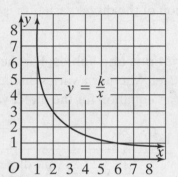

y varies [ ] with *x*.

y is [ ] proportional to *x*.

The [ ] $\frac{y}{x}$ is constant.

y varies [ ] with *x*.

y is [ ] proportional to *x*.

The [ ] xy is constant.

An equation in the form $xy = k$ or $y = \frac{k}{x}$, where $k \neq 0$, is an [ ] variation. The constant of variation is [ ].

Examples

① **Finding the Missing Coordinate** The points $(5, 6)$ and $(3, y)$ are two points on the graph of an inverse variation. Find the missing value.

$x_1 \cdot y_1 = x_2 \cdot y_2$ **Use the equation $x_1 \cdot y_1 = x_2 \cdot y_2$ since you know coordinates but not the constant of variation.**

$\boxed{}(\boxed{}) = \boxed{}y_2$ **Substitute** $\boxed{}$ **for x_1,** $\boxed{}$ **for y_1, and** $\boxed{}$ **for x_2.**

$\boxed{} = \boxed{}y_2$ **Simplify.**

$\boxed{} = y_2$ **Solve for y_2.**

The missing value is $\boxed{}$. The point $(3, \boxed{})$ is on the graph of the inverse variation that includes the point $(5, 6)$.

❷ Determining Direct or Inverse Variation Decide whether each data set represents a direct variation or an inverse variation. Then write an equation to model the data.

a.

x	y
3	10
5	6
10	3

The values of y seem to vary [ ] with the values of x. Check each product xy.

xy: $3(10) = 30$ $5(6) = 30$ $10(3) = 30$

The product of xy is the same for all pairs of data.

So, this is an [ ] variation, and $k = $ [ ].

The equation is [ ].

b.

x	y
2	3
4	6
8	12

The values of y seem to vary [ ] with the values of x. Check each ratio $\frac{y}{x}$.

$\frac{y}{x} \to$ $\frac{3}{2} = 1.5$ $\frac{6}{4} = 1.5$ $\frac{12}{8} = 1.5$

The ratio $\frac{y}{x}$ is the same for all pairs of data. So, this is a

[ ] variation, and $k = $ [ ].

The equation is [ ].

Quick Check

1. Each pair of points is on the graph of an inverse variation. Find the missing values.

a. $(3, y)$ and $(5, 9)$

b. $(75, 0.2)$ and $(x, 3)$

2. Determine whether the data in each table represent a direct variation or an inverse variation. Write an equation to model the data in each table.

a.

x	y
3	12
6	6
9	4

b.

x	y
3	12
5	20
8	32

Lesson 5-7

Describing Number Patterns

Lesson Objectives	NAEP 2005 Strand: Algebra
1 Use inductive reasoning in continuing number pattterns	**Topic:** Patterns, Relations, and Functions
2 Write rules for arithmetic sequences	**Local Standards:** _____

Vocabulary and Key Concepts

Arithmetic Sequence

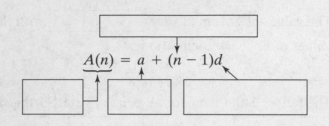

$$A(n) = a + (n - 1)d$$

A _____ is a number pattern.

A term of a sequence is _____

An _____ is a number sequence formed by adding a fixed number to each

previous term.

A common difference is _____

_____ is making conclusions based on observed patterns.

A conjecture is _____

Examples

1 **Extending Number Patterns** Use inductive reasoning to describe the pattern.
Then find the next two numbers in the pattern.

a.

The pattern is "multiply the previous term by [ ]." To find the next two

numbers, you [_____]: $9 \times$ [ ] $= 27$ and

$27 \times$ [ ] $= 81$.

b. $1, 9, 25, 49, \ldots$

The pattern is "squares of consecutive odd integers." To find the next two

numbers, square the next two consecutive odd integers: $9^2 =$ [ ] and

[ ]$^2 =$ [ ].

❷ Finding the Common Difference Find the common difference of each arithmetic sequence.

a. 5, 2, −1, −4, . . .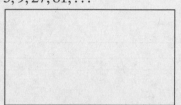

The common difference is ⬚.

b. 8, 11, 14, 17, . . .

The common difference is ⬚.

❸ Finding Terms of a Sequence Find the first, fifth, and tenth terms of the sequence that has the rule $A(n) = 15 + (n − 1)(5)$.

first term: $A\left(\boxed{}\right) = 15 + \left(\boxed{} − 1\right)(5) = 15 + \boxed{}(5) = \boxed{}$

fifth term: $A\left(\boxed{}\right) = 15 + \left(\boxed{} − 1\right)(5) = 15 + \boxed{}(5) = \boxed{}$

tenth term: $A\left(\boxed{}\right) = 15 + \left(\boxed{} − 1\right)(5) = 15 + \boxed{}(5) = \boxed{}$

Quick Check

1. Use inductive reasoning to describe each pattern. Then find the next two numbers in each pattern.

   a. 3, 9, 27, 81, . . .

   b. 9, 15, 21, 27, . . .

2. Find the common difference of each sequence.

   a. 11, 23, 35, 47, . . .

   b. 8, 3, −2, −7, . . .

3. Find the first, sixth, and twelfth terms of each sequence.

   a. $A(n) = −5 + (n − 1)(3)$

   b. $A(n) = 6.3 + (n − 1)(5)$

Name_____ Class_____ Date_____

Lesson 6-1
Rate of Change and Slope

Lesson Objectives	NAEP 2005 Strand: Algebra
▼ 1 Find rates of change from tables and graphs	**Topic:** Algebraic Representations
▼ 2 Find slope	**Local Standards:** _____

Vocabulary and Key Concepts

$$\text{Slope} = \frac{\text{vertical change}}{\text{horizontal change}} = \frac{\text{rise}}{\text{run}} = \frac{y_2 - y_1}{x_2 - x_1}, \text{ where } x_2 - x_1 \neq 0$$

Slopes of Lines

 A line with [____] slope slants upward from left to right.

 A line with [____] slope slants downward from left to right.

 A line with a slope of 0 is [____].

 A line with an undefined slope is [____].

$$\text{Rate of change} = \frac{\text{change in the } \boxed{} \text{ variable}}{\text{change in the } \boxed{} \text{ variable}}$$

Examples

① Finding Rate of Change Using a Table For the data in the table, is the rate of change the same?

Fee for Miles Driven	
Miles	**Fee**
100	$30
150	$42
200	$54

Find the rate of change for each pair of consecutive mileage amounts.

$$\frac{\text{rate of}}{\text{change}} = \frac{\text{change in cost}}{\text{change in number of miles}} \quad \begin{array}{l}\textbf{Cost depends on the}\\ \textbf{number of miles.}\end{array}$$

$$\frac{42 - 30}{150 - 100} = \frac{\boxed{}}{\boxed{}} = \frac{\boxed{}}{\boxed{}}$$

$$\frac{\boxed{} - 42}{200 - \boxed{}} = \frac{\boxed{}}{\boxed{}} = \frac{\boxed{}}{\boxed{}}$$

The rate of change for each pair of consecutive mileage amounts is
$ [____] per [____] miles. The rate of change is the same for all the data.

Daily Notetaking Guide [L1]

Name_____ Class_____ Date _____

❷ Finding Slope Using a Graph Find the slope of the line.

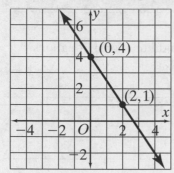

$$\text{slope} = \frac{\text{rise}}{\text{run}}$$

$$= \frac{\boxed{} - 1}{0 - \boxed{}} = -\frac{\boxed{}}{\boxed{}}$$

The slope of the line is $\boxed{}$.

❸ Finding Slope Using Points Find the slope of the line through $E(3, -2)$ and $F(-2, -1)$.

$$\text{slope} = \frac{y_2 - y_1}{x_2 - x_1}$$

$$= \frac{\boxed{} - (-2)}{-2 - \boxed{}}$$ **Substitute** $\left(\boxed{}, \boxed{}\right)$ **for** (x_2, y_2) **and** $\left(\boxed{}, \boxed{}\right)$ **for** (x_1, y_1).

$$= \frac{1}{\boxed{}} = -\frac{\boxed{}}{\boxed{}}$$ **Simplify.**

The slope of $\overleftrightarrow{EF}$ is $\boxed{}$.

Quick Check

1. Using the table in Example 1, find the rate of change using mileage amounts 100 and 200.

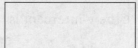

2. Find the slope of each line.

a.

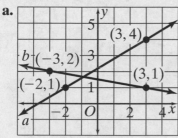

3. Find the slope of the line through each pair of points.

a. $C(2, 5)$ and $D(4, 7)$

b. $P(-1, 4)$ and $Q(3, -2)$

Lesson 6-2

Slope-Intercept Form

<table>
<tr>
<td>

Lesson Objectives

 Write linear equations in slope-intercept form

 Graph linear equations

</td>
<td>

NAEP 2005 Strand:

Topics: Patterns, Relations, and Functions; Equations and Inequalities

Local Standards: _____

</td>
</tr>
</table>

Vocabulary and Key Concepts

Slope-Intercept Form of a Linear Equation

The slope-intercept form of a linear equation is $y = mx + b$.

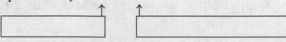

A _____ is an equation whose graph forms a straight line.

The y-intercept is _____

_____

Example

1 **Identifying Slope and *y*-Intercept** What are the slope and *y*-intercept of $y = 2x - 3$?

$y = mx + b$ **Use slope-intercept form.**

$y = \boxed{}x + \boxed{}$

The slope is $\boxed{}$; the *y*-intercept is $\boxed{}$.

Quick Check

1. Find the slope and *y*-intercept of each equation.

a. $y = -2x + 1$

b. $y = -\frac{4}{5}x$

Examples

❷ Writing an Equation From a Graph Write the equation for the line.

Step 1 Find the slope. Two points on the line are $(0, 1)$ and $(3, -1)$.

slope = $\dfrac{\boxed{}}{\boxed{}}$

= $\boxed{}$

Step 2 Write an equation in slope-intercept form. The y-intercept is $\boxed{}$.

$y = mx + b$

$y = \boxed{}x + \boxed{}$ **Substitute** $\boxed{}$ **for m and** $\boxed{}$ **for b.**

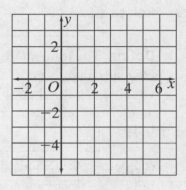

❸ Graphing Equations Graph $y = \frac{1}{3}x - 2$.

Step 1 The y-intercept is $\boxed{}$. So plot a point at $\left(\boxed{}, \boxed{}\right)$.

Step 2 The slope is $\boxed{}$. Use the slope to plot a second point.

Step 3 Draw a line through the two points.

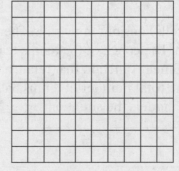

Quick Check

2. Write the equation of the line.

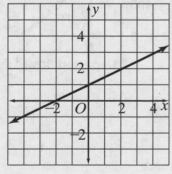

3. Graph $y = \frac{3}{2}x - 2$.

Lesson 6-3

Applying Linear Functions

Lesson Objectives	NAEP 2005 Strand: Algebra
▽ Interpret Linear Graphs	**Topic:** Algebraic Representations, Variables, Expressions and Operations, Equations and Inequalities
	Local Standards: _____

Example

① **Social Science** After a hurricane, 1045 people came to a shelter. They are to be moved by bus to housing. Each bus can carry 55 passengers. Assuming that every bus leaves with a full load, write a linear function that relates the number of busloads already gone to the number of people remaining at the shelter. Graph the function that models the situation.

Relate [　　　　] equals [　　] minus [　　] times [　　　　]

Define The total <u>number of people remaining</u> depends on <u>the number of busloads already gone</u>. So <u>number of people remaining</u> is the dependent variable and <u>number of busloads already gone</u> is the independent variable.

Let x = [　　　　　　　　]　　　　Let y = [　　　　　　　　]

Write y = [　　　] − [　　　] · x

The domain is the whole numbers 0 through 19 because the number of buses cannot [　　　　　].

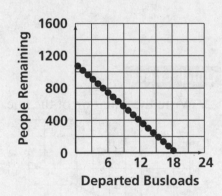

Quick Check

1. A sporting goods store sells cans of tennis balls. There are 3 tennis balls in each can. The coach of the tennis team is buying supplies. Write a linear function that relates the number of cans to the total number of tennis balls. Graph the function that models the situation.

t = [　　　　　　　]　　　　n = [　　　　　　　]

The function is [　　　　　　　].

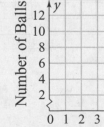

Name_____ Class_____ Date _____

Example

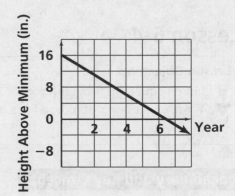

❷ **Engineering** One thing that affects the ability of soil to support the weight of man-made structures is the amount of water below the soil surface. The graph illustrates the changing water table in an urban area, due to water being pumped from drilled wells. The present time is designated as time $t = 0$.

a. What do the slope and the y-intercept mean for the given situation?

The slope is ⬚ . This means that the water level is ⬚

at a rate of ⬚ inches per year.

The y-intercept is ⬚ . This means that at present, the level is

⬚ the minimum.

b. If the graph had the same slope but a y-intercept of 26, what could you conclude about the water table?

You could conclude that the water table was ⬚

minimum. It would take ⬚

for the water to drop to the minimum level.

c. If the graph had a slope of −4.5 in./yr, what could you conclude about the water table?

You could conclude that the water table was ⬚ , at

⬚ .

Quick Check

2. a. Suppose you drew the following graph to represent how far you ride your bike at a steady rate. What is your rate?

⬚

b. If the graph had a slope of 10, what could you conclude about your bike ride?

⬚

Distance Traveled

Name_____ Class_____ Date_____

Lesson 6-4   **Standard Form**

<table>
<tr><td>

Lesson Objectives

 Graph equations using intercepts

 Write equations in standard form

</td><td>

NAEP 2005 Strand: Algebra

Topic: Patterns, Relations, and Functions

Local Standards: _____

</td></tr>
</table>

Vocabulary and Key Concepts

Standard Form of a Linear Equation

The standard form of a linear equation is [   ] , where A, B, and C are real numbers, and A and B are not both zero.

The _____ is the x-coordinate of the point where a line crosses the x-axis.

Example

❶ **Finding x- and y-Intercepts** Find the x- and y-intercepts of $2x + 5y = 6$.

Step 1 To find the x-intercept,
substitute 0 for y and solve for x.

$$2x + 5y = 6$$
$$2x + 5(0) = 6$$

[   ] $x =$ [   ]

$x =$ [   ]

The x-intercept is [   ] .

Step 2 To find the y-intercept,
substitute 0 for x and solve for y.

$$2x + 5y = 6$$
$$2(0) + 5y = 6$$

[   ] $y =$ [   ]

$y =$ [   ]

The y-intercept is [   ] .

Quick Check

1. Find the x- and y-intercepts of $4x - 9y = -12$.

Examples

❷ Graphing Lines Using Intercepts Graph $3x + 5y = 15$ using intercepts.

Step 1 Find the intercepts.

$3x + 5y = 15$

$3x + 5(\boxed{}) = 15$ — Substitute $\boxed{}$ for *y*.

$\boxed{}x = \boxed{}$ — Solve for *x*.

$x = \boxed{}$

$3x + 5y = 15$

$3(\boxed{}) + 5y = 15$ — Substitute $\boxed{}$ for *x*.

$\boxed{}y = \boxed{}$ — Solve for *y*.

$y = \boxed{}$

Step 2 Plot $\left(\boxed{}, 0\right)$ and $\left(0, \boxed{}\right)$. Draw a line through the points.

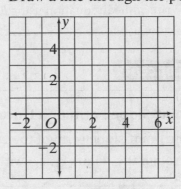

❸ Transforming to Standard Form Write $y = \frac{2}{3}x + 6$ in standard form using integers.

$y = \frac{2}{3}x + 6$

$\boxed{}y = \boxed{}\left(\frac{2}{3}x + 6\right)$ — **Multiply each side by** $\boxed{}$.

$\boxed{}y = \boxed{}x + \boxed{}$ — **Use the Distributive Property.**

$\boxed{} + 3y = \boxed{}$ — **Subtract** $\boxed{}$ **from each side.**

The equation in standard form is $\boxed{}$.

Quick Check

2. Graph $5x + 2y = -10$ using the *x*- and *y*-intercepts.

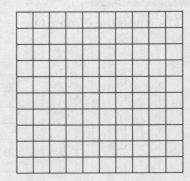

3. Write $y = -\frac{2}{5}x + 1$ in standard form using integers.

Lesson 6-5

Point-Slope Form and Writing Linear Equations

Lesson Objectives	**NAEP 2005 Strand:**
▼ Graph and write linear equations using point-slope form	**Topics:** Patterns, Relations, and Functions; Variables, Expressions, and Operations
▼ Write a linear equation using data	**Local Standards:** _____

Key Concepts

Point-Slope Form of a Linear Equation

The point-slope form of the equation of a nonvertical line that passes through the point (x_1, y_1) with slope m is [   ].

Example

❶ **Graphing Using Point-Slope Form** Graph the equation $y - 2 = \frac{1}{3}(x - 1)$.

The equation shows that the line passes through ([ ], [ ]) with slope [ ].

Start at ([ ], [ ]).

Using the slope, go up [ ] unit and right [ ] units to ([ ], [ ]).

Draw a line through the two points.

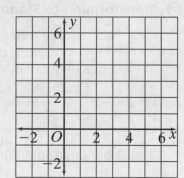

Quick Check

1. Graph the equation $y - 5 = -\frac{2}{3}(x + 2)$.

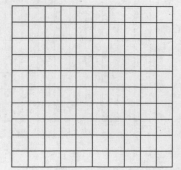

Examples

❷ **Writing an Equation in Point-Slope Form** Write the equation of the line with slope -2 that passes through the point $(3, -3)$.

$y - y_1 = m(x - x_1)$ **Use point-slope form.**

$y - \left(\boxed{}\right) = \boxed{}\left(x - \boxed{}\right)$ **Substitute** $\left(\boxed{}, \boxed{}\right)$ **for** (x_1, y_1) **and** $\boxed{}$ **for** m.

$y + \boxed{} = \boxed{}\left(x - \boxed{}\right)$ **Simplify.**

The equation is $\boxed{}$.

❸ **Using Two Points to Write an Equation** Write equations for the line in point-slope form.

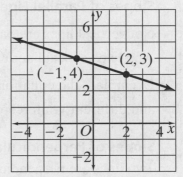

$\dfrac{y_2 - y_1}{x_2 - x_1} = m$ **Find the slope.**

$\dfrac{\boxed{} - \boxed{}}{\boxed{} - \boxed{}} = \boxed{}$ **Substitute** $\left(\boxed{}, \boxed{}\right)$ **and** $\left(\boxed{}, \boxed{}\right)$ **for** (x_2, y_2) **and** (x_1, y_1).

The slope is $\boxed{}$.

$y - y_1 = m(x - x_1)$ **Use point** $(-1, 4)$ **to write the equation.**

$y - \boxed{} = \boxed{}\left(x - \left(\boxed{}\right)\right)$ **Substitute** $\left(\boxed{}, \boxed{}\right)$ **for** (x, y) **and** $\boxed{}$ **for** m.

The equation is $\boxed{}$

Quick Check

2. Write the equation of the line with slope $\frac{2}{5}$ that passes through the point $(10, -8)$.

3. Write an equation for the line in Example 3 in point-slope form using point $(2, 3)$.

Lesson 6-6

Parallel and Perpendicular Lines

Lesson Objectives	NAEP 2005 Strand: Geometry
▼ Determine whether lines are parallel	**Topics:** Algebraic Representations; Relationships Among Geometric Figures
▼ Determine whether lines are perpendicular	**Local Standards:** _____

Vocabulary and Key Concepts

Slopes of Parallel Lines

Nonvertical lines are parallel if _____

Any two vertical lines are parallel.

Example   The equations $y = \frac{2}{3}x + 1$ and $y = \frac{2}{3}x - 3$ have the same slope, $\frac{2}{3}$,

and different y-intercepts. The graphs of the two equations are parallel.

Slopes of Perpendicular Lines

Two lines are perpendicular if the product of their slopes is $\boxed{}$.
A vertical and a horizontal line are also perpendicular.

Example   The slope of $y = -\frac{1}{4}x - 1$ is $-\frac{1}{4}$. The slope of $y = 4x + 2$ is 4.

Since $-\frac{1}{4} \cdot 4 = -1$, the graphs of the two equations are perpendicular.

_____ are lines in the same plane that never intersect.

Perpendicular lines are _____

The product of a number and its negative reciprocal is _____

Example

❶ **Writing Equations of Parallel Lines** Write an equation for the line that
contains $(-2, 3)$ and is parallel to $y = \frac{5}{2}x - 4$.

Step 1 Identify the slope of the given line. The slope of $y = \frac{5}{2}x - 4$ is $\boxed{}$.

Step 2 Write the equation of the line through $(-2, 3)$ using point-slope form.

$y - y_1 = m(x - x_1)$	Use point-slope form.
$y - \boxed{} = \boxed{}\left(x - \boxed{}\right)$	Substitute $\left(\boxed{}, \boxed{}\right)$ for (x_1, y_1) and $\boxed{}$ for m.
$y - \boxed{} = \boxed{}x - \boxed{}\left(\boxed{}\right)$	Use the Distributive Property.
$y - \boxed{} = \boxed{}x + \boxed{}$	Simplify.
$y = \boxed{}x + \boxed{}$	Add $\boxed{}$ to each side and simplify.

Example

❷ Writing Equations for Perpendicular Lines The line in the graph represents the street in front of a house. The sidewalk from the front door is perpendicular to the street. Write an equation representing the sidewalk.

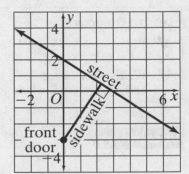

Step 1 Find the slope m of the street.

$$m = \frac{y_2 - y_1}{x_2 - x_1} = \frac{\boxed{} - \boxed{}}{\boxed{} - \boxed{}} = \frac{\boxed{}}{\boxed{}} = -\frac{\boxed{}}{\boxed{}}$$

Points (0, 2) and (3, 0) are on the street.

Step 2 Find the negative reciprocal of the slope.

The negative reciprocal of $-\frac{2}{3}$ is $\boxed{}$, so the slope of the

sidewalk is $\boxed{}$.

The y-intercept is $\boxed{}$.

The equation for the sidewalk is $\boxed{}$.

Quick Check

1. Write an equation for the line that contains $(2, -6)$ and is parallel to $y = 3x + 9$.

2. Write an equation of the line that contains $(1, 8)$ and is perpendicular to $y = \frac{3}{4}x + 1$.

3. Using the diagram in Example 2, write an equation in slope-intercept form for a new sidewalk perpendicular to the street from a front door at $(-1, -1)$.

Lesson 6-7

Scatter Plots and Equations of Lines

Lesson Objectives	NAEP 2005 Strand: Algebra; Data Analysis and Probability
▼ Write an equation for a trend line and use it to make predictions	**Topics:** Algebraic Representations; Characteristics of Data Sets
▼ Write an equation for a line of best fit and use it to make predictions	**Local Standards:** _____

Vocabulary

The _____ is the trend line that shows the relationship between two sets of data most accurately.

The correlation coefficient, r, tells you _____

_____

Examples

1 **Trend Line** Make a scatter plot to represent the data. Draw a trend line and write an equation for the trend line. Use the equation to predict the time needed to travel 32 miles on a bicycle.

Speed on a Bicycle Trip

Miles	5	10	14	18	22
Time (min)	27	46	71	78	107

Step 1 Draw a scatter plot of the data.
Use a straightedge to draw a trend line.
Estimate two points on the line.
Two points are $(5, 27)$ and $(25, 120)$.

Step 2 Write an equation of the trend line.

$$m = \frac{y_2 - y_1}{x_2 - x_1} = \frac{\boxed{} - \boxed{}}{\boxed{} - \boxed{}} = \frac{\boxed{}}{\boxed{}} \approx \boxed{}$$

$$y - y_1 = m(x - x_1) \quad \textbf{Use point-slope form.}$$

$$y - \boxed{} = \boxed{}\left(x - \boxed{}\right) \quad \textbf{Substitute } \boxed{} \textbf{ for } m \textbf{ and } \left(\boxed{}, \boxed{}\right) \textbf{ for } (x_1, y_1).$$

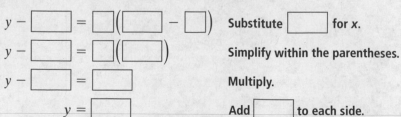

Step 3 Predict the time needed to travel 32 miles.

$$y - \boxed{} = \boxed{}\left(\boxed{} - \boxed{}\right) \quad \textbf{Substitute } \boxed{} \textbf{ for } x.$$

$$y - \boxed{} = \boxed{}\left(\boxed{}\right) \quad \textbf{Simplify within the parentheses.}$$

$$y - \boxed{} = \boxed{} \quad \textbf{Multiply.}$$

$$y = \boxed{} \quad \textbf{Add } \boxed{} \textbf{ to each side.}$$

The time needed to travel 32 miles is about $\boxed{}$ minutes.

❷ Line of Best Fit Find the equation of the line of best fit for the data at right. What is the correlation coefficient?

Use the EDIT feature of the ▨STAT▨ screen on your graphing calculator. Let 95 correspond to 1995. Enter the data for years and then enter the data for crimes.

LinReg

$y = ax + b$	
$a = -248.55$	**slope**
$b = 28945.07$	**y-intercept**
$r^2 = .9711922459$	
$r = -.9854908654$	**correlation coefficient**

U.S. Crime Rate (per 100,000 inhabitants)

Year	No. of Crimes
1995	5275.9
1996	5086.6
1997	4930.0
1998	4619.3
1999	4266.8

Source: *Crime in the United States*

Use the CALC feature of the ▨STAT▨ screen. Find the equation for the line of best fit.

The equation for the line of best fit is ⬚⬚⬚⬚⬚⬚⬚⬚⬚⬚ for values *a* and *b* rounded to the nearest hundredth. The value of the correlation coefficient is ⬚⬚⬚⬚⬚⬚⬚ .

Quick Check

1. Graph the data below and draw a trend line. Find an equation for the trend line. Estimate the number of calories in a fast-food meal that has 14 g of fat.

Calories and Fat in Selected Fast-Food Meals

Fat (g)	6	7	10	19	20	27	36
Calories	276	260	220	388	430	550	633

2. Find the equation of the line of best fit. Let 91 correspond to 1991. What is the correlation coefficient?

Yearly Box Office Gross for Movies (billions)

1991 $4.8	1992 $4.9	1993 $5.2	1994 $5.4	1995 $5.5	1996 $6.0	1997 $6.4	1998 $7.0	1999 $7.4

Lesson 6-8

Graphing Absolute Value Equations

Lesson Objective	**NAEP 2005 Strand:** Algebra
▼ Translate the graph of an absolute value equation	**Topic:** Algebraic Representations
	Local Standards: _____

Vocabulary

The graph of an absolute value equation forms a ___ that opens ___ or _____.

A _____ is a shift of a graph horizontally, vertically, or both.

Examples

❶ **Graphing a Vertical Translation** Graph $y = |x| - 3$
by translating $y = |x|$. Start with a graph of $y = |x|$.
Translate the graph down [   ] units.

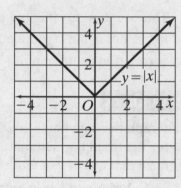

❷ **Writing an Absolute Value Equation** Write an equation for each translation of $y = |x|$.
 a. 9 units down
   The equation is [   ].

 b. 13 units up
   The equation is [   ].

❸ **Graphing a Horizontal Translation** Graph each equation by translating $y = |x|$.
 a. $y = |x + 2.5|$

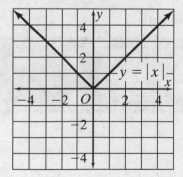

 b. $y = |x - 2.5|$

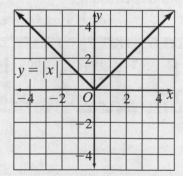

Start with a graph of $y = |x|$.
Translate the graph [   ] 2.5 units.

Start with a graph of $y = |x|$.
Translate the graph [   ] 2.5 units.

Daily Notetaking Guide [L1]

Name_____ Class_____ Date _____

Example

④ **Writing an Absolute Value Equation** Write an equation for each translation of $y = |x|$.

  a. 10 units left

    The equation is [＿＿＿＿＿＿＿].

  b. 7 units right

    The equation is [＿＿＿＿＿＿＿].

Quick Check

1. Graph each function by translating $y = |x|$.

  a. $y = |x| + 4$

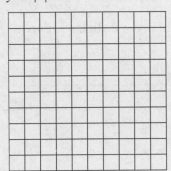

  b. $y = |x| - 5$

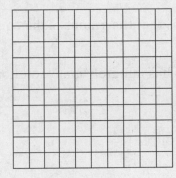

2. For each translation of $y = |x|$, write an equation.

  a. 2 units up

  b. 5 units down

3. Graph each function by translating $y = |x|$.

  a. $y = |x - 4|$

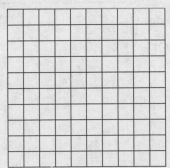

  b. $y = |x + 1|$

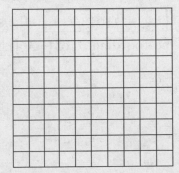

4. Write an equation for each translation of $y = |x|$.

  a. 5 units right

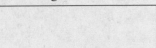

  b. 7 units left

Lesson 7-1

Solving Systems by Graphing

Lesson Objectives	NAEP 2005 Strand: Algebra
▼1 Solve systems by graphing	**Topics:** Equations and Inequalities
▼2 Analyze special types of systems	**Local Standards:** _____

Vocabulary

A _____ is two or more linear equations using the same variables.

A solution of a system of linear equations is _____

_____

_____ means that the graphs of the equations in a system are parallel, with no

point of intersection.

A system of equations has infinitely many solutions when _____

_____

Examples

① **Solving a System of Equations** Solve by graphing. $y = -x + 1$
$y = -2x - 2$

Graph both equations on the same coordinate plane.

$y = -x + 1$ The slope is ☐.

The y-intercept is ☐.

$y = -2x - 2$ The slope is ☐.

The y-intercept is ☐.

The graphs intersect at ☐, so ☐ is the solution of the system.

Check by substituting the coordinates of $(-3, 4)$ into each equation.

❷ Systems With No Solution Solve by graphing. $y = 3x + 2$
$y = 3x - 2$

Graph both equations on the same coordinate plane.

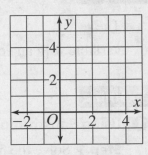

$y = 3x + 2$ **The slope is** ☐. **The y-intercept is** ☐.

$y = 3x - 2$ **The slope is** ☐. **The y-intercept is** ☐.

The lines are ☐, so there are ☐ solutions.

❸ Systems With Infinitely Many Solutions Solve by graphing.
$3x + 4y = 12$

$y = -\frac{3}{4}x + 3$

Graph both equations on the same coordinate plane.

$3x + 4y = 12$ **The y-intercept is** ☐. **The x-intercept is** ☐.

$y = -\frac{3}{4}x + 3$ **The slope is** ☐. **The y-intercept is** ☐.

The graphs are ☐ line, so the solutions are an

☐ of ordered pairs (x, y), such that $y = -\frac{3}{4}x + 3$.

Quick Check

1. Solve by graphing. Check your solution.

a. $y = x + 5$
$y = -4x$

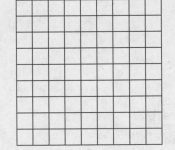

b. $y = \frac{1}{5}x + 4$
$5y = x + 20$

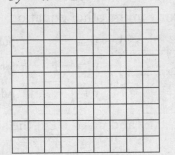

2. Without graphing, how can you tell if a system has no solution?
Give an example.

Lesson 7-2

Solving Systems Using Substitution

Lesson Objective	NAEP 2005 Strand: Algebra
▼ Solve systems using substitution	**Topics:** Equations and Inequalities
	Local Standards: _____

Vocabulary

The _____ is a method of solving a system of equations by replacing one variable with an equivalent expression containing the other variable.

Example

❶ Using Substitution and the Distributive Property Solve using substitution.

$$-2x + y = -1$$
$$4x + 2y = 12$$

Step 1 Solve the first equation for y because it has a coefficient of 1.

$$-2x + y = -1$$

$y = \boxed{}$ **Add** $\boxed{}$ **to each side.**

Step 2 Write an equation containing only one variable and solve.

$4x + 2y = 12$ **Start with the other equation.**

$4x + 2\left(\boxed{}\right) = 12$ **Substitute** $\boxed{}$ **for y in that equation.**

$4x + \boxed{} = 12$ **Use the Distributive Property.**

$\boxed{} = \boxed{}$ **Combine like terms and add** $\boxed{}$ **to each side.**

$x = \boxed{}$ **Divide each side by** $\boxed{}$.

Step 3 Solve for y in the other equation.

$-2\left(\boxed{}\right) + y = -1$ **Substitute** $\boxed{}$ **for x.**

$\boxed{} + y = -1$ **Simplify.**

$y = \boxed{}$ **Add** $\boxed{}$ **to each side.**

Since $x = \boxed{}$ and $y = \boxed{}$, the solution is $\left(\boxed{}\right)$.

Quick Check

1. Solve using substitution. Check your solution.

a. $y = 2x$
      $7x - y = 15$

b. $6y + 8x = 28$
      $3 = 2x - y$

Example

❷ **Using Substitution** A class with 26 students is going to the zoo. Five chaperones will each drive a van or a car. Each van seats 7 persons, including the driver. Each car seats 5 persons, including the driver. How many vans and cars will be needed?

Let $\boxed{v}$ = number of vans and $\boxed{c}$ = number of cars.

drivers $\quad \boxed{v} + \boxed{c} = 5$

people $\quad 7\boxed{v} + 5\boxed{c} = 31$

Solve using substitution.

Step 1 Write an equation containing only one variable.

$v + c = 5 \qquad$ **Solve the first equation for c.**

$c = \boxed{} + 5$

Step 2 Write and solve an equation containing the variable v.

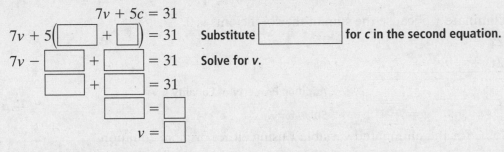

$7v + 5c = 31$

$7v + 5\left(\boxed{} + \boxed{}\right) = 31 \qquad$ **Substitute** $\boxed{}$ **for c in the second equation.**

$7v - \boxed{} + \boxed{} = 31 \qquad$ **Solve for v.**

$\boxed{} + \boxed{} = 31$

$\boxed{} = \boxed{}$

$v = \boxed{}$

Step 3 Solve for c in either equation.

$\boxed{} + c = 5 \qquad$ **Substitute 3 for v in the first equation.**

$c = \boxed{}$

$\boxed{}$ vans and $\boxed{}$ cars are needed to transport 31 persons.

Quick Check

2. A rectangle is 4 times longer than it is wide. The perimeter of the rectangle is 30 cm. Find the dimensions of the rectangle.

Lesson 7-3

Solving Systems Using Elimination

Lesson Objectives	NAEP 2005 Strand: Algebra
▼ Solve systems by adding or subtracting	**Topics:** Equations and Inequalities
▼ Multiply first when solving systems	**Local Standards:** _____

Vocabulary

The _____ is a method for solving a system of linear equations in which you add or subtract the equations to eliminate a variable.

Example

❶ **Adding Equations** Solve by elimination. $2x + 3y = 11$
$-2x + 9y = 1$

Step 1 Eliminate x because the sum of the coefficients is 0.

$$2x + 3y = 11$$
$$\underline{-2x + 9y = 1}$$
$$\boxed{} + \boxed{} = \boxed{} \qquad \text{Addition Property of Equality}$$
$$y = \boxed{} \qquad \text{Solve for } y.$$

Step 2 Solve for the eliminated variable x using either original equation.

$$2x + 3y = 11 \qquad \text{Choose the first equation.}$$
$$2x + 3\left(\boxed{}\right) = 11 \qquad \text{Substitute } \boxed{} \text{ for } y.$$
$$2x + \boxed{} = 11 \qquad \text{Solve for } x.$$
$$2x = \boxed{}$$
$$x = \boxed{}$$

Since $x = \boxed{}$ and $y = \boxed{}$, the solution is $\left(\boxed{}, \boxed{}\right)$.

Check See if $(4, 1)$ makes the equation *not* used in Step 2 true.

$$-2\left(\boxed{}\right) + 9\left(\boxed{}\right) \stackrel{?}{=} 1 \qquad \text{Substitute } \boxed{} \text{ for } x \text{ and } \boxed{} \text{ for } y \text{ into the second equation.}$$
$$\boxed{} + \boxed{} \stackrel{?}{=} 1$$
$$\boxed{} = 1 ✔$$

Example

❷ **Multiplying Both Equations** Solve by elimination. $3x + 5y = 10$
$5x + 7y = 10$

Step 1 Eliminate one variable.

| **Start with the given system.** | **To prepare to eliminate x, multiply one equation by ☐ and the other equation by ☐.** | **Subtract the equations to eliminate x.** |

$3x + 5y = 10$ → ☐$(3x + 5y = 10)$ → $15x + \ 25y \ = \ 50$

$\underline{5x + 7y = 10}$ → $\underline{☐(5x + 7y = 10)}$ → $\underline{15x + \ 21y \ = \ 30}$

☐ + ☐ = ☐

Step 2 Solve for y.

☐y = ☐

y = ☐

Step 3 Solve for the eliminated variable x using either of the original equations.

$3x + 5y = 10$ **Use the first equation.**

$3x + 5($☐$) = 10$ **Substitute** ☐ **for y.**

$3x +$ ☐ $= 10$

$3x =$ ☐

$x =$ ☐

The solution is ☐.

Quick Check

Solve by elimination.

1. $6x - 3y = 3$
     $-6x + 5y = 3$

2. $15x + 3y = \ \ 9$
    $10x + 7y = -4$

Lesson 7-4

Applications of Linear Systems

Lesson Objective ▼ Write systems of linear equations	NAEP 2005 Strand: Algebra Topics: Equations and Inequalities Local Standards: _____

Key Concepts

Methods for Solving Systems of Linear Equations

Graphing   Use graphing for solving systems that are easily graphed. If the point of intersection does not have integers for coordinates, find the exact solution by using one of the methods below or by using a graphing calculator.

Substitution   Use substitution when one variable has a coefficient of 1 or -1.

Elimination   Use elimination for solving any system.

Example

1 **Writing Systems** A chemist has one solution that is 50% acid. She has another solution that is 25% acid. How many liters of each type of acid solution should she combine to get 10 liters of a 40% acid solution?

Define Let $\boxed{a}$ = volume of the 50% solution.

Let $\boxed{b}$ = volume of the 25% solution.

Relate volume of solution   amount of acid

Write $\boxed{} + \boxed{} = 10$ $\boxed{}a + \boxed{}b = \boxed{}(10)$

Step 1 Choose one of the equations and solve for a variable.

$a + b = 10$ **Solve for a.**

$a = 10 - \boxed{}$ **Subtract** $\boxed{}$ **from each side.**

Step 2 Find b.

$\boxed{}a + \boxed{}b = \boxed{}(10)$

$0.5(\boxed{}) + 0.25b = 0.4(10)$ **Substitute** $\boxed{}$ **for a. Use parentheses.**

$5 - \boxed{} + 0.25b = 0.4(10)$ **Use the Distributive Property.**

$5 - \boxed{} = \boxed{}$ **Simplify.**

$-0.25b = \boxed{}$ **Subtract** $\boxed{}$ **from each side.**

$b = \boxed{}$ **Divide each side by** $\boxed{}$.

Step 3 Find a. Substitute $\boxed{}$ for b in either equation.

$a + \boxed{} = 10$ **Solve for a.**

$a = \boxed{}$ **Subtract** $\boxed{}$ **from each side.**

To make 10 L of 40% acid solution, you need $\boxed{}$ L of 50% solution and $\boxed{}$ L of 25% solution.

Example

❷ **Finding a Break-Even Point** Suppose you have a typing service. You buy a personal computer for $1,750 on which to do your typing. You charge $5.50 per page for typing. Expenses are $.50 per page for ink, paper, electricity, and other expenses. How many pages must you type to break even?

Define Let $\boxed{p}$ = the number of pages.

Let $\boxed{d}$ = the amount of dollars of expenses or income.

Relate

Expenses are per-page expenses plus computer purchase.	Income is price times pages typed.

Write $\boxed{} = 0.5\boxed{} + 1{,}750$ $\boxed{} = 5.5\boxed{}$

Choose a method to solve this system. Use substitution since it is easy to substitute for *d* with these equations.

$d = 0.5p + 1{,}750$ **Start with one equation.**

$\boxed{} = 0.5p + 1{,}750$ **Substitute** $\boxed{}$ **for *d*.**

$\boxed{} = 1{,}750$ **Solve for *p*.**

$p = \boxed{}$

To break even, you must type 350 pages.

Quick Check

1. Suppose a chemist combines a 25% acid solution and a 50% acid solution to make 40 L of 45% acid solution. How many liters of each solution did she use?

2. Suppose an antique car club publishes a newsletter. Expenses are $.35 for printing and mailing each copy, plus $770 total for research and writing. The price of the newsletter is $.55 per copy. How many copies of the newsletter must the club sell to break even?

Lesson 7-5

Linear Inequalities

Lesson Objectives	NAEP 2005 Strand: Algebra
▼ Graph linear inequalities ▼ Write and use linear inequalities when modeling real-world situations	**Topics:** Variables, Expressions, and Operations; Equations and Inequalities **Local Standards:** _____

Vocabulary

A _____ is a mathematical sentence that describes a region of the coordinate

plane having a boundary line.

Each point in the region is a [   ] of the inequality.

The solutions of an inequality are _____

_____

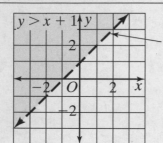

Each point on a *dashed* boundary line is not a solution.

Each point on a *solid* boundary line is a solution.

Example

① **Rewriting to Graph an Inequality** Graph $4x - 3y \geq 6$.
Solve $4x - 3y \geq 6$ for y.
$4x - 3y \geq 6$

$-3y \geq \boxed{} + 6$ **Subtract** [   ] **from each side.**

$y \boxed{} \boxed{} x - 2$ **Divide each side by** [   ]. **Reverse the inequality symbol.**

Graph $y = \boxed{} x - \boxed{}$. The coordinates of the points on the

boundary line make the inequality true. So, use a [   ] line.

Since $y \leq \boxed{} x - \boxed{}$, shade [   ] the boundary line.

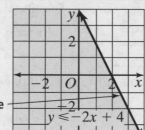

Quick Check

1. a. Graph $y \geq 3x - 1$.

b. Graph $6x + 8y \geq 12$.

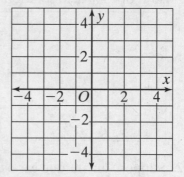

Daily Notetaking Guide L1

Example

❷ **Making a Budget** Suppose your budget allows you to spend no more than $24 for decorations for a party. Streamers cost $2 a roll and tablecloths cost $6 each. Use intercepts to graph the inequality that represents the situation. Find three possible combinations of streamers and tablecloths you can buy.

Relate | cost of streamers | plus | cost of tablecloths | is less than or equal to | total budget |

Define Let $\boxed{s}$ = the number of rolls of streamers.

Let $\boxed{t}$ = the number of tablecloths.

Write $\quad 2\boxed{} \quad + \quad 6\boxed{} \quad\quad \le \quad\quad \boxed{}$

Graph $2s + 6t = 24$ by graphing the intercepts $\left(\boxed{},\boxed{}\right)$

and $\left(\boxed{},\boxed{}\right)$. The coordinates of the points on the boundary

line make the inequality true. So, use a $\boxed{}$ line.

Graph only in Quadrant I, since you cannot buy a negative amount of decorations.

Test the point $(0, 0)$.

$$2s + 6t \le 24$$

$2\left(\boxed{}\right) + 6\left(\boxed{}\right) \le 24$ **Substitute (0, 0) for (s, t).**

$\boxed{} \le 24$ **Since the inequality is true, (0, 0) is a solution.**

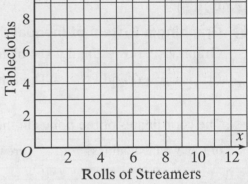

Shade the region containing $(0, 0)$.

Since the boundary line is included in the graph, the intercepts are also solutions

to the inequality. The solution $(9, 1)$ means that if you buy $\boxed{}$ rolls of streamers,

you can buy $\boxed{}$ tablecloth. Three solutions are $(9, 1)$, $\left(\boxed{},\boxed{}\right)$, and $\left(\boxed{},\boxed{}\right)$.

Quick Check

2. Suppose you plan to spend no more than $24 on meat for a cookout. Hamburger costs $3.00/lb and chicken wings cost $2.40/lb. Write and graph an equation to find three possible combinations of hamburger and chicken wings you can buy.

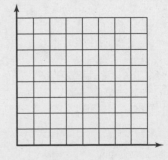

Lesson 7-6

Systems of Linear Inequalities

Lesson Objectives	**NAEP 2005 Strand:** Algebra
1 Solve systems of linear inequalities by graphing	**Topics:** Equations and Inequalities
2 Model real-world situations using systems of linear inequalities	**Local Standards:** _____

Vocabulary

A _____ is two or more inequalities using the same variables.

A solution of a system of linear inequalities is _____

_____

Example

1 Graphing a System of Inequalities Solve by graphing.

Graph $y < -\frac{1}{2}x + 2$ and $y < 4$ by first graphing the boundaries

$y \boxed{} -\frac{1}{2}x + 2$ and $y \boxed{} 4$. Then shade the appropriate regions.

The coordinates of the points in the region where the $\boxed{}$

of the two inequalities $\boxed{}$ are the $\boxed{}$ of the system.

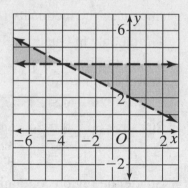

Quick Check

1. Solve by graphing.

$y \geq -x + 2$

$2x + 4y < 4$

Name_____ Class_____ Date _____

Example

❷ **Graphing Inequalities** Suppose you have two jobs, babysitting for $5 per hour and sacking groceries for $6 per hour. You can work no more than 20 hours each week, but you need to earn at least $90 per week. How many hours can you work at each job?

Define Let $\boxed{b}$ = hours of babysitting.

Let $\boxed{s}$ = hours of sacking groceries.

Relate

| the number of hours worked | is less than or equal to | $\boxed{20}$ | the amount earned | is at least | $\boxed{90}$ |

Write $\boxed{} + \boxed{}$ $\le$ $\boxed{}$ $5\boxed{} + 6\boxed{}$ $\ge$ $\boxed{}$

Solve by graphing. $b + s \le 20$
$5b + 6s \ge 90$

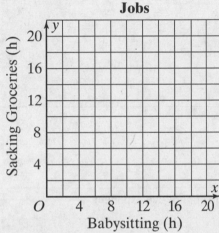

Jobs

The solutions are all the coordinates of the points that are nonnegative numbers in the shaded region and on the lines $b + s = 20$ and $5b + 6s = 90$.

Quick Check

2. **a.** Give two solutions from the graph in Example 2.

   b. Critical Thinking Why are the solutions to the problem only nonnegative numbers?

Name_____ Class_____ Date_____

Lesson 8-1

Zero and Negative Exponents

<table>
<tr><td>

Lesson Objectives

▼ ① Simplify expressions with zero and negative exponents

▼ ② Evaluate exponential expressions

</td><td>

NAEP 2005 Strand: Number Properties and Operations

Topics: Number Sense; Properties of Number and Operations

Local Standards: _____

</td></tr>
</table>

Key Concepts

Zero as an Exponent

For every nonzero number a, $a^0 = 1$.

Examples $5^0 = 1$ $(-2)^0 = \square$ $(1.02)^0 = \square$ $\left(\frac{1}{3}\right)^0 = \square$

Negative Exponent

For every nonzero number a and integer n, $a^{-n} = \frac{1}{a^n}$.

Examples $6^{-4} = \frac{1}{6^4}$ $(-8)^{-1} = \frac{1}{(-8)^1}$

Examples

❶ **Simplifying a Power** Simplify:

a. $3^{-2} = \boxed{}$ **Use the definition of negative exponent.**

$\phantom{3^{-2}} = \boxed{}$ **Simplify.**

b. $(-22.4)^0 = \square$ **Use the definition of zero as an exponent.**

❷ **Simplifying an Exponential Expression** Simplify the expression.

$\frac{1}{x^{-3}} = 1 \div x^{-3}$ **Rewrite using a division symbol.**

$= 1 \div \dfrac{1}{\boxed{}}$ **Use the definition of negative exponent.**

$= 1 \cdot \boxed{}$ **Multiply by the reciprocal of $\frac{1}{x^3}$, which is $\boxed{}$.**

$= \boxed{}$ **Identity Property of Multiplication**

Quick Check

1. Simplify each expression.

a. 3^{-4}

b. $(-7)^0$

Example

❸ Evaluating an Exponential Expression Evaluate $4x^2y^{-3}$ for $x = 3$ and $y = -2$.

$$4x^2y^{-3} = 4\left(\boxed{}\right)^2\left(\boxed{}\right)^{-3}$$ **Substitute** $\boxed{}$ **for** x **and** $\boxed{}$ **for** y.

$$= \frac{4\left(\boxed{}\right)^2}{\left(\boxed{}\right)^3}$$ **Use the definition of negative exponent.**

$$= \frac{36}{-8} = \boxed{}$$ **Simplify.**

Quick Check

2. Simplify each expression.

   a. $11m^{-5}$ **b.** $7s^{-4}t^2$

   c. $\dfrac{2}{a^{-3}}$ **d.** $\dfrac{n^{-5}}{v^2}$

3. Evaluate each expression for $n = -2$ and $w = 5$.

   a. $n^{-3}w^0$ **b.** $\dfrac{n^{-1}}{w^2}$

   c. $\dfrac{w^0}{n^4}$ **d.** $\dfrac{1}{nw^{-2}}$

Lesson 8-2

Scientific Notation

Lesson Objectives	NAEP 2005 Strand: Number Properties and Operations
▼ Write numbers in scientific and standard notation	**Topics:** Number Sense; Estimation
▼ Use scientific notation	**Local Standards:** _____

Key Concepts

Scientific Notation

A number in scientific notation is written as the product of two factors in the form $a \times 10^n$, where n is an integer and $1 \le a < 10$.

Examples 3.4×10^6 5.43×10^{13} 2.1×10^{-10}

Examples

❶ Writing a Number in Scientific Notation Write each number in scientific notation.

a. 234,000,000

$234,000,000 = \boxed{} \times 10^{\boxed{}}$ **Move the decimal point** $\boxed{}$ **places to the left and use** $\boxed{}$ **as an exponent. Drop the zeros after the 4.**

b. 0.000063

$0.000063 = \boxed{} \times 10^{\boxed{}}$ **Move the decimal point** $\boxed{}$ **places to the right and use** $\boxed{}$ **as an exponent. Drop the zeros before the 6.**

❷ Writing a Number in Standard Notation Write each number in standard notation.

a. elephant's mass: 8.8×10^4 kg

$8.8 \times 10^4 = \boxed{}$

$= \boxed{}$ kg

A positive exponent indicates a number greater than 10. Move the decimal point $\boxed{}$ **places to the right.**

b. ant's mass: 7.3×10^{-5} kg

$7.3 \times 10^{-5} = \boxed{}$

$= \boxed{}$ kg

A negative exponent indicates a number between 0 and 1. Move the decimal point $\boxed{}$ **places to the left.**

Example

❸ **Multiplying a Number in Scientific Notation** Simplify. Write each answer using scientific notation.

a. $6(8 \times 10^{-4}) = (\boxed{} \cdot \boxed{}) \times 10^{-4}$ **Associative Property of Multiplication**

$\phantom{6(8 \times 10^{-4})} = \boxed{} \times 10^{-4}$ **Simplify inside the parentheses.**

$\phantom{6(8 \times 10^{-4})} = \boxed{} \times 10^{\boxed{}}$ **Write the product in scientific notation.**

b. $0.3(1.3 \times 10^{3}) = (\boxed{} \cdot \boxed{}) \times 10^{3}$ **Associative Property of Multiplication**

$\phantom{0.3(1.3 \times 10^{3})} = \boxed{} \times 10^{3}$ **Simplify inside the parentheses.**

$\phantom{0.3(1.3 \times 10^{3})} = \boxed{} \times 10^{\boxed{}}$ **Write the product in scientific notation.**

Quick Check

1. Write each number in scientific notation.

a. 0.0000325

b. 46,205,000

2. Write each number in standard notation.

a. 5.07×10^{4}

b. 8.3×10^{-2}

3. Simplify. Write each answer using scientific notation.

a. $2.5(6 \times 10^{3})$

b. $0.4(2 \times 10^{-9})$

Lesson 8-3

Multiplication Properties of Exponents

Lesson Objectives	**NAEP 2005 Strand:** Number Properties and Operations
▼ Multiply powers	**Topics:** Number Sense; Estimation
▼ Work with scientific notation	**Local Standards:** _____

Key Concepts

Multiplying Powers With the Same Base

For every nonzero number a and integers m and n, $a^m \cdot a^n = a^{m+n}$.

Example $3^5 \cdot 3^4 = 3^{5+4} = 3^{\boxed{}}$

Examples

❶ **Multiplying Powers** Rewrite the expression using each base only once.

$7^3 \cdot 7^2 = 7^{3\boxed{}2}$ ⬚ $\boxed{}$ exponents of powers with the same base.

$= \boxed{}$ Simplify the sum of the exponents.

❷ **Multiplying Powers in an Algebraic Expression** Simplify the expression.

$4x^6 \cdot 5x^{-4} = (\boxed{} \cdot \boxed{})(x^6 \cdot x^{-4})$ $\boxed{}$ **Property of Multiplication**

$= \boxed{}\left(x^{\boxed{}+\left(\boxed{}\right)}\right)$ Add exponents of powers with the same base.

$= \boxed{}$ Simplify.

Quick Check

1. Rewrite each expression using each base only once.

a. $5^3 \cdot 5^6$ **b.** $2^4 \cdot 2^{-3}$ **c.** $7^{-3} \cdot 7^2 \cdot 7^6$

Example

❸ **Multiplying Numbers in Scientific Notation** Simplify $(3 \times 10^{-3})(7 \times 10^{-5})$. Write the answer in scientific notation.

$(3 \times 10^{-3})(7 \times 10^{-5}) = \left(3 \cdot \boxed{}\right)\left(10^{\boxed{}} \cdot 10^{\boxed{}}\right)$ **Commutative and Associative Properties of Multiplication**

$\qquad = \boxed{} \times 10^{\boxed{}}$ **Simplify.**

$\qquad = 2.1 \times 10^{\boxed{}} \cdot 10^{\boxed{}}$ **Write 21 in scientific notation.**

$\qquad = 2.1 \times 10^{\boxed{} + \boxed{}}$ **Add exponents of powers with the same base.**

$\qquad = 2.1 \times 10^{\boxed{}}$ **Simplify.**

Quick Check

2. Simplify each expression.

a. $n^2 \cdot n^3 \cdot 7n$

b. $2y^3 \cdot 7x^2 \cdot 2y^4$

c. $m^2 \cdot n^{-2} \cdot 7m$

3. Simplify each expression. Write each answer in scientific notation.

a. $(2.5 \times 10^8)(6 \times 10^3)$

b. $(1.5 \times 10^{-2})(3 \times 10^4)$

c. $(9 \times 10^{-6})(7 \times 10^{-9})$

Lesson 8-4

More Multiplication Properties of Exponents

Lesson Objectives	NAEP 2005 Strand: Number Properties and Operations
▼ Raise a power to a power ▼ Raise a product to a power	Topic: Properties of Number and Operations Local Standards: _____

Key Concepts

Raising a Power to a Power

For every nonzero number a and integers m and n, $(a^m)^n = a^{mn}$.

Examples $(5^4)^2 = 5^{4 \cdot 2} = 5^8$ $\qquad (n^2)^5 = n^{2 \cdot 5} = n^{10}$

Raising a Product to a Power

For every nonzero number a and b and integer n, $(ab)^n = a^n b^n$.

Example $(3x)^4 = 3^4 x^4 = 81x^4$

Examples

❶ **Simplifying a Power Raised to a Power** Simplify $(a^3)^4$.

$(a^3)^4 = a^3 \boxed{} 4$ $\boxed{}$ exponents when raising a power to a power.

$\qquad = a^{\boxed{}}$ **Simplify.**

❷ **Simplifying an Expression With Powers** Simplify $b^2(b^3)^{-2}$.

$b^2(b^3)^{-2} = b^2 \cdot b^3 \boxed{} (-2)$ $\boxed{}$ exponents in $(b^3)^{-2}$.

$\qquad = b^2 \cdot b^{\boxed{}}$ **Simplify.**

$\qquad = b^2 \boxed{} (-6)$ $\boxed{}$ exponents when multiplying powers of the same base.

$\qquad = b^{\boxed{}}$ **Simplify.**

$\qquad = \boxed{}$ **Write using only positive exponents.**

Quick Check

Simplify.

1. $(a^4)^7$

2a. $(a^{-4})^7$

2b. $(n^4)^3 \cdot n^5$

Name_____ Class_____ Date _____

Examples

❸ **Simplifying a Product Raised to a Power** Simplify $(4xy^3)^2(x^3)^{-3}$.

$(4xy^3)^2(x^3)^{-3} = 4^{\square}x^{\square}(y^3)^{\square} \cdot (x^3)^{-3}$ **Raise the three factors to the second power.**

$= 4^2 \cdot x^2 \cdot y^{\square} \cdot x^{\boxed{}}$ $\boxed{}$ **exponents of a power raised to a power.**

$= 4^2 \cdot x^2 \cdot x^{\boxed{}} \cdot y^{\square}$ **Use the Commutative Property of Multiplication.**

$= 4^2 \cdot x^{\boxed{}} \cdot y^6$ **Add exponents of powers with the same base.**

$= \boxed{}$ **Simplify.**

❹ **Applying Multiplication Properties of Exponents** An object has a mass of 10^2 kg. The expression $10^2 \cdot (3 \times 10^8)^2$ describes the amount of resting energy in joules the object contains. Simplify the expression.

$10^2 \cdot (3 \times 10^8)^2 = 10^{\square} \cdot 3^{\square} \cdot (10^8)^{\square}$ **Raise each factor within parentheses to the second power.**

$= 10^{\square} \cdot 3^{\square} \cdot 10^{\boxed{}}$ **Simplify $(10^8)^2$.**

$= 3^{\square} \cdot 10^{\square} \cdot 10^{\boxed{}}$ **Use the Commutative Property of Multiplication.**

$= 3^{\square} \cdot 10^{\square + \boxed{}}$ **Add exponents of powers with the same base.**

$= \square \times 10^{\boxed{}}$ **Simplify. Write in scientific notation.**

Quick Check

3. Simplify each expression.

   a. $(2z)^4$ **b.** $(4g^5)^{-2}$ **c.** $(2a^3)^5(3ab^2)^3$

4. An hour of television use consumes 1.45×10^{-1} kWh (kilowatt-hour) of electricity. Each kilowatt-hour of electricity use is equivalent to 3.6×10^6 joules of energy. Simplify the expression $(1.45 \times 10^{-1})(3.6 \times 10^6)$ to find how many joules a television uses in 1 hour.

Name_____ Class_____ Date_____

Lesson 8-5   **Division Properties of Exponents**

<table>
<tr><td>

Lesson Objectives
▼ 1 Divide powers with the same base
▼ 2 Raise a quotient to a power

</td><td>

NAEP 2005 Strand: Number Properties and Operations
Topic: Properties of Number and Operations
Local Standards: _____

</td></tr>
</table>

Key Concepts

Dividing Powers With the Same Base

For every nonzero number a and integers m and n, $\frac{a^m}{a^n} = a^{m-n}$.

Example $\frac{3^7}{3^3} = 3^{7-3} = 3^{\boxed{}}$

Raising a Quotient to a Power

For every nonzero number a and b and integer n, $\left(\frac{a}{b}\right)^n = \frac{a^n}{b^n}$.

Example $\left(\frac{4}{5}\right)^3 = \frac{4^3}{5^3} = \boxed{}$

Examples

❶ **Simplifying an Algebraic Expression** Simplify.

$\frac{p^3 j^{-4}}{p^{-3} j^6} = p^{3-\left(\boxed{}\right)} j^{-4\boxed{}6}$ $\boxed{}$ exponents when dividing powers with the same base.

$= p^{\boxed{}} j^{\boxed{}}$ **Simplify.**

$= \boxed{}$ **Rewrite using positive exponents.**

❷ **Raising a Quotient to a Power** Simplify $\left(\frac{3}{y^3}\right)^4$.

$\left(\frac{3}{y^3}\right)^4 = \frac{3^{\boxed{}}}{(y^3)^{\boxed{}}}$ **Raise the numerator and the denominator to the $\boxed{}$ power.**

$= \frac{3^4}{y^{\boxed{}}}$ **Multiply the exponent in the denominator.**

$= \boxed{}$ **Simplify.**

Example

❸ Simplifying an Exponential Expression

Simplify $\left(\frac{2}{3}\right)^{-3}$.

$\left(\frac{2}{3}\right)^{-3} = \left(\boxed{}\right)^{\boxed{}}$ **Rewrite using the reciprocal of $\frac{2}{3}$.**

$= \dfrac{3^{\boxed{}}}{2^{\boxed{}}}$ **Raise the numerator and the denominator to the $\boxed{}$ power.**

$= \boxed{}$ or $\boxed{}$ **Simplify.**

Quick Check

1. Simplify each expression.

a. $\dfrac{b^4}{b^9}$

b. $\dfrac{a^2 b}{a^4 b^3}$

c. $\dfrac{m^{-1} n^2}{m^3 n}$

2. Simplify each expression.

a. $\left(\dfrac{3}{x^2}\right)^2$

b. $\left(\dfrac{x}{y^2}\right)^3$

c. $\left(\dfrac{t^7}{2^3}\right)^2$

3. Simplify each expression.

a. $\left(\dfrac{3}{4}\right)^{-3}$

b. $\left(\dfrac{-1}{2}\right)^{-5}$

c. $\left(\dfrac{2r}{s}\right)^{-1}$

Lesson 8-6

Geometric Sequences

Lesson Objectives	NAEP 2005 Strand: Algebra
▼ 1 Form geometric sequences ▼ 2 Use formulas when describing geometric sequences	**Topic:** Patterns, Relations, and Functions **Local Standards:** _____

Vocabulary and Key Concepts

Geometric Sequence

$$A(n) = a \cdot r^{n-1}$$

nth term   first term   common ratio   term number

A _____ is a number sequence formed by multiplying a term in a sequence by a fixed number to find the next term.

A common ratio is _____

Example

1 **Finding the Common Ratio** Find the common ratio of each sequence.

a. $3, -15, 75, -375, \ldots$

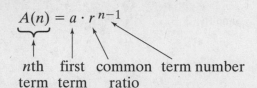

The common ratio is ☐.

b. $3, \frac{3}{2}, \frac{3}{4}, \frac{3}{8}, \ldots$

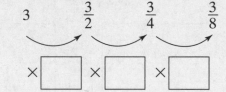

The common ratio is ☐.

Quick Check

1. Find the common ratio of each sequence.

a. $750, 150, 30, 6, \ldots$

b. $-3, -6, -12, -24, \ldots$

Name_____ Class_____ Date _____

Examples

❷ Arithmetic or Geometric Sequence Determine whether each sequence is arithmetic or geometric.

a. 162, 54, 18, 6, . . .

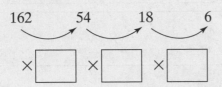

162　　54　　18　　6

× ☐　× ☐　× ☐

The sequence has a ☐☐☐☐☐

ratio. The sequence is ☐☐☐☐☐ .

b. 98, 101, 104, 107, . . .

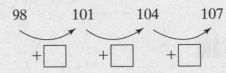

98　　101　　104　　107

+ ☐　+ ☐　+ ☐

The sequence has a ☐☐☐☐☐

difference. The sequence is ☐☐☐☐☐ .

❸ Finding Terms of a Sequence Find the first, fifth, and tenth terms of the sequence that has the rule $A(n) = -3(2)^{n-1}$.

first term: $A(1) = -3(2)^{\boxed{}-1} = -3(2)^{\boxed{}} = -3(1) = \boxed{}$

fifth term: $A(5) = -3(2)^{\boxed{}-1} = -3(2)^{\boxed{}} = -3(16) = \boxed{}$

tenth term: $A(10) = -3(2)^{\boxed{}-1} = -3(2)^{\boxed{}} = -3(512) = \boxed{}$

Quick Check

2. Determine whether each sequence is arithmetic or geometric.

a. 2, 4, 6, 8, . . .

b. 2, 4, 8, 16, . . .

c. 1, 3, 5, 7, . . .

3. Find the first, sixth, and twelfth terms of each sequence.

a. $A(n) = 4 \cdot 3^{n-1}$

b. $A(n) = -2 \cdot 5^{n-1}$

Name_____ Class_____ Date_____

Lesson 8-7

Exponential Functions

Lesson Objectives
▼ Evaluate exponential functions
▼ Graph exponential functions

NAEP 2005 Strand: Algebra

Topics: Patterns, Relations, and Functions

Local Standards: _____

Key Concepts

Exponential Function

An exponential function is a function in the form of $y = a \cdot b^x$, where a is a nonzero constant, b is greater than 0 and not equal to 1, and x is a real number.

Examples $y = 0.5 \cdot 2^x$ $f(x) = -2 \cdot 0.5^x$

Examples

❶ Evaluating an Exponential Function Evaluate the exponential function $y = 3^x$ for $x = 2, 3, 4$.

x	$y = 3^x$	y
2	$3^{\square} = 9$	$\square$
3	$3^{\square} = 27$	$\square$
4	$3^{\square} = 81$	$\square$

❷ Applying Exponential Functions Suppose two mice live in a barn. The number of mice quadruples every 3 months. The function $f(x) = 2 \cdot 4^x$ models this situation. How many mice will be in the barn after 2 years?

$f(x) = \boxed{} \cdot \boxed{}^x$

$f(x) = \boxed{} \cdot \boxed{}^{\boxed{}}$ **In two years, there are** $\boxed{}$ **three-month time periods.**

$f(x) = 2 \cdot \boxed{}$ **Simplify powers.**

$f(x) = \boxed{}$ **Simplify.**

Example

❸ Applying Exponential Functions The function $f(x) = 1.25^x$ models the increase in size of an image being copied over and over at 125% on a photocopier. Graph the function.

x	$f(x) = 1.25^x$	(x, f(x))
1	$1.25^\square = 1.25 \approx \square$	$(\square, \square)$
2	$1.25^\square = 1.5625 \approx \square$	$(\square, \square)$
3	$1.25^\square \approx 1.9531 \approx \square$	$(\square, \square)$
4	$1.25^\square \approx 2.4414 \approx \square$	$(\square, \square)$
5	$1.25^\square \approx 3.0518 \approx \square$	$(\square, \square)$

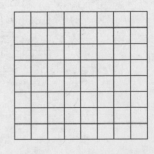

Quick Check

1. Evaluate each exponential function for the domain $\{-2, 0, 3\}$.

   a. $y = 4^x$

   b. $f(x) = 10 \cdot 5^x$

   c. $g(x) = -2 \cdot 3^x$

2. Suppose the population of 10 animals quadruples every year. Use the function $f(x) = 10 \cdot 4^x$. How many animals would there be after 6 years?

3. Consider Example 3. You can also make images that are smaller than the original. The function $y = 0.9^x$ models the new size of an image being copied over and over at 90%. Graph the function.

Lesson 8-8

Exponential Growth and Decay

Lesson Objectives	NAEP 2005 Strand: Algebra
1 Model exponential growth **2** Model exponential decay	**Topic:** Algebraic Representations **Local Standards:** _____

Vocabulary and Key Concepts

Exponential Growth

Exponential growth can be modeled with the function $y = a \cdot b^x$ for $a > 0$ and $b > 1$.

starting amount (when $x = 0$)

$\downarrow$

$y = a \cdot b^x \leftarrow$ **exponent**

$\uparrow$

The [____], which is greater than 1, is the growth factor.

Exponential Decay

The function $y = a \cdot b^x$ models exponential decay for $a > 0$ and $0 < b < 1$.

starting amount (when $x = 0$)

$\downarrow$

$y = a \cdot b^x \leftarrow$ **exponent**

$\uparrow$

The [____], which is between 0 and 1, is the decay factor.

_____ is interest paid on both the principal and the interest that has already been earned.

The interest period is the _____

Examples

1 Compound Interest Suppose you deposit $1000 in a fund that pays 7.2% interest compounded annually. Find the account balance after 5 years.

Relate [y] = [a] $\cdot$ [b^x]   **Use an exponential function.**

Define Let [x] = the number of interest periods.

Let [y] = the balance.

Let [a] = the [_____] deposit, $1000.

Let [b] = 100% + 7.2% = 107.2% = [_____].

Write y = [_____] $\cdot$ [_____]^x

= [_____] $\cdot$ [_____]$^{[\ ]}$ **Once a year for [ ] years is [ ] interest periods. Substitute [ ] for x.**

$\approx$ [_____]

Use a calculator. Round to the nearest cent.

The balance after 5 years will be $[_____].

❷ Modeling Exponential Decay Suppose the population of a certain endangered species has decreased 2.4% each year. Suppose there were 60 of these animals in a given area in 1999.

a. Write an equation to model the number of animals in this species that remain alive in that area.

Relate $\boxed{y}$ $=$ $\boxed{a}$ $\cdot$ $\boxed{b^x}$ **Use an exponential function.**

Define Let $\boxed{x}$ $=$ the number of years since 1999.

Let $\boxed{y}$ $=$ the number of animals that remain.

Let $\boxed{a}$ $=$ $\boxed{}$, the initial population in 1999.

Let $\boxed{b}$ $=$ the decay factor, which is $100\% - 2.4\% = 97.6\% = \boxed{}$.

Write y $=$ $\boxed{}$ $\cdot$ $\boxed{}^x$

b. Use your equation to find the approximate number of animals remaining in 2005.

$y = 60 \cdot 0.976^x$

$y = 60 \cdot 0.976^{\boxed{}}$ **2005 is** $\boxed{}$ **years after 1999, so substitute** $\boxed{}$ **for** *x.*

≈ 52 **Use a calculator. Round to the nearest whole number.**

The approximate number of animals of this endangered species remaining in the area in 2005 is $\boxed{}$.

Quick Check

1. Suppose the interest rate on the account in Example 1 was 8%. How much would be in the account after 18 years?

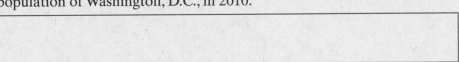

2. Statistics In 1990, the population of Washington, D.C., was about 604,000 people. Since then the population has decreased about 1.8% per year. The equation that models the population since 1990 is $y = 604{,}000 \cdot (0.982)^x$. Suppose the current trend in population change continues. Predict the population of Washington, D.C., in 2010.

Lesson 9-1

Adding and Subtracting Polynomials

Lesson Objectives	NAEP 2005 Strand: Algebra
▼ Describe polynomials	**Topic:** Variables, Expressions, and Operations
▼ Add and subtract polynomials	**Local Standards:** _____

Vocabulary

A _____ is an expression that is a number, a variable, or a product of a number and one or more variables.

The degree of a monomial is _____

_____

The degree of a polynomial is _____

_____

A binomial is _____

A trinomial is _____

Example

❶ **Degree of a Monomial** Find the degree of each monomial.

a. 18   Degree: ☐   The degree of a nonzero constant is ☐ .

b. $3xy^3$ Degree: ☐   The exponents are ☐ and ☐ . Their sum is ☐ .

c. $6c$ Degree: ☐ $6c = 6c^1$. The exponent is ☐ .

❷ **Adding Polynomials** Simplify $(6x^2 + 3x + 7) + (2x^2 - 6x - 4)$.

Line up like terms. Then add the coefficients.

$$\begin{array}{cccccc} 6x^2 & + & 3x & + & 7 \\ 2x^2 & - & 6x & - & 4 \\ \hline \boxed{} & - & \boxed{} & + & \boxed{} \end{array}$$

Daily Notetaking Guide   L1

Name_____ Class_____ Date _____

❸ Subtracting Polynomials Simplify $(2x^3 + 4x^2 - 6) - (5x^3 + 2x - 2)$.

Subtract horizontally.

$(2x^3 + 4x^2 - 6) - (5x^3 + 2x - 2)$

$= 2x^3 + 4x^2 - 6 \boxed{} 5x^3 \boxed{} \boxed{} + 2$ **Write the opposite of each term in the polynomial being subtracted.**

$= \left(2x^3 - \boxed{}\right) + 4x^2 - 2x + \left(\boxed{} + 2\right)$ **Group like terms.**

$= \boxed{} + 4x^2 - \boxed{} - \boxed{}$ **Simplify.**

Quick Check

1. Critical Thinking What is the degree of $9x^0$? Explain.

2. Simplify each sum.

    a. $(t^2 - 6) + (3t^2 + 11)$

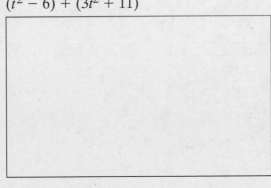

    b. $(2p^3 + 6p^2 + 10p) + (9p^3 + 11p^2 + 3p)$

3. Simplify each difference.

    a. $(v^3 + 6v^2 - v) - (9v^3 - 7v^2 + 3v)$

    b. $(4x^2 + 5x + 1) - (6x^2 + x + 8)$

Lesson 9-2

Multiplying and Factoring

Lesson Objectives	NAEP 2005 Strand: Algebra
▼ Multiply a polynomial by a monomial	**Topic:** Variables, Expressions, and Operations
▼ Factor a monomial from a polynomial	**Local Standards:** _____

Examples

❶ Multiplying a Monomial and a Trinomial Simplify $-2g^2(3g^3 + 6g - 5)$.

$-2g^2(3g^3 + 6g - 5)$

$= \boxed{}(3g^3) - 2g^2(\boxed{}) - 2g^2(\boxed{})$ **Use the Distributive Property.**

$= -6g^{2+3} - 12g^{2+\square} + \boxed{}$ **Multiply the coefficients and add the exponents of powers with the same base.**

$= \boxed{} - \boxed{} + 10g^2$ **Simplify.**

❷ Finding the Greatest Common Factor Find the GCF of $2x^4 + 10x^2 - 6x$.

List the prime factors of each term. Identify the factors common to all terms.

$2x^4 = 2 \cdot x \cdot \boxed{} \cdot x \cdot \boxed{}$

$10x^2 = 2 \cdot \boxed{} \cdot x \cdot \boxed{}$

$6x = \boxed{} \cdot 3 \cdot x$

The GCF is $\boxed{}$.

❸ Factoring Out a Monomial Factor $4x^3 + 12x^2 - 16x$.

Step 1 Find the GCF.

$4x^3 = 2 \cdot \boxed{} \cdot x \cdot \boxed{} \cdot \boxed{}$

$12x^2 = 2 \cdot 2 \cdot \boxed{} \cdot x \cdot x$

$16x = 2 \cdot \boxed{} \cdot 2 \cdot \boxed{} \cdot x$

The GCF is $\boxed{}$.

Step 2 Factor out the GCF.

$4x^3 + 12x^2 - 16x$

$= 4x(\boxed{}) + \boxed{}(3x) + 4x(-4)$

$= \boxed{}(x^2 + \boxed{} - \boxed{})$

Name_____ Class_____ Date _____

Quick Check

1. Simplify each product.

   a. $4b(5b^2 + b + 6)$

       b. $2x(x^2 - 6x + 5)$

2. Find the GCF of the terms of each polynomial.

   a. $5v^5 + 10v^3$

       b. $3t^2 - 18$

3. Use the GCF to factor each polynomial.

   a. $8x^2 - 12x$

       b. $5d^3 + 10d$

Name_____ Class_____ Date_____

Lesson 9-3

Multiplying Binomials

Lesson Objectives	NAEP 2005 Strand: Algebra
▼ Multiply binomials using FOIL	**Topic:** Variables, Expressions, and Operations
▼ Multiply trinomials by binomials	**Local Standards:** _____

Examples

❶ Using the Distributive Property Simplify $(3x + 4)(x + 7)$.

$(3x + 4)(x + 7) = \boxed{}(x + 7) + \boxed{}(x + 7)$ **Distribute x + 7.**

$= 3x^2 + \boxed{} + 4x + \boxed{}$ **Now distribute 3x and 4.**

$= \boxed{} + \boxed{} + \boxed{}$ **Simplify.**

❷ Multiplying Using FOIL Simplify $(4x + 2)(3x - 6)$.

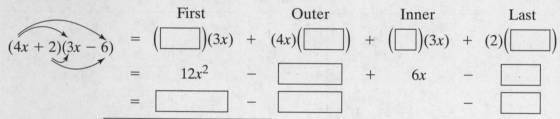

The product is $\boxed{}$.

Quick Check

1. Simplify each product.

   a. $(6h - 7)(2h + 3)$

   b. $(5m + 2)(8m - 1)$

2. Simplify each product using FOIL.

   a. $(3x + 4)(2x + 5)$

   b. $(3x - 4)(2x + 5)$

Example

❸ Multiplying a Trinomial and a Binomial Simplify the product $(3x^2 - 2x + 3)(2x + 7)$.

Method 1 Multiply using the vertical method.

$$
\begin{array}{ccccccc}
 & 3x^2 & - & 2x & + & 3 & \\
 & & & 2x & + & 7 & \\
\hline
\boxed{} & - & 14x & + & \boxed{} & & \text{Multiply by } \boxed{}. \\
\boxed{} & - & 4x^2 & + & \boxed{} & & \text{Multiply by } \boxed{}. \\
\hline
\boxed{} & + & 17x^2 & - & \boxed{} & + & \boxed{} \quad \text{Add like terms.}
\end{array}
$$

Method 2 Multiply using the horizontal method.

$(2x + 7)(3x^2 - 2x + 3)$

$= \left(\boxed{}\right)(3x^2) - (2x)\left(\boxed{}\right) + \left(\boxed{}\right)(3) + (7)\left(\boxed{}\right) - \left(\boxed{}\right)(2x) + (7)\left(\boxed{}\right)$

$= 6x^3 - \boxed{} + 6x + \boxed{} - 14x + \boxed{}$

$= \boxed{} + 17x^2 - \boxed{} + 21$

The product is $\boxed{}$.

Quick Check

3. Simplify $(6n - 8)(2n^2 + n + 7)$ using both methods shown in Example 3.

Lesson 9-4

Lesson Objectives	**NAEP 2005 Strand:** Algebra
▼ Find the square of a binomial	**Topic:** Variables, Expressions, and Operations
▼ Find the difference of squares	**Local Standards:** _____

Key Concepts

The Square of a Binomial

$(a + b)^2 =$ ☐

$(a - b)^2 =$ ☐

The square of a binomial is the square of the first term plus twice the product of the two terms plus the square of the last term.

The Difference of Squares

$(a + b)(a - b) =$ ☐

The product of the sum and difference of the same two terms is the difference of their squares.

Example

1 Squaring a Binomial

a. Find $(y + 11)^2$.

$(y + 11)^2 = y^2 + $ ☐ $(11) + 11^2$ Square the binomial.

$= $ ☐ $ + $ ☐ $ + $ ☐   Simplify.

b. Find $(3w - 6)^2$.

$(3w - 6)^2 = ($☐$)^2 - $☐$(3w)($☐$) + 6^2$ Square the binomial.

$= $ ☐ $ - $ ☐ $w + $ ☐   Simplify.

Quick Check

1. Find each square.

a. $(t + 6)^2$

b. $(5y + 1)^2$

c. $(7m - 2p)^2$

Examples

❷ Mental Math

a. Find 81^2 using mental math.

$$81^2 = \left(80 + \boxed{}\right)^2$$

$$= 80^2 + \boxed{}\left(\boxed{} \cdot 1\right) + \boxed{}^2 \qquad \text{Square the binomial.}$$

$$= \boxed{} + 160 + \boxed{} = \boxed{} \qquad \text{Simplify.}$$

b. Find 59^2 using mental math.

$$59^2 = \left(60 - \boxed{}\right)^2$$

$$= \boxed{} - 2\left(\boxed{} \cdot 1\right) + 1^2 \qquad \text{Square the binomial.}$$

$$= \boxed{} - \boxed{} + 1 = \boxed{} \qquad \text{Simplify.}$$

❸ Finding the Difference of Squares Find $(p^4 - 8)(p^4 + 8)$.

$$(p^4 - 8)(p^4 + 8) = (p^4)^{\boxed{}} - (\boxed{})^2 \qquad \text{Find the difference of squares.}$$

$$= \boxed{} - \boxed{} \qquad \text{Simplify.}$$

❹ Mental Math Find $43 \cdot 37$.

$$43 \cdot 37 = \left(40 + \boxed{}\right)\left(40 - \boxed{}\right) \qquad \text{Express each factor using 40 and 3.}$$

$$= \boxed{}^2 - \boxed{} \qquad \text{Find the difference of squares.}$$

$$= \boxed{} - 9 = \boxed{} \qquad \text{Simplify.}$$

Quick Check

2. Use mental math.

a. 31^2

b. 29^2

3. Find each product.

a. $(d + 11)(d - 11)$

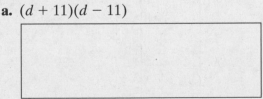

b. $(c^2 + 8)(c^2 - 8)$

Lesson 9-5

Factoring Trinomials of the Type $x^2 + bx + c$

Lesson Objective	NAEP 2005 Strand: Algebra
▼ Factor trinomials	**Topic:** Variables, Expressions, and Operations
	Local Standards: _____

Examples

❶ Factoring $x^2 + bx + c$ Factor $x^2 + 8x + 15$.

Find the factors of 15. Identify the pair that has a sum of 8.

$x^2 + 8x + 15 = \left(x + \boxed{}\right)\left(x + \boxed{}\right)$

Check $\quad x^2 + 8x + 15 \stackrel{?}{=} \left(x + \boxed{}\right)(x + \boxed{})$

$\qquad = \boxed{} + 5x + 3x + \boxed{}$

$\qquad = x^2 + 8x + 15$

Factors of 15	Sum of Factors
1 and ☐	☐
☐ and 5	☐

❷ Factoring $x^2 - bx + c$ Factor $c^2 - 9c + 20$.

Since the middle term is negative, find the negative factors of 20. Identify the pair that has a sum of −9.

$c^2 - 9c + 20 = \left(c - \boxed{}\right)\left(c - \boxed{}\right)$

Factors of 20	Sum of Factors
☐ and −20	☐
☐ and −10	☐
☐ and ☐	☐

Quick Check

1. Factor each expression. Check your answer.

   a. $g^2 + 7g + 10$ **b.** $v^2 + 21v + 20$ **c.** $a^2 + 13a + 30$

2. **a.** $k^2 - 10k + 25$ **b.** $x^2 - 11x + 18$ **c.** $q^2 - 15q + 36$

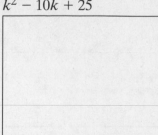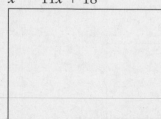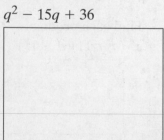

Examples

❸ Factoring Trinomials With a Negative c

a. Factor $x^2 + 13x - 48$.

Identify the pair of factors of ☐ that has a sum of ☐.

Factors of −48	Sum of Factors
☐ and −48	☐
48 and ☐	☐
☐ and −24	☐
24 and ☐	☐
☐ and −16	☐
16 and ☐	☐

$x^2 + 13x - 48 = (x + \boxed{})(x - \boxed{})$

b. Factor $n^2 - 5n - 24$.

Identify the pair of factors of ☐ that has a sum of ☐.

Factors of −24	Sum of Factors
☐ and −24	☐
24 and ☐	☐
☐ and −12	☐
12 and ☐	☐
☐ and −8	☐

$n^2 - 5n - 24 = (n + \boxed{})(n - \boxed{})$

Quick Check

3. Factor each expression.

a. $m^2 + 8m - 20$

b. $p^2 - 3p - 40$

c. $y^2 - y - 56$

Lesson 9-6

Factoring Trinomials
of the Type $ax^2 + bx + c$

Lesson Objective	NAEP 2005 Strand: Algebra
▼ Factor trinomials of the type $ax^2 + bx + c$	**Topic:** Variables, Expressions, and Operations
	Local Standards: _____

Key Concepts

FOIL = first, outer, inner, last

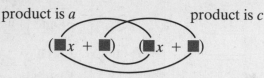

product is a product is c

$(\blacksquare x + \blacksquare)(\blacksquare x + \blacksquare)$

sum of products is b

Examples

1 **c Is Positive** Factor $20x^2 + 17x + 3$.

$$20x^2 \qquad\qquad + 17x \qquad\qquad + 3$$

$$\boxed{\text{F}} \qquad\qquad \boxed{\text{O}} \quad \boxed{\text{I}} \qquad\qquad \boxed{\text{L}}$$

factors of a $\left(\boxed{}\right)(20)$ $(1)(3) + (1)(20) = \boxed{}$ $(1)(3)$ **factors of c**

$(1)(1) + (3)(20) = \boxed{}$ $(3)(1)$

$(2)\left(\boxed{}\right)$ $(2)\left(\boxed{}\right) + \left(\boxed{}\right)(10) = \boxed{}$ $(1)(3)$

$(2)(1) + (3)(10) = \boxed{}$ $(3)(1)$

$\left(\boxed{}\right)(5)$ $\left(\boxed{}\right)(3) + (1)(5) = \boxed{}$ $(1)(3)$

$$20x^2 + 17x + 3 = \left(\boxed{} + 1\right)\left(\boxed{} + 3\right)$$

2 **c Is Negative** Factor $3n^2 - 7n - 6$.

$$3n^2 \qquad\qquad -7n \qquad\qquad -6$$

$(1)(3)$ $(1)(-6) + \left(\boxed{}\right)(3) = \boxed{}$ $(1)(-6)$

$\left(\boxed{}\right)(1) + (-6)(3) = \boxed{}$ $(-6)(1)$

$(1)(-3) + \left(\boxed{}\right)(3) = \boxed{}$ $(2)(-3)$

$(1)\left(\boxed{}\right) + (-3)(3) = \boxed{}$ $(-3)(2)$

$$3n^2 - 7n - 6 = \left(\boxed{} - 3\right)\left(\boxed{} + 2\right)$$

Name_____ Class_____ Date _____

❸ Factoring Out a Monomial First Factor $18x^2 + 33x - 30$ completely.

$18x^2 + 33x - 30 = \boxed{}\left(6x^2 + \boxed{}x - \boxed{}\right)$ **Factor out the GCF.**

Factor $6x^2 + 11x - 10$.

$6x^2$	$+ 11x$	$- 10$
$(2)(3)$	$(2)(-10) + (1)(\boxed{}) = \boxed{}$	$(1)(-10)$
	$(\boxed{})(1) + (-10)(3) = \boxed{}$	$(-10)(1)$
	$(2)(-5) + (\boxed{})(3) = \boxed{}$	$(2)(-5)$
	$(2)(2) + (-5)(3) = \boxed{}$	$(-5)(2)$
	$(2)(\boxed{}) + (5)(\boxed{}) = \boxed{}$	$(5)(-2)$

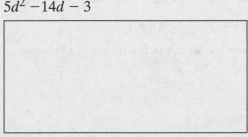

$6x^2 + 11x - 10 = \left(\boxed{} + 5\right)\left(\boxed{} - 2\right)$

$18x^2 + 33x - 30 = \boxed{}\left(2x + \boxed{}\right)\left(3x - \boxed{}\right)$ **Include the GCF in your final answer.**

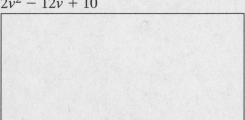

Quick Check

1. Factor each expression.

   a. $2y^2 + 5y + 2$ **b.** $6n^2 - 23n + 7$

2. a. $5d^2 - 14d - 3$ **b.** $2n^2 + n - 3$

3. a. $2v^2 - 12v + 10$ **b.** $4y^2 + 14y + 6$

Lesson 9-7

Factoring Special Cases

Lesson Objectives	NAEP 2005 Strand: Algebra
▼1 Factor perfect-square trinomials ▼2 Factor the difference of squares	Topic: Variables, Expressions, and Operations Local Standards: _____

Vocabulary and Key Concepts

Perfect-Square Trinomials

For every real number a and b:

$a^2 + 2ab + b^2 = (a + b)(a + b) = $ ☐

$a^2 - 2ab + b^2 = (a - b)(a - b) = $ ☐

Difference of Two Squares

For every real number a and b:

$a^2 - b^2 = $ ☐

Examples

❶ Factoring a Perfect-Square Trinomial with $a = 1$ Factor $m^2 - 6m + 9$.

$m^2 - 6m + 9 = m \cdot m - 6m + 3 \cdot 3$ **Rewrite first and last terms.**

$\qquad = m \cdot m - \boxed{}\left(m \cdot \boxed{}\right) + 3 \cdot 3$ **Does the middle term equal 2ab? 6m = ** $\boxed{}$.

$\qquad = \left(m - \boxed{}\right)^2$ **Write the factors as the square of a binomial.**

❷ Factoring a Perfect-Square Trinomial with $a \neq 1$ The area of a square is $(16h^2 + 40h + 25)$ in.^{2}. Find the length of a side.

$16h^2 + 40h + 25 = \left(\boxed{}\right)^2 + 40h + \boxed{}^2$ **Write $16h^2$ as $\left(\boxed{}\right)^2$ and 25 as $\boxed{}^2$.**

$\qquad = (4h)^2 + 2\left(\boxed{}\right)(5) + 5^2$ **Does the middle term equal 2ab?**

$\qquad\qquad\qquad\qquad\qquad\qquad\qquad$ **$40h = 2\left(\boxed{}\right)(5)$ ✔**

$\qquad = \left(\boxed{} + \boxed{}\right)^2$ **Write the factors as the square of a binomial.**

The side of the square has a length of $\boxed{}$ in.

❸ The Difference of Two Squares for $a = 1$ Factor $a^2 - 16$.

$a^2 - 16 = a^2 - \boxed{}^2$ **Rewrite 16 as $\boxed{}^2$.**

$\qquad = \left(a + \boxed{}\right)\left(a - \boxed{}\right)$ **Factor.**

Check   Use FOIL to multiply.

$\qquad \left(a + \boxed{}\right)\left(a - \boxed{}\right)$

$\qquad a^2 - \boxed{} + 4a - \boxed{}$

$\qquad a^2 - \boxed{}$ ✔

Name_____ Class_____ Date_____

Examples

❹ **The Difference of Two Squares for $a \neq 1$** Factor $9b^2 - 25$.

$9b^2 - 25 = \left(\boxed{}\right)^2 - \boxed{}^2$ **Rewrite $9b^2$ as $\left(\boxed{}\right)^2$ and 25 as $\boxed{}^2$.**

$ = \left(3b + \boxed{}\right)\left(\boxed{} - 5\right)$ **Factor.**

❺ **Factoring Out a Common Factor** Factor $5x^2 - 80$.

$5x^2 - 80 = \boxed{}\left(x^2 - \boxed{}\right)$ **Factor out the GCF of $\boxed{}$.**

$ = \boxed{}\left(x + \boxed{}\right)\left(x - \boxed{}\right)$ **Factor $(x^2 - 16)$.**

Check Use FOIL to multiply the binomials. Then multiply by the GCF.

$\boxed{}\left(x + \boxed{}\right)\left(x - \boxed{}\right)$

$5\left(x^2 - \boxed{}\right)$

$5x^2 - 80 \checkmark$

Quick Check

Factor each expression.

1. $x^2 + 8x + 16$

2a. $n^2 + 16n + 64$

2b. $9g^2 - 12g + 4$

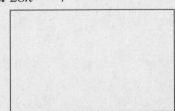

Factor each expression. Check your answer.

3a. $x^2 - 36$

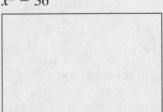

3b. $m^2 - 100$

4. $9v^2 - 4$

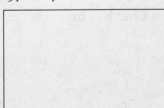

Factor each expression.

5a. $8y^2 - 50$

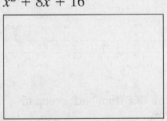

5b. $3c^2 - 75$

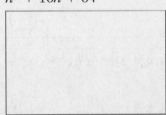

5c. $28k^2 - 7$

Lesson 9-8

Factoring by Grouping

Lesson Objectives	NAEP 2005 Strand: Algebra
1 Factor polynomials with four terms	**Topic:** Variables, Expressions, and Operations
2 Factor trinomials by grouping	**Local Standards:** _____

Vocabulary and Key Concepts

Factoring Polynomials
1. Factor out the greatest common factor (GCF).
2. If the polynomial has two terms or three terms, look for a difference of two squares, a product of two squares, or a pair of binomial factors.
3. If there are four or more terms, group terms and factor to find common binomial factors.
4. As a final check, make sure there are no common factors other than 1.

Factor by grouping is _____

_____

Examples

1 **Factoring a Four-Term Polynomial** Factor $6x^3 + 3x^2 - 4x - 2$.

$6x^3 + 3x^2 - 4x - 2 = \boxed{}(2x + 1) - 2(\boxed{})$ **Factor the GCF from each group of two terms.**

$= (\boxed{})(3x^2 - 2)$ **Factor out $(\boxed{})$.**

Check $6x^3 + 3x^2 - 4x - 2 \overset{?}{=} (\boxed{})(3x^2 - 2)$

$= 6x^3 - \boxed{} + \boxed{} - 2$ **Use FOIL.**

$= 6x^3 + 3x^2 - 4x - 2$ ✔   **Write in standard form.**

2 **Factoring Completely** Factor $8t^4 + 12t^3 + 16t + 24$.

$8t^4 + 12t^3 + 16t + 24 = \boxed{}(2\boxed{} + 3t^3 + \boxed{} + 6)$ **Factor out the GCF, $\boxed{}$.**

$= 4[\boxed{}(2t + \boxed{}) + 2(\boxed{} + 3)]$ **Factor by grouping.**

$= 4(2t + 3)(\boxed{} + 2)$ **Factor again.**

Quick Check

1. Factor each expression. Check your answer.

   a. $5t^4 + 20t^3 + 6t + 24$

   b. $2w^3 + w^2 - 14w - 7$

2. Factor completely.

   $45m^4 - 9m^3 + 30m^2 - 6m$

Lesson 10-1

Exploring Quadratic Graphs

Lesson Objectives	NAEP 2005 Strand: Algebra
▼ Graph quadratic functions of the form $y = ax^2$	**Topics:** Patterns, Relations, and Functions; Algebraic Representations
✔ Graph quadratic functions of the form $y = ax^2 + c$	**Local Standards:** _____

Vocabulary and Key Concepts

Standard Form of a Quadratic Function

A quadratic function is a function that can be written in the form

$y =$ [_____], where $a \neq 0$. This form is called the

[_____] form of a quadratic function.

Examples $y = 5x^2$ $y = x^2 + 7$ $y = x^2 - x - 3$

A _____ is the graph of a quadratic function.

The axis of symmetry is _____

_____

A _____ is the highest or lowest point of a parabola.

The minimum is _____

_____

The _____ is the y-coordinate of the vertex of a parabola that opens downward.

Examples

❶ Identifying a Vertex Identify the vertex of each graph. Tell whether it is a minimum or a maximum.

a.

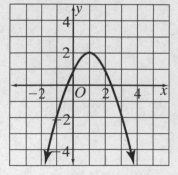

b.

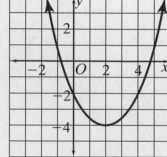

The vertex is [_____].   The vertex is [_____].

It is a [_____].   It is a [_____].

Name_____ Class_____ Date_____

❷ Graphing $y = ax^2 + c$ Graph the quadratic functions $y = 3x^2$ and $y = 3x^2 - 2$.
Compare the graphs.

x	$y = 3x^2$	$y = 3x^2 - 2$
2	12	☐
1	☐	1
0	0	☐
−1	☐	1
−2	12	☐

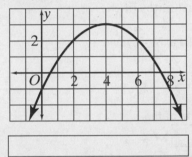

The graph of $y = 3x^2 - 2$ has the same shape as the graph of $y = 3x^2$,
but is shifted down ☐ units.

Quick Check

1. Identify the vertex of each graph. Tell whether it is a minimum or maximum.

a.

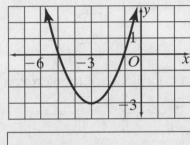

b.

2. a. Graph $y = x^2$ and $y = x^2 - 4$. Compare the graphs.

b. Critical Thinking Describe what positive and negative values of
c do to the position of the vertex of $y = x^2$.

Lesson 10-2

Quadratic Functions

Lesson Objectives	**NAEP 2005 Strand:** Algebra
▼ Graph quadratic functions of the form $y = ax^2 + bx + c$ ▼ Graph quadratic inequalities	**Topics:** Patterns, Relations, and Functions; Algebraic Representations; Equations and Inequalities **Local Standards:** _____

Key Concepts

Graph of a Quadratic Function

The graph of $y = ax^2 + bx + c$, where $a \neq 0$, has the line $x = \boxed{}$ as its axis of symmetry. The x-coordinate of the vertex is $\boxed{}$.

Examples

❶ Graphing $y = ax^2 + bx + c$ Graph the function $y = 2x^2 + 4x - 3$.

Step 1 Find the equation of the axis of symmetry and the coordinates of the vertex.

$$x = -\frac{b}{2a} = -\frac{\boxed{}}{2(\boxed{})} = \boxed{}$$ **Find the equation of the axis of symmetry.**

The x-coordinate of the vertex is $\boxed{}$.

$y = 2x^2 + 4x - 3$

$y = 2\left(\boxed{}\right)^2 + 4\left(\boxed{}\right) - 3$ **To find the y-coordinate of the vertex, substitute $\boxed{}$ for x.**

$= \boxed{}$

The vertex is $\boxed{}$.

Step 2 Find two other points.
Use the y-intercept.

For $x = 0$, $y = \boxed{}$, so one point is $\boxed{}$.

Choose a value for x on the same side of the vertex.
Let $x = 1$

$y = 2(\boxed{})^2 + 4(\boxed{}) - 3$ **Find the y-coordinate for $x = 1$.**

$= \boxed{}$

For $x = 1$, $y = \boxed{}$, so another point is $\boxed{}$.

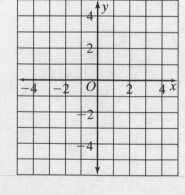

Step 3 Reflect $(0, -3)$ and $(1, 3)$ across the axis of symmetry to get two more points. Then draw the parabola.

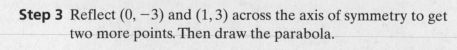

Daily Notetaking Guide   L1

❷ Graphing Quadratic Inequalities Graph the quadratic inequality
$y > -x^2 + 6x - 5$.

Graph the boundary curve, $y \boxed{} -x^2 + 6x - 5$.

Use a $\boxed{}$ curve because the solution of the inequality
$y > -x^2 + 6x - 5$ does not include the boundary.

Shade $\boxed{}$ the curve.

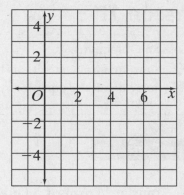

Quick Check

1. Graph $f(x) = x^2 - 6x + 9$. Label the axis of symmetry and the vertex.

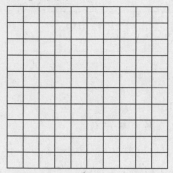

2. Graph each quadratic inequality.

a. $y \leq x^2 + 2x - 5$

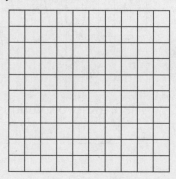

b. $y > x^2 + x + 1$

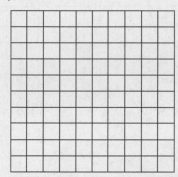

Lesson 10-3

Solving Quadratic Equations

Lesson Objectives	NAEP 2005 Strand: Algebra
▼ 1 Solve quadratic equations by graphing	**Topic:** Equations and Inequalities
▼ 2 Solve quadratic equations using square roots	**Local Standards:** _____

Key Concepts

Standard Form of a Quadratic Equation

A quadratic equation is an equation that can be written in the form [   ]

where $a \neq 0$. This form is called the [   ] form of a quadratic equation.

Example

1 Solving by Graphing Solve each equation by graphing the related function.

a. $2x^2 = 0$

Graph $y = 2x^2$

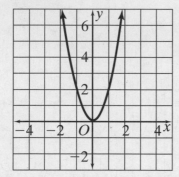

There is one solution,

$x = $ [ ].

b. $2x^2 + 2 = 0$

Graph $y = 2x^2 + 2$

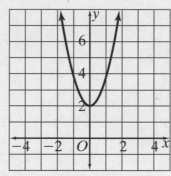

There is [ ] solution.

c. $2x^2 - 2 = 0$

Graph $y = 2x^2 - 2$

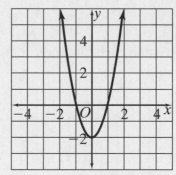

There are two solutions,

$x = $ [ ] and $x = $ [ ].

Quick Check

1. Solve each equation by graphing the related function.

a . $x^2 - 1 = 0$

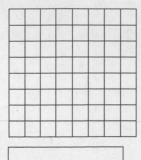

b. $2x^2 + 4 = 0$

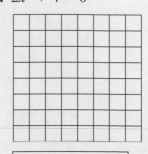

Examples

❷ Using Square Roots Solve $3x^2 - 75 = 0$.

$3x^2 - 75 +$ ⬜ $= 0 +$ ⬜　　**Add** ⬜ **to each side.**

$3x^2 =$ ⬜

$x^2 =$ ⬜　　**Divide each side by** ⬜.

$x = \pm\sqrt{\rule{2em}{0pt}}$　　**Find the square roots.**

$x =$ ⬜　　**Simplify.**

❸ Applying Quadratic Equations A museum is planning an exhibit that will contain a large globe. The surface area of the globe will be 315 ft². Find the radius of the sphere. Use the equation $S = 4\pi r^2$, where S is the surface area and r is the radius.

$S = 4\pi r^2$

⬜ $= 4\pi r^2$　　**Substitute** ⬜ **for S.**

$\dfrac{\rule{2em}{0pt}}{4\pi} = r^2$　　**Put in calculator-ready form.**

$\sqrt{\dfrac{\rule{2em}{0pt}}{4\pi}} = r$　　**Find the principal square root.**

⬜ $\approx r$　　**Use a calculator.**

The radius of the sphere is about ⬜ ft.

Quick Check

2. Solve each equation.

   a. $t^2 - 25 = 0$　　　　**b.** $3n^2 + 12 = 12$　　　　**c.** $2g^2 + 32 = 0$

　　　　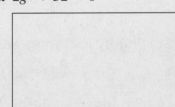

3. A city is planning a circular fountain. The depth of the fountain will be 3 ft. The maximum volume will be 1800 ft.³ Find the radius of the fountain using the equation $V = \pi r^2 h$, where V is the volume, r is the radius, and h is the depth.

Lesson 10-4

Factoring to Solve Quadratic Equations

Lesson Objective	NAEP 2005 Strand: Algebra
▼ Solve quadratic equations by factoring	**Topic:** Equations and Inequalities
	Local Standards: _____

Key Concepts

Zero-Product Property

For every real number a and b, if $ab = 0$, then $a = \boxed{}$ or $b = \boxed{}$.

Example   If $(x + 3)(x + 2) = 0$, then $\boxed{} = 0$ or $\boxed{} = 0$.

Examples

❶ Using the Zero-Product Property Solve $(2x + 3)(x - 4) = 0$ by using the Zero-Product Property.

$(2x + 3)(x - 4) = 0$

$2x + 3 = 0$ or $x - 4 = 0$ **Use the Zero-Product Property.**

$2x = \boxed{}$ **Solve for x.**

$x = \boxed{}$ or $x = \boxed{}$

Check   Substitute $\boxed{}$ for x.   Substitute $\boxed{}$ for x.

$(2x + 3)(x - 4) = 0$ $(2x + 3)(x - 4) = 0$

$[2(\boxed{}) + 3](\boxed{} - 4) \stackrel{?}{=} 0$ $[2(\boxed{}) + 3](\boxed{} - 4) \stackrel{?}{=} 0$

$(0)(-5\frac{1}{2}) = 0$ ✓ $(\boxed{})(0) = 0$ ✓

❷ Solving by Factoring Solve $x^2 + x - 42 = 0$ by factoring.

$x^2 + x - 42 = 0$

$\left(x + \boxed{}\right)\left(x - \boxed{}\right) = 0$ **Factor $x^2 + x - 42$.**

$x + \boxed{} = 0$ or $x - \boxed{} = 0$ **Use the Zero-Product Property.**

$x = \boxed{}$ or $x = \boxed{}$ **Solve for x.**

Name_____ Class_____ Date _____

Quick Check

1. Solve each equation.

   a. $(x + 7)(x - 4) = 0$

   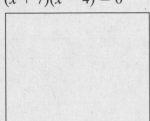

   b. $(3y - 5)(y - 2) = 0.$

   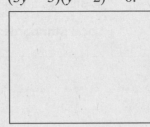

   c. $(6k + 9)(4k - 11) = 0$

   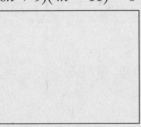

   d. $(5h + 1)(h + 6) = 0$

   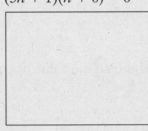

2. Solve $x^2 - 8x - 48 = 0$ by factoring.

Name_____ Class_____ Date_____

Lesson 10-5

Lesson Objective	NAEP 2005 Strand: Algebra
▼ Solve quadratic equations by completing the square	Topic: Equations and Inequalities
	Local Standards: _____

Vocabulary

Completing the square is _____

_____

Examples

❶ **Finding n to Complete the Square** Find the value of c to complete the square for $x^2 - 16x + c$.

The value of b in the expression $x^2 - 16x + c$ is $\boxed{}$.

The term to add to $x^2 - 16x$ is $\boxed{}$.

❷ **Solving $x^2 + bx = c$** Solve the equation $x^2 + 5x = 50$ by completing the square.

Step 1 Write the left side of $x^2 + 5x = 50$ as a perfect square.

$$x^2 + 5x = 50$$

$$x^2 + 5x + \left(\boxed{}\right)^2 = 50 + \left(\boxed{}\right)^2 \quad \text{Add } \left(\boxed{}\right)^2 \text{, or } \frac{25}{4} \text{, to each side.}$$

$$\left(x + \frac{5}{2}\right)^2 = \frac{\boxed{}}{4} + \frac{\boxed{}}{4} \quad \text{Write } x^2 + 5x + \left(\frac{5}{2}\right)^2 \text{ as a square.}$$

$$\left(x + \frac{5}{2}\right)^2 = \frac{\boxed{}}{4} \quad \text{Simplify.}$$

Step 2 Solve the equation.

$$\left(x + \frac{5}{2}\right) = \pm\sqrt{\frac{225}{4}} \quad \text{Find the square root of each side.}$$

$$x + \frac{5}{2} = \pm\frac{\boxed{}}{2} \quad \text{Simplify.}$$

$$x + \frac{5}{2} = \boxed{} \text{ or } x + \frac{5}{2} = \boxed{} \quad \text{Write as two equations.}$$

$$x = \boxed{} \text{ or } x = \boxed{} \quad \text{Solve for x.}$$

Quick Check

1. Find the value of n such that $x^2 + 22x + n$ is a perfect square trinomial.

Example

❸ **Solving** $x^2 + bx + c = 0$ Solve $x^2 + 10x - 16 = 0$ by completing the square. Round to the nearest hundredth.

Step 1 Rewrite the equation in the form $x^2 + bx = c$ and complete the square.

$$x^2 + 10x - 16 = 0$$

$x^2 + 10x = \boxed{}$ **Add** $\boxed{}$ **to each side of the equation.**

$x^2 + 10x + \boxed{} = 16 + \boxed{}$ **Add** $\left(\boxed{}\right)^2$**, or** $\boxed{}$**, to each side of the equation.**

$\left(x + \boxed{}\right)^2 = \boxed{}$ **Write** $x^2 + 10x + 25$ **as a square.**

Step 2 Solve the equation.

$x + 5 = \pm \sqrt{\boxed{}}$ **Find the square root of each side.**

$x + 5 \approx \pm \boxed{}$ **Use a calculator.**

$x + 5 \approx \boxed{}$ or $x + 5 \approx \boxed{}$ **Write as two equations.**

$x \approx \boxed{} - \boxed{}$ or $x \approx \boxed{} - \boxed{}$ **Subtract** $\boxed{}$ **from each side.**

$x \approx \boxed{}$ or $x \approx \boxed{}$ **Simplify.**

Quick Check

2. Solve the equation $m^2 - 6m = 247$.

3. Solve each equation. Round to the nearest hundredth.

a. $x^2 + 5x + 3 = 0$

b. $x^2 - 14x + 16 = 0$

Name_____ Class_____ Date_____

Lesson 10-6

Using the Quadratic Formula

Lesson Objectives	**NAEP 2005 Strand:** Algebra
▼ Use the quadratic formula when solving quadratic equations ▼ Choose an appropriate method for solving a quadratic equation	**Topic:** Equations and Inequalities **Local Standards:** _____

Key Concepts

Quadratic Formula

If $ax^2 + bx + c = 0$, and $a \neq 0$, then $x = \dfrac{-b \,\square\, \sqrt{\square^2 - 4\,\square\,\square}}{2\,\square}$.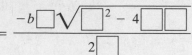

Example

❶ **Using the Quadratic Formula** Solve $x^2 + 2 = -3x$ using the quadratic formula.

$x^2 + 3x + 2 = 0$ Add [   ] to each side and write in standard form.

$x =$ [   ]   Use the quadratic formula.

$x = \dfrac{-\square \pm \sqrt{(\square)^2 - 4(\square)(\square)}}{2(\square)}$ Substitute [ ] for a, [ ] for b, and [ ] for c.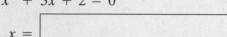

$x = \dfrac{\square \pm \sqrt{\square}}{\square}$ Simplify.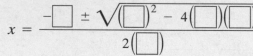

$x = \dfrac{-3 + \square}{2}$ or $x = \dfrac{-3 - \square}{2}$ Write two solutions.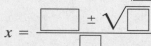

$x =$ [   ]   or $x =$ [   ]   Simplify.

Check   for $x =$ [   ]   for $x =$ [   ]

$(\square)^2 + 3(\square) + 2 \stackrel{?}{=} 0$ $(\square)^2 + 3(\square) + 2 \stackrel{?}{=} 0$

$1 - 3 + 2 \stackrel{?}{=} 0$ $4 - 6 + 2 \stackrel{?}{=} 0$

$0 = 0$ ✓ $0 = 0$ ✓

Quick Check

1. Use the quadratic formula to solve each equation.

a. $x^2 - 2x - 8 = 0$ **b.** $x^2 - 4x = 117$

❷ Choosing an Appropriate Method Which method(s) would you choose
to solve each equation? Justify your reasoning.

a. $5x^2 + 8x - 14 = 0$ [_____] ; the equation
[_____] be factored easily.

b. $25x^2 - 169 = 0$ Square [_____] ; there is no x term.

c. $x^2 - 2x - 3 = 0$ [_____] ; the equation [_____]
easily factorable.

d. $x^2 - 5x + 3 = 0$ [_____] , completing
the square, or graphing; the x^2 term is 1, but
the equation [_____] factorable.

Quick Check

2. Which method(s) would you choose to solve each equation? Justify your reasoning.

a. $13x^2 - 5x + 21 = 0$ **b.** $x^2 - x - 30 = 0$ **c.** $144x^2 = 25$

  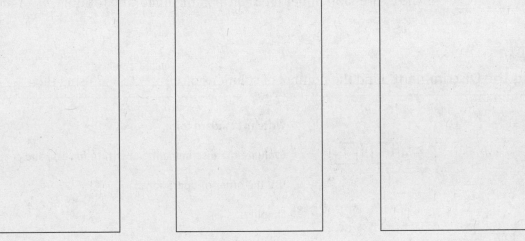

Lesson 10-7

Lesson Objective	NAEP 2005 Strand: Algebra
▼ Find the number of solutions of a quadratic equation	Topic: Equations and Inequalities
	Local Standards: _____

Vocabulary and Key Concepts

Property of the Discriminant

For the quadratic equation $ax^2 + bx + c = 0$, where $a \neq 0$, you can use the value of the discriminant to determine the number of solutions.

If $b^2 - 4ac > 0$, there are [ ] solutions.

If $b^2 - 4ac = 0$, there is [ ] solution.

If $b^2 - 4ac < 0$, there are [ ] solutions.

The _____ is the expression under the radical in the quadratic formula, $b^2 - 4ac$.

Example

1 **Using the Discriminant** Find the number of solutions of $x^2 = -3x - 7$ using the discriminant.

$x^2 + 3x + 7 = 0$	**Write in standard form.**
$b^2 - 4ac = \boxed{}^2 - 4(\boxed{})(\boxed{})$	**Evaluate the discriminant. Substitute for a, b, and c.**
$= 9 - \boxed{}$	**Use the order of operations.**
$= \boxed{}$	**Simplify.**

Since $\boxed{} < 0$, the equation has $\boxed{}$ solution.

Quick Check

1. Find the number of solutions for each equation.

   a. $x^2 = 2x - 3$ **b.** $3x^2 - 4x = 7$

Example

2 **Applying the Discriminant** A football is kicked from a starting height of 3 ft with an initial upward velocity of 40 ft/s. Will the football ever reach a height of 30 ft? Use the vertical motion formula $h = -16t^2 + vt + c$, where $h = 30$, $v =$ velocity, $c =$ starting height, and $t =$ time to land.

$h = -16t^2 + vt + c$ **Use the vertical motion formula.**

$\boxed{} = -16t^2 + \boxed{} t + 3$ **Substitute** $\boxed{}$ **for h,** $\boxed{}$ **for v, and** $\boxed{}$ **for c.**

$0 = -16t^2 + 40t - \boxed{}$ **Write in standard form.**

$b^2 - 4ac = (40)^2 - 4\left(\boxed{}\right)\left(\boxed{}\right)$ **Evaluate the discriminant.**

$= \boxed{} - 1{,}728$ **Use the order of operations.**

$= \boxed{}$ **Simplify.**

The discriminant is $\boxed{}$. The football $\boxed{}$ reach a height of 30 ft.

Quick Check

2. A construction worker on the ground tosses an apple to a fellow worker who is 20 ft above the ground. The starting height of the apple is 5 ft with an initial upward velocity of 32 ft/s. Will the apple reach the worker? Use the vertical motion formula.

Lesson 10-8

Choosing a Linear, Quadratic, or Exponential Model

Lesson Objective	**NAEP 2005 Strand:** Algebra
▼ Choose a linear, quadratic, or exponential model for data	**Topic:** Algebraic Representations
	Local Standards: _____

Key Concepts

Linear, Quadratic, and Exponential Functions

Linear

$y =$ [   ]

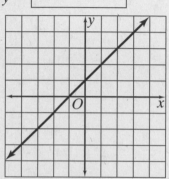

Quadratic

$y =$ [   ]

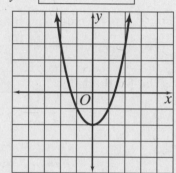

Exponential

$y =$ [   ]

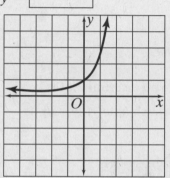

Examples

❶ Choosing a Model by Graphing Graph each set of points. Which model is most appropriate for each set?

a. $(-2, 2.25), (0, 3),$
$(1, 4), (2, 6)$

b. $(-2, -2), (0, 2),$
$(1, 4), (2, 6)$

c. $(-1, 5), (2, 11), (0, 3),$
$(1, 5), (-2, 11)$

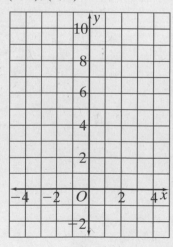

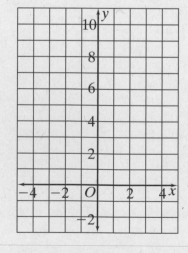

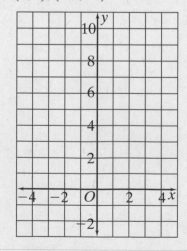

[   ]   [   ]   [   ]

Name_____ Class_____ Date _____

Quick Check

1. a. Graph this set of points: $(-1.5, -2), (0, 2), (1, 4), (2, 6)$.
   Which model is most appropriate?

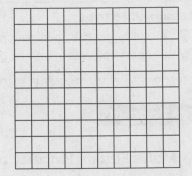

b. Which kind of function best models the data in
   the table? Write an equation to model the data.

x	y
0	4
1	4.4
2	4.84
3	5.324
4	5.8564

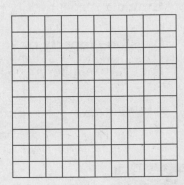

Lesson 11-1

Simplifying Radicals

Lesson Objectives	NAEP 2005 Strand: Algebra
▼ Simplify radicals involving products ▼ Simplify radicals involving quotients	**Topic:** Variables, Expressions, and Operations **Local Standards:** _____

Key Concepts

Multiplication Property of Square Roots

For every number $a \geq 0$ and $b \geq 0$, $\sqrt{ab} = \boxed{} \cdot \boxed{}$.

Example $\sqrt{54} = \boxed{} \cdot \boxed{} = \boxed{} \cdot \sqrt{6} = 3\sqrt{6}$

Division Property of Square Roots

For every number $a \geq 0$ and $b > 0$, $\sqrt{\dfrac{a}{b}} = \dfrac{\boxed{}}{\boxed{}}$.

Example $\sqrt{\dfrac{16}{25}} = \dfrac{\boxed{}}{\boxed{}} = \dfrac{4}{5}$

Examples

❶ **Removing Variable Factors** Simplify $\sqrt{28x^7}$.

$\sqrt{28x^7} = \sqrt{\boxed{}^{\boxed{}} \cdot 7x}$ $\boxed{}^{\boxed{}}$ is a perfect square and a factor of $28x^7$.

$= \sqrt{\boxed{}^{\boxed{}}} \cdot \sqrt{7x}$ Use the Multiplication Property of Square Roots.

$= \boxed{}^{\boxed{}} \sqrt{7x}$ Simplify $\sqrt{\boxed{}^{\boxed{}}}$.

❷ **Multiplying Two Radicals** Simplify each radical expression.

a. $\sqrt{12} \cdot \sqrt{32} = \sqrt{\boxed{} \cdot \boxed{}}$ Use the Multiplication Property of Square Roots.

$= \sqrt{\boxed{}}$ Simplify under the radical.

$= \sqrt{\boxed{} \cdot 6}$ $\boxed{}$ is a perfect square and a factor of 384.

$= \sqrt{\boxed{}} \cdot \sqrt{6}$ Use the Multiplication Property of Square Roots.

$= \boxed{} \sqrt{6}$ Simplify $\sqrt{\boxed{}}$.

❸ **Simplifying Radicals by Dividing** Simplify $\sqrt{\dfrac{75x^5}{48x}}$.

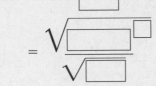 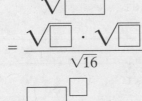 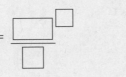

$\sqrt{\dfrac{75x^5}{48x}} = \sqrt{\dfrac{\boxed{}^{\boxed{}}}{\boxed{}}}$ **Divide the numerator and denominator by** $\boxed{}$.

$= \dfrac{\sqrt{\boxed{}^{\boxed{}}}}{\sqrt{\boxed{}}}$ **Use the Division Property of Square Roots.**

$= \dfrac{\sqrt{\boxed{}} \cdot \sqrt{\boxed{}}}{\sqrt{16}}$ **Use the Multiplication Property of Square Roots.**

$= \dfrac{\boxed{}^{\boxed{}}}{\boxed{}}$ **Simplify** $\sqrt{\boxed{}}, \sqrt{\boxed{}}$ **, and** $\sqrt{\boxed{}}$.

Quick Check

1. Simplify each expression.

    a. $\sqrt{27n^2}$ **b.** $-a\sqrt{60a^7}$

2. Simplify each expression.

    a. $\sqrt{13} \cdot \sqrt{52}$ **b.** $5\sqrt{3c} \cdot \sqrt{6c}$

3. Simplify each radical expression.

    a. $\sqrt{\dfrac{90}{5}}$ **b.** $\sqrt{\dfrac{48}{75}}$

Lesson 11-2

Operations With Radical Expressions

Lesson Objectives	NAEP 2005 Strand: Algebra
▼ 1 Simplify sums and differences	**Topic:** Variables, Expressions and Operations
▼ 2 Simplify products and quotients	**Local Standards:** _____

Vocabulary

Like _____ are radical expressions with the same radicands.

Unlike radicals are _____

_____

_____ are the sum and the difference of the same two terms.

Examples

❶ Combining Like Radicals Simplify $4\sqrt{3} + \sqrt{3}$.

$4\sqrt{3} + \sqrt{3} = \boxed{}\sqrt{3} + \boxed{}\sqrt{3}$ **Both terms contain** $\sqrt{\boxed{}}$.

$\phantom{4\sqrt{3} + \sqrt{3}} = (\boxed{} + \boxed{})\sqrt{3}$ **Use the Distributive Property to combine like radicals.**

$\phantom{4\sqrt{3} + \sqrt{3}} = \boxed{}\sqrt{3}$ **Simplify.**

❷ Simplifying to Combine Like Radicals Simplify $8\sqrt{5} - \sqrt{45}$.

$8\sqrt{5} - \sqrt{45} = 8\sqrt{5} - \sqrt{\boxed{} \cdot 5}$ $\boxed{}$ **is a perfect square and a factor of 45.**

$\phantom{8\sqrt{5} - \sqrt{45}} = 8\sqrt{5} - \sqrt{\boxed{}} \cdot \sqrt{5}$ **Use the Multiplication Property of Square Roots.**

$\phantom{8\sqrt{5} - \sqrt{45}} = \boxed{}\sqrt{5} - \boxed{}\sqrt{5}$ **Simplify** $\sqrt{\boxed{}}$.

$\phantom{8\sqrt{5} - \sqrt{45}} = (\boxed{} - \boxed{})\sqrt{5}$ **Use the Distributive Property to combine like terms.**

$\phantom{8\sqrt{5} - \sqrt{45}} = \boxed{}\sqrt{5}$ **Simplify.**

Quick Check

1. Simplify each expression.
   a. $-3\sqrt{5} - 4\sqrt{5}$
   b. $\sqrt{10} - 5\sqrt{10}$

Examples

❸ Using the Distributive Property Simplify $\sqrt{5}\left(\sqrt{8}+9\right)$.

$\sqrt{5}\left(\sqrt{8}+9\right) = \sqrt{\boxed{}} + \boxed{}\sqrt{5}$ — Use the Distributive Property.

$\qquad = \sqrt{\boxed{}} \cdot \sqrt{\boxed{}} + \boxed{}\sqrt{5}$ — Use the Multiplication Property of Square Roots.

$\qquad = \boxed{}\sqrt{\boxed{}} + \boxed{}\sqrt{5}$ — Simplify.

❹ Simplifying Using FOIL Simplify $\left(\sqrt{6}-3\sqrt{21}\right)\left(\sqrt{6}+\sqrt{21}\right)$.

$\left(\sqrt{6}-3\sqrt{21}\right)\left(\sqrt{6}+\sqrt{21}\right)$

$= \sqrt{\boxed{}} + \sqrt{\boxed{}} - 3\sqrt{\boxed{}} - 3\sqrt{\boxed{}}$ — Use FOIL.

$= \boxed{} - \boxed{}\sqrt{126} - 3\left(\boxed{}\right)$ — Combine like radicals and simplify $\sqrt{36}$ and $\sqrt{441}$.

$= \boxed{} - 2\sqrt{\boxed{} \cdot 14} - \boxed{}$ — $\boxed{}$ is a perfect-square factor of 126.

$= \boxed{} - 2\sqrt{\boxed{}} \cdot \sqrt{\boxed{}} - 63$ — Use the Multiplication Property of Square Roots.

$= \boxed{} - \boxed{}\sqrt{\boxed{}} - 63$ — Simplify $\sqrt{9}$.

$= \boxed{} - \boxed{}\sqrt{14}$ — Simplify.

Quick Check

Simplify each expression.

2. a. $3\sqrt{20} + 2\sqrt{5}$

b. $3\sqrt{3} - 2\sqrt{27}$

3. a. $\sqrt{5}(2 + \sqrt{10})$

b. $\sqrt{2x}\left(\sqrt{6x} - 11\right)$

4. a. $(2\sqrt{6} + 3\sqrt{3})(\sqrt{6} - 5\sqrt{3})$

b. $(\sqrt{7} + 4)^2$

Name_____ Class_____ Date_____

Lesson 11-3

Solving Radical Equations

Lesson Objectives	NAEP 2005 Strand: Algebra
▼ Solve equations containing radicals	**Topic:** Variables, Expressions, and Operations
▼ Identify extraneous solutions	**Local Standards:** _____

Vocabulary

A _____ is an equation that has a variable in a radicand.

An extraneous solution is _____

_____

Example

❶ **Solving by Isolating the Radical** Solve the equation and check your solution.

$\sqrt{x} - 5 = 4$

$\sqrt{x} = \boxed{}$　　　　　　　Isolate the radical on the left side of the equation.

$(\sqrt{x})^2 = \boxed{}^2$　　　　　Square each side.

$x = \boxed{}$

Check　　　$\sqrt{x} - 5 = 4$

$\sqrt{\boxed{}} - 5 \overset{?}{=} 4$　　　**Substitute** $\boxed{}$ **for x.**

$\boxed{} - 5 \overset{?}{=} 4$

$4 = 4 ✓$

Quick Check

1. Solve each equation. Check your solutions.

a. $\sqrt{x} + 7 = 12$　　　　**b.** $\sqrt{a} - 4 = 5$　　　　**c.** $\sqrt{c - 2} = 6$

Examples

❷ **Solving with Radical Expressions on Both Sides** Solve $\sqrt{3x - 4} = \sqrt{2x + 3}$.

$\left(\sqrt{3x - 4}\right)^2 = \left(\sqrt{2x + 3}\right)^2$ **Square both sides.**

$\quad 3x - 4 = 2x + 3$ **Simplify.**

$\quad\quad 3x = 2x + \boxed{}$ **Add** $\boxed{}$ **to each side.**

$\quad\quad \boxed{} = 7$ **Subtract** $\boxed{}$ **from each side.**

Check $\sqrt{3x - 4} = \sqrt{2x + 3}$

$\sqrt{3\left(\boxed{}\right) - 4} \overset{?}{=} \sqrt{2\left(\boxed{}\right) + 3}$ **Substitute** $\boxed{}$ **for** *x*.

$\sqrt{\boxed{}} = \sqrt{\boxed{}}$ ✓

The solution is $\boxed{}$.

Quick Check

2. Solve $\sqrt{3t + 4} = \sqrt{5t - 6}$. Check your answer.

Lesson 11-4

Graphing Square Root Functions

Lesson Objectives	NAEP 2005 Strand: Algebra
V Graph square root functions **2** Translate graphs of square root functions	**Topic:** Algebraic Representations **Local Standards:** _____

Vocabulary

A _____ function is a function that contains the independent variable in the radicand.

Examples

1 **Finding the Domain of a Square Root Function** Find the domain of each function.

a. $y = \sqrt{x + 5}$

$x + \boxed{} \geq 0$ **Make the radicand greater**

$x \geq \boxed{}$ **than or equal to 0.**

The domain is the set of all numbers greater than or equal to $\boxed{}$.

b. $y = 6\sqrt{4x - 12}$

$4x - 12 \geq \boxed{}$ **Make the radicand greater**

$4x \geq \boxed{}$ **than or equal to $\boxed{}$.**

$x \geq \boxed{}$

The domain is the set of all numbers greater than or equal to $\boxed{}$.

2 **Measurement** The size of a television screen is the length of the screen's diagonal d in inches. The equation $d = \sqrt{2A}$ estimates the length of a diagonal of a television with screen area A. Graph the function.

Domain
$2A \geq 0$

Screen Area (sq. in.)	Length of Diagonal (in.)
$A \geq 0 \rightarrow$ 0	
50	
100	
200	
300	
400	

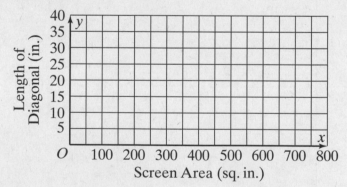

Quick Check

1. Find the domain of $y = \sqrt{x - 7}$.

❸ Graphing a Vertical Translation Graph $y = \sqrt{x} + 4$
by translating the graph of $y = \sqrt{x}$.

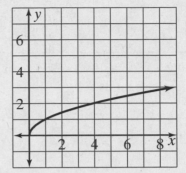

For the graph **$y = \sqrt{x} + 4$**, the graph of
$y = \sqrt{x}$ is shifted ☐ units ☐ .

❹ Graphing a Horizontal Translation Graph
$f(x) = \sqrt{x + 3}$ by translating the graph of $y = \sqrt{x}$.

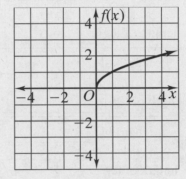

For the graph **$f(x) = \sqrt{x + 3}$**, the graph of
$y = \sqrt{x}$ is shifted ☐ units to the ☐ .

Quick Check

2. Critical Thinking What is the area of a television screen with a diagonal length of
45 inches?

3. Graph $f(x) = \sqrt{x} - 4$ by translating
the graph of $f(x) = \sqrt{x}$.

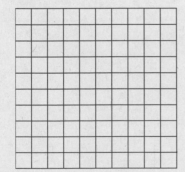

4. Graph $f(x) = \sqrt{x - 3}$ by translating
the graph of $f(x) = \sqrt{x}$.

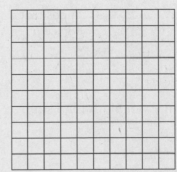

Lesson 11-5

Trigonometric Ratios

Lesson Objective	NAEP 2005 Strand: Measurement
▼ Find trigonometric ratios	Topic: Measuring Physical Attributes
	Local Standards: _____

Vocabulary

Ratios of the sides of a right triangle are called [_____] ratios.

$\sin A = \dfrac{\text{length of leg } [] \angle A}{\text{length of } []} = \dfrac{\square}{\square}$

$\cos A = \dfrac{\text{length of leg } [] \text{ to } \angle A}{\text{length of } []} = \dfrac{\square}{\square}$

$\tan A = \dfrac{\text{length of leg } [] \angle A}{\text{length of leg } [] \text{ to } \angle A} = \dfrac{\square}{\square}$

Right triangle with vertices A, B, C; right angle at C; side c opposite B, side a, side b.

Example

❶ Finding Trigonometric Ratios Use the triangle. Find sin A, cos A, and tan A.

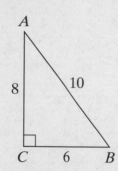

$\sin A = \dfrac{\text{opposite leg}}{\text{hypotenuse}} = \dfrac{\square}{\square} = \dfrac{3}{\square}$

$\cos A = \dfrac{\text{adjacent leg}}{\text{hypotenuse}} = \dfrac{\square}{\square} = \dfrac{\square}{\square}$

$\tan A = \dfrac{\text{opposite leg}}{\text{adjacent leg}} = \dfrac{\square}{\square} = \dfrac{\square}{\square}$

Quick Check

1. Use the triangle in Example 1. Find sin B, cos B, and tan B.

Example

❷ **Finding Missing Side Lengths** Find the value of *x* in the triangle.

Step 1 Decide which trigonometric ratio to use.

You know the angle and the length of the [   ].

You are trying to find the [   ] side.

Use the [   ].

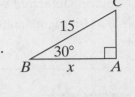

Step 2 Write an equation and solve.

$$\cos 30° = \frac{\boxed{}}{\boxed{}}$$

$$\cos 30° = \frac{\boxed{}}{\boxed{}}$$ **Substitute** [ ] **for adjacent leg and**

[ ] **for hypotenuse.**

$$x = \boxed{}\left(\cos \boxed{}°\right)$$ **Solve for x.**

[ ] ✕ COS [ ] ENTER 12.99038106 **Use a calculator.**

$$x \approx \boxed{}$$ **Round to the nearest tenth.**

The value of *x* is about [ ].

Quick Check

2. Find the value of *x* in each triangle. Round to the nearest tenth.

a.

b.
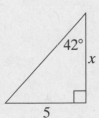

Lesson 11-6

Angles of Elevation and Depression

Lesson Objective	**NAEP 2005 Strand:** Measurement
▼ Use trigonometric ratios	**Topic:** Measuring Physical Attributes
	Local Standards: _____

Vocabulary

An angle of _____ is an angle from the horizontal up to a line of sight.

An angle of depression is measured _____

_____

Examples

1 **Using Angle of Elevation** Suppose the angle of elevation from a rowboat to the top of a lighthouse is 70°. The lighthouse is 70 ft tall. How far from the lighthouse is the rowboat? Round your answer to the nearest foot.

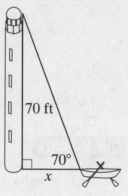

Relate You know the [   ] and the [   ]. You are trying to find the [   ]. Use the [   ].

Define Let $\boxed{x}$ = the distance from the boat to the lighthouse.

Write $\tan A = \dfrac{}{}$

$\tan 70° = \dfrac{\boxed{}}{\boxed{}}$ **Substitute for the angle and the sides.**

$x = \dfrac{\boxed{}}{\boxed{}}$ **Solve for *x*.**

$x \approx \boxed{}$ **Use a calculator.**

$x \approx \boxed{}$ **Round to the nearest unit.**

The rowboat is about $\boxed{}$ feet from the lighthouse.

Name_____ Class_____ Date _____

❷ Using Angle of Depression

A pilot is flying a plane 15,000 ft above the ground. The pilot begins a 3° descent to an airport runway. How far is the airplane from the start of the runway (in ground distance)?

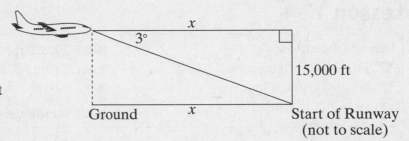

15,000 ft

Ground x Start of Runway (not to scale)

$$\tan A = \frac{\boxed{}}{\boxed{}}$$

$$\tan \boxed{}° = \frac{\boxed{}}{\boxed{}}$$ **Substitute for the angle and the sides.**

$$\boxed{} \, (\tan \boxed{}°) = \boxed{}$$ **Multiply each side by** $\boxed{}$.

$$x = \frac{15,000}{\boxed{}}$$ **Divide each side by** $\boxed{}$.

$$x \approx \boxed{}$$ **Use a calculator.**

$$x \approx \boxed{}$$ **Round to the nearest 10,000 feet.**

The airplane is about $\boxed{}$ ft (about $\boxed{}$ mi) from the start of the runway.

Quick Check

1. The angle of elevation from a point on the ground 300 ft from a tower is 42°. How tall is the tower?

2. Suppose the pilot in Example 2 is at an altitude of 26,000 ft when the airplane begins a 2° descent. How far is the airplane from the start of the runway?

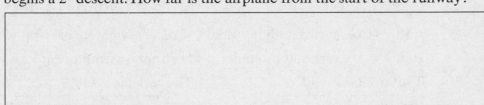

Name_____ Class_____ Date_____

Lesson 12-1

Graphing Rational Functions

Lesson Objectives	**NAEP 2005 Strand:** Algebra
▼ Graph rational functions ▼ Identify types of functions	**Topics:** Patterns, Relations, and Functions; Algebraic Representations **Local Standards:** _____

Vocabulary and Key Concepts

Families of Functions

[_____] **function**

$y = mx + b$

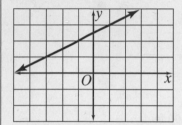

slope = [   ]

y-intercept = [   ]

The greatest exponent is 1.

[_____] **value function**

$y = |x - a| + b$

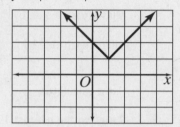

shift $y = |x|$ horizontally [   ] units

shift $y = |x|$ vertically [   ] units

vertex at [   ]

The greatest exponent is [   ].

[_____] **function**

$y = ax^2 + bx + c$

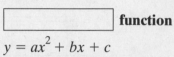

[_____] with axis

of symmetry at $x =$ [   ]

The greatest exponent is [   ].

[_____] **function**

$y = ab^x$

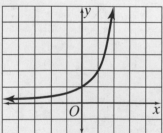

growth for $b >$ [   ]

decay for [   ] $< b <$ [   ]

The variable is

the [_____].

[_____] **function**

$y = \sqrt{x - b} + c$

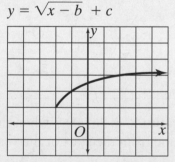

shift $y = \sqrt{x}$ horizontally [   ] units

shift $y = \sqrt{x}$ vertically [   ] units

The variable is under

the [_____].

[_____] **function**

$y = \dfrac{a}{x - b} + c$

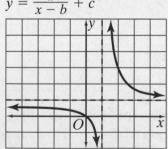

vertical asymptote at $x =$ [   ]

horizontal asymptote at $y =$ [   ]

The variable is in

the [_____].

Name_____ Class_____ Date _____

Example

❶ Identifying Functions Describe the graph of each function.

a. $y = \frac{x}{6}$

The graph is a line with slope ⬚ and y-intercept ⬚.

b. $y = 6^x$

The graph is of ⬚ growth.

c. $y = 6x^2$

The graph is a ⬚ with axis of symmetry at ⬚.

d. $y = |x - 6|$

The graph is an ⬚ function with a vertex at (⬚, ⬚).

e. $y = \frac{6}{x}$

The graph is a ⬚ with vertical asymptote at ⬚ and horizontal asymptote at ⬚.

f. $y = \sqrt{x - 6}$

The graph is the ⬚ function ⬚ shifted right ⬚ units.

Quick Check

1. Describe the graph of each function.

a. $g(x) = |x + 4|$

b. $f(x) = 8 \cdot 2^x$

c. $h(x) = \frac{2}{x + 1}$

Lesson 12-2

Simplifying Rational Expressions

Lesson Objective ▼ Simplify rational expressions	**NAEP 2005 Strand:** Algebra **Topic:** Variables, Expressions, and Operations **Local Standards:** _____

Vocabulary

A _____ is an expression with a variable in the denominator.

Examples

❶ Simplifying a Rational Expression Simplify $\dfrac{4x - 20}{x^2 - 9x + 20}$.

$$\frac{4x - 20}{x^2 - 9x + 20} = \frac{\boxed{}(x - 5)}{\left(x - \boxed{}\right)\left(\boxed{} - \boxed{}\right)}$$ Factor the numerator and the denominator.

$$= \frac{4(x - 5)^{\boxed{}}}{(x - 4)(x - 5)_{\boxed{}}}$$ Divide out the common factor $\boxed{}$.

$$= \frac{\boxed{}}{\boxed{}}$$ Simplify.

❷ Recognizing Opposite Factors Simplify $\dfrac{3x - 27}{81 - x^2}$.

$$\frac{3x - 27}{81 - x^2} = \frac{3\left(\boxed{}\right)}{(9 - x)\left(\boxed{}\right)}$$ Factor the numerator and the denominator.

$$= \frac{3(x - 9)}{-1\left(\boxed{}\right)(9 + x)}$$ Factor $\boxed{}$ from $9 - x$.

$$= \frac{3(x - 9)^{\boxed{}}}{-1\boxed{}(x - 9)(9 + x)}$$ Divide out the common factor $\boxed{}$.

$$= -\frac{\boxed{}}{\boxed{}}$$ Simplify.

❸ Evaluating a Rational Expression The baking time for bread depends, in part, on its size and shape. A good approximation for the baking time, in minutes, of a cylindrical loaf is $\frac{60 \cdot \text{volume}}{\text{surface area}}$, or $\frac{30rh}{r + h}$, where the radius r and the length h of the baked loaf are in inches. Find the baking time for a loaf that is 8 inches long and has a radius of 3 inches. Round your answer to the nearest minute.

 $\frac{30rh}{r + h} = \frac{30(\boxed{})(\boxed{})}{\boxed{} + \boxed{}}$ **Substitute** $\boxed{}$ **for r and** $\boxed{}$ **for h.**

$= \dfrac{\boxed{}}{\boxed{}}$ **Simplify.**

$\approx \boxed{}$ **Round to the nearest whole number.**

The baking time is approximately $\boxed{}$ minutes.

Quick Check

1. Simplify each expression.

   a. $\dfrac{12c^2}{3c + 6}$

   $\boxed{}$

   b. $\dfrac{c^2 - c - 6}{c^2 + 5c + 6}$

   $\boxed{}$

2. Simplify each expression.

   a. $\dfrac{x - 4}{4 - x}$

   $\boxed{}$

   b. $\dfrac{8 - 4r}{r^2 + 2r - 8}$

   $\boxed{}$

3. Find the baking time for a loaf that is 4 inches long and has a radius of 3 inches. Round your answer to the nearest minute.

   $\boxed{}$

Lesson 12-3

Multiplying and Dividing Rational Expressions

Lesson Objectives	**NAEP 2005 Strand:** Algebra
▼ 1 Multiply rational expressions ▼ 2 Divide rational expressions	**Topic:** Variables, Expressions, and Operations **Local Standards:** _____

Examples

❶ Using Factoring Multiply $\dfrac{3x + 1}{4}$ and $\dfrac{8x}{9x^2 - 1}$.

$$\dfrac{3x + 1}{4} \cdot \dfrac{8x}{9x^2 - 1} = \dfrac{3x + 1}{4} \cdot \dfrac{8x}{(3x - 1)(\boxed{} + \boxed{})}$$ Factor the denominator.

$$= \dfrac{3x + 1\,\boxed{}}{\boxed{}4} \cdot \dfrac{8\boxed{}x}{(3x - 1)(3x + 1)}\boxed{}$$ Divide out the common factors: $\left(\boxed{}\right)$ and 4.

$$= \dfrac{\boxed{}}{3x - 1}$$ Simplify.

❷ Multiplying a Rational Expression by a Polynomial

Multiply $\dfrac{5x + 1}{3x + 12}$ and $x^2 + 7x + 12$.

$$\dfrac{5x + 1}{3x + 12} \cdot (x^2 + 7x + 12) = \dfrac{5x + 1}{3\left(\boxed{}\right)} \cdot \dfrac{\left(\boxed{}\right)\left(\boxed{}\right)}{1}$$ Factor.

$$= \dfrac{5x + 1}{3(x + 4)\,\boxed{}} \cdot \dfrac{(x + 3)(x + 4)\,\boxed{}}{1}$$ Divide out the common factor $\boxed{}$.

$$= \dfrac{(5x + 1)(x + 3)}{\boxed{}}$$ Leave in factored form.

❸ Dividing Rational Expressions Divide $\dfrac{x^2 + 13x + 40}{x - 7}$ by $\dfrac{x + 8}{x^2 - 49}$.

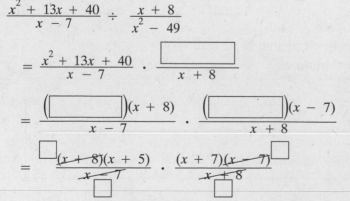

$$\dfrac{x^2 + 13x + 40}{x - 7} \div \dfrac{x + 8}{x^2 - 49}$$

$$= \dfrac{x^2 + 13x + 40}{x - 7} \cdot \dfrac{\boxed{}}{x + 8}$$ Multiply by $\dfrac{x^2 - 49}{x + 8}$, the $\boxed{}$ of $\dfrac{x + 8}{x^2 - 49}$.

$$= \dfrac{\left(\boxed{}\right)(x + 8)}{x - 7} \cdot \dfrac{\left(\boxed{}\right)(x - 7)}{x + 8}$$ Factor.

$$= \dfrac{\boxed{}(x + 8)(x + 5)}{x - 7\,\boxed{}} \cdot \dfrac{(x + 7)(x - 7)\,\boxed{}}{x + 8\,\boxed{}}$$ Divide out the common factors $\boxed{}$ and $\boxed{}$.

$$= \left(\boxed{}\right)\left(\boxed{}\right)$$ Leave in factored form.

❹ Dividing a Rational Expression by a Polynomial

Divide $\dfrac{x^2 + 9x + 14}{11x}$ by $(8x^2 + 16x)$.

$$\dfrac{x^2 + 9x + 14}{11x} \div \dfrac{8x^2 + 16x}{1}$$

$$= \dfrac{x^2 + 9x + 14}{11x} \cdot \dfrac{1}{\boxed{}}$$
$\qquad$ Multiply by the $\boxed{}$ of $8x^2 + 16x$.

$$= \dfrac{(x + 7)\left(\boxed{}\right)}{11x} \cdot \dfrac{1}{\boxed{}(x + 2)}$$
$\qquad$ Factor.

$$= \dfrac{(x + 7)\cancel{(x + 2)}^{\boxed{}}}{11x} \cdot \dfrac{1}{8x\cancel{(x + 2)}_{\boxed{}}}$$
$\qquad$ Divide out the common factor $\boxed{}$.

$$= \dfrac{\boxed{}}{\boxed{}}$$
$\qquad$ Simplify.

Quick Check

Multiply.

1. $\dfrac{x - 2}{8x} \cdot \dfrac{-8x - 16}{x^2 - 4}$

2. $\dfrac{3}{c} \cdot (c^3 - c)$

Divide.

3. $\dfrac{a - 2}{ab} \div \dfrac{a - 2}{a}$

4. $\dfrac{z^2 + 2z - 15}{z^2 + 9z + 20} \div (z - 3)$

Name_____ Class_____ Date_____

Lesson 12-4 **Dividing Polynomials**

Lesson Objective	NAEP 2005 Strand: Algebra
▼ Divide polynomials	Topic: Variables, Expressions, and Operations
	Local Standards: _____

Key Concepts

Dividing a Polynomial by a Polynomial

Step 1 Arrange the terms of the dividend and divisor in [   ] form.

Step 2 Divide the first term of the dividend by the first term of the divisor. This is the first term of the [   ].

Step 3 Multiply the first term of the quotient by the divisor and place the [   ] under the dividend.

Step 4 Subtract this product from the [   ].

Step 5 Bring down the next term.
Repeat Steps 2–5 as necessary until the degree of the remainder is less than the degree of the divisor.

Examples

❶ Dividing a Polynomial by a Monomial Divide $18x^3 + 9x^2 - 15x$ by $3x^2$.

$$(18x^3 + 9x^2 - 15x) \div 3x^2 = (18x^3 + 9x^2 - 15x) \cdot \frac{1}{\boxed{}}$$ Multiply by the reciprocal of $\boxed{}$.

$$= \frac{18x^3}{\boxed{}} + \frac{9x^2}{\boxed{}} - \frac{15x}{\boxed{}}$$ Use the $\boxed{}$ Property.

$$= 6x^1 + \boxed{}x^{\boxed{}} - \frac{5}{x}$$ Use the division rules for exponents.

$$= \boxed{}$$ Simplify.

❷ Dividing a Polynomial by a Binomial Divide $5x^2 + 2x - 3$ by $x + 2$.

Step 1 Begin the long division process.

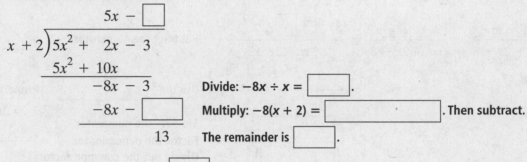

Align terms by their degrees.
Put 5x above 2x of the dividend.

$$x + 2 \overline{)5x^2 + \boxed{}x - 3}$$

Divide: Think $5x^2 \div x = \boxed{}$.

$5x^2 + \boxed{}x$

Multiply: $5x(x + 2) = \boxed{}$. **Then subtract.**

$\boxed{}x - 3$ **Bring down −3.**

Step 2 Repeat the process: Divide, multiply, subtract, bring down.

$$
\begin{array}{r}
5x - \boxed{} \\
x + 2 \overline{)5x^2 + 2x - 3} \\
5x^2 + 10x \\
\hline
-8x - 3 \\
-8x - \boxed{} \\
\hline
13
\end{array}
$$

Divide: $-8x \div x = \boxed{}$.

Multiply: $-8(x + 2) = \boxed{}$. **Then subtract.**

The remainder is $\boxed{}$.

The answer is $\boxed{} - \boxed{} + \dfrac{\boxed{}}{\boxed{}}$.

Quick Check

Divide.

1. $(3m^3 - 6m^2 + m) \div 3m^2$

2. $(2b^2 - b - 3) \div (b + 1)$

Lesson 12-5

Adding and Subtracting Rational Expressions

Lesson Objectives	NAEP 2005 Strand: Algebra
▼ Add and subtract rational expressions with like denominators	**Topic:** Variables, Expressions, and Operations
❷ Add and subtract rational expressions with unlike denominators	**Local Standards:** _____

Examples

❶ Subtracting Expressions With Like Denominators

Subtract $\dfrac{3x + 5}{3x^2 + 2x - 8}$ from $\dfrac{4x + 7}{3x^2 + 2x - 8}$.

$$\dfrac{4x + 7}{3x^2 + 2x - 8} - \dfrac{3x + 5}{3x^2 + 2x - 8} = \dfrac{4x + 7 \;\boxed{}\; (3x + 5)}{3x^2 + 2x - 8} \qquad \text{Subtract the numerators.}$$

$$= \dfrac{4x + 7\; - 3x - \boxed{}}{3x^2 + 2x - 8} \qquad \text{Use the } \boxed{} \text{ Property.}$$

$$= \dfrac{\boxed{}\;\boxed{}}{\left(\boxed{}\right)(x + 2)\;\boxed{}} \qquad \begin{array}{l}\text{Simplify the numerator.}\\ \text{Factor the denominator.}\\ \text{Divide out the common factor } \boxed{}.\end{array}$$

$$= \dfrac{\boxed{}}{\boxed{}} \qquad \text{Simplify.}$$

❷ Adding Expressions With Monomial Denominators Add $\dfrac{3}{4x} + \dfrac{1}{8}$.

Step 1 Find the LCD of $\dfrac{3}{4x}$ and $\dfrac{1}{8}$.

$$4x = 2 \cdot 2 \cdot \boxed{}$$
$$8 = 2 \cdot 2 \cdot \boxed{} \qquad \text{Factor each denominator.}$$
$$\text{LCD} = 2 \cdot 2 \cdot 2 \cdot x = \boxed{}$$

Step 2 Rewrite using the LCD and add.

$$\dfrac{3}{4x} + \dfrac{1}{8} = \dfrac{\boxed{} \cdot 3}{\boxed{} \cdot 4x} + \dfrac{1 \cdot \boxed{}}{8 \cdot x} \qquad \text{Rewrite each fraction using the LCD.}$$

$$= \dfrac{\boxed{}}{8x} + \dfrac{x}{\boxed{}} \qquad \text{Simplify numerators and denominators.}$$

$$= \dfrac{\boxed{}}{\boxed{}} \qquad \text{Add the numerators.}$$

Daily Notetaking Guide L1

❸ Adding Expressions With Polynomial Denominators

Add $\dfrac{7}{x+4}$ and $\dfrac{3}{x-5}$.

Step 1 Find the LCD of $x + 4$ and $x - 5$. Since there are no common factors,

the LCD is $(x+4)\left(\boxed{}\right)$.

Step 2 Rewrite using the LCD, and add.

$$\dfrac{7}{x+4} + \dfrac{3}{x-5} = \dfrac{7\left(\boxed{}\right)}{(x+4)(x-5)} + \dfrac{3\left(\boxed{}\right)}{(x+4)(x-5)}$$ Rewrite the fractions using the $\boxed{}$.

$$= \dfrac{7x - \boxed{}}{(x+4)(x-5)} + \dfrac{\boxed{} + \boxed{}}{(x+4)(x-5)}$$ Simplify each numerator.

$$= \dfrac{7x - 35 + \boxed{} + \boxed{}}{(x+4)(x-5)}$$ Add the numerators.

$$= \dfrac{\boxed{} - \boxed{}}{(x+4)(x-5)}$$ Simplify the numerator.

Quick Check

Add or subtract.

1. a. $\dfrac{4}{t-2} - \dfrac{5}{t-2}$

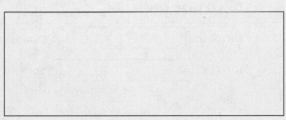

b. $\dfrac{2c+1}{5m+2} - \dfrac{3c-4}{5m+2}$

2. a. $\dfrac{3}{7y^4} + \dfrac{2}{3y^2}$

b. $\dfrac{5}{12b} + \dfrac{15}{36b^2}$

3. a. $\dfrac{5}{t+4} + \dfrac{3}{t-1}$

b. $\dfrac{-2}{a+2} + \dfrac{3a}{2a-1}$

Name_____ Class_____ Date_____

Lesson 12-6   **Solving Rational Equations**

Lesson Objectives	NAEP 2005 Strand: Algebra
▼ 1 Solve rational equations	**Topics:** Algebraic Representations; Equations and Inequalities
▼ 2 Solve proportions	**Local Standards:** _____

Vocabulary

A rational equation is _____

Example

1 Solving by Factoring Solve $\frac{6}{x^2} = \frac{5}{x} - 1$. Check the solution.

$$\boxed{}\left(\frac{6}{x^2}\right) = \boxed{}\left(\frac{5}{x} - 1\right) \qquad \text{Multiply each side by the LCD, } \boxed{}.$$

$$\frac{\boxed{}}{\boxed{}}\left(\frac{6}{x^2}\right) = \frac{\boxed{}}{\boxed{}}\left(\frac{5}{x}\right) - \boxed{}(1) \qquad \text{Use the } \boxed{} \text{ Property.}$$

$$6 = \boxed{}x - \boxed{} \qquad \text{Simplify.}$$

$$x^2 - \boxed{} + \boxed{} = 0 \qquad \text{Collect terms on one side.}$$

$$\left(\boxed{}\right)\left(\boxed{}\right) = 0 \qquad \text{Factor the } \boxed{} \text{ expression.}$$

$$\boxed{} - \boxed{} = 0 \text{ or } \boxed{} - \boxed{} = 0 \qquad \text{Use the } \boxed{} \text{ Property.}$$

$$x = \boxed{} \text{ or } \qquad x = \boxed{} \qquad \text{Solve.}$$

Check $\quad \frac{6}{\boxed{}^2} \overset{?}{=} \frac{5}{\boxed{}} - 1 \qquad \frac{6}{\boxed{}^2} \overset{?}{=} \frac{5}{\boxed{}} - 1$

$\qquad\qquad \frac{\boxed{}}{\boxed{}} = \frac{\boxed{}}{\boxed{}} \checkmark \qquad\qquad \frac{\boxed{}}{\boxed{}} = \frac{\boxed{}}{\boxed{}} \checkmark$

Quick Check

1. Solve each equation. Check your solution.

a. $\frac{1}{3} + \frac{1}{3x} = \frac{1}{6}$

b. $\frac{5}{m} = \frac{2}{m^2} + 2$

Daily Notetaking Guide   L1

Name _____ Class _____ Date _____

Example

② **Checking to Find an Extraneous Solution** Solve $\dfrac{x+3}{x-1} = \dfrac{4}{x-1}$.

$(x + 3)\left(\boxed{} - \boxed{}\right) = \boxed{}(x - 1)$ **Write cross products.**

$\boxed{} - x + \boxed{} - 3 = 4x - \boxed{}$ **Use the** \boxed{} **Property.**

$x^2 + \boxed{} - \boxed{} = 4x - \boxed{}$ **Combine** \boxed{} **terms.**

$x^2 - \boxed{} + \boxed{} = \boxed{}$ **Subtract** \boxed{} **from each side.**

$\left(x - \boxed{}\right)\left(x - \boxed{}\right) = 0$ **Factor.**

$\boxed{} - \boxed{} = 0$ **Use the Zero-Product Property.**

$\boxed{} = \boxed{}$ **Simplify.**

Check 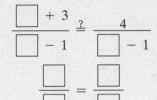 $\dfrac{\boxed{} + 3}{\boxed{} - 1} \overset{?}{=} \dfrac{4}{\boxed{} - 1}$

$\dfrac{\boxed{}}{\boxed{}} = \dfrac{\boxed{}}{\boxed{}}$ **Undefined! There is no division by** $\boxed{}$.

The equation has no solution because $\boxed{}$ makes the denominator equal $\boxed{}$.

Quick Check

2. Solve each equation. Check your solution.

a. $\dfrac{3}{a} = \dfrac{5}{a - 2}$

b. $\dfrac{n}{5} = \dfrac{4}{n + 1}$

c. $\dfrac{2}{c^2} = \dfrac{2}{c^2 + 1}$

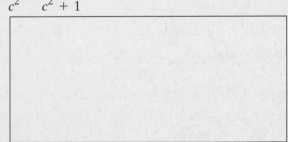

d. $\dfrac{w^2}{w - 1} = \dfrac{1}{w - 1}$

Name_____ Class_____ Date_____

Lesson 12-7

Counting Methods and Permutations

Lesson Objectives	NAEP 2005 Strand: Data Analysis and Probability
▼ Use the multiplication counting principle	Topic: Probability
② Find permutations	Local Standards: _____

Vocabulary

A _____ is an arrangement of objects in a specific order.

Examples

❶ **Using a Tree Diagram** Suppose you have three shirts and three ties that coordinate. Make a tree diagram to find the number of possible outfits you have.

There are [   ] possible outfits.

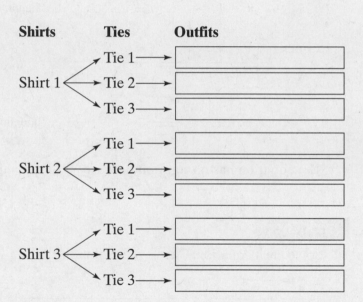

❷ **Using the Multiplication Counting Principle** Suppose there are two routes you can drive to get from Austin, Texas, to Dallas, Texas, and four routes from Dallas, Texas, to Tulsa, Oklahoma. How many possible routes are there from Austin to Tulsa through Dallas?

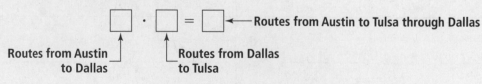

There are [   ] possible routes from Austin to Tulsa.

❸ Counting Permutations In how many ways can 11 students enter a classroom? There are 11 choices for the first student, ☐ for the second, ☐ for the third, and so on.

11 · ☐ · ☐ · ☐ · ☐ · ☐ · ☐ · ☐ · ☐ · ☐ · ☐   **Use a calculator.**

= ☐

There are ☐ possible ways in which the students can enter the classroom.

❹ Using Permutation Notation Simplify $_8P_5$.
Use pencil and paper.

$_8P_5$ = ☐ · ☐ · ☐ · ☐ · ☐   The first factor is ☐, and there are ☐ factors.

= ☐   **Simplify.**

Quick Check

1. Suppose you have two T-shirts and four pairs of shorts you could bring for gym class. Make a tree diagram to find the number of possible outfits for the gym.

2. At the neighborhood pizza shop, there are five vegetable toppings and three meat toppings for a pizza. How many different pizzas can you order with one meat and one vegetable topping?

3. A swimming pool has eight lanes. In how many ways can eight swimmers be assigned lanes for a race?

4. Simplify each expression.

   a. $_9P_3$ **b.** $_7P_3$

Lesson 12-8

Combinations

Lesson Objectives	NAEP 2005 Strand: Data Analysis and Probability
▼ Find combinations	**Topic:** Probability
▼ Find probability with counting techniques	**Local Standards:** _____

Vocabulary

A _____ is a collection of objects without regard to order.

Example

1 **Counting Combinations** Eighteen people enter a talent contest. Awards will be given to the top ten finishers. How many different groups of ten winners can be chosen?

The order in which the top ten winners are listed once they are chosen does not distinguish one group of winners from another. You need the number of combinations of 18 potential winners chosen 10 at a time.

$_{18}C_{10} = \dfrac{\boxed{}}{_{10}P_{10}}$ **Write using permutation notation.**

$= \dfrac{18 \cdot \boxed{} \cdot \boxed{} \cdot \boxed{} \cdot \boxed{} \cdot \boxed{} \cdot \boxed{} \cdot \boxed{} \cdot \boxed{} \cdot \boxed{}}{10 \cdot \boxed{} \cdot \boxed{} \cdot \boxed{} \cdot \boxed{} \cdot \boxed{} \cdot \boxed{} \cdot \boxed{} \cdot \boxed{} \cdot \boxed{}}$

$= \boxed{}$ **Use a calculator.**

Quick Check

1. a. For your history report, you can choose to write about two of a list of five presidents of the United States. Use $_nC_r$ notation to write the number of combinations possible for your report.

b. Calculate the number of combinations of presidents on whom you could report.

Example

② **Using Combinations in Probability** Suppose you have eight red pens and four black pens in a box. You choose five pens without looking. What is the probability that all the pens you choose are red?

There are 12 pens in all. Eight of the pens are red.

number of favorable outcomes = $_8C_{\square}$ **number of ways to choose 5 pens from the** $\boxed{}$ **red pens**

number of possible outcomes = $_{\square}C_5$ **number of ways to choose 5 pens from the** $\boxed{}$ **possible pens**

$P(5 \text{ red pens}) = \dfrac{\text{number of } \boxed{} \text{ outcomes}}{\text{total number of outcomes}}$ **Use the definition of probability.**

$= \dfrac{\boxed{}}{_{12}C_5}$ **Substitute.**

$= \dfrac{56}{\boxed{}} = \dfrac{\boxed{}}{\boxed{}}$ **Simplify each expression. Simplify the fractions.**

The probability that you will choose five red pens is $\dfrac{\boxed{}}{\boxed{}}$, or about $\boxed{}$%.

Quick Check

2. a. Suppose you have the pens in Example 2. You choose eight pens at random. How many combinations are possible?

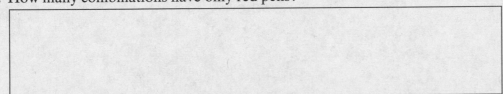

  b. How many combinations have only red pens?

  c. What is the probability that all of the pens are red?

A Note to the Student:

This section of your workbook contains a series of pages that support your mathematics understandings for each chapter and lesson presented in your student edition.

- Practice pages provide additional practice for every lesson.

- Guided Problem Solving pages lead you through a step-by-step solution to an application problem in each lesson.

- Vocabulary pages contain a variety of activities to increase your reading and math understanding, ranging from graphic organizers to vocabulary review puzzles.

Practice 1-1

Using Variables

Write an algebraic expression for each phrase.

1. 7 increased by x

_____

2. p multiplied by 3

_____

3. 10 decreased by m

_____

4. n less than 7

_____

5. the product of 2 and q

_____

6. 3 more than m

_____

Write a phrase for each algebraic expression.

7. $\frac{8}{a}$

_____

8. $s - 10$

_____

9. $x + 13$

_____

Define a variable and write an algebraic expression for each phrase.

10. the difference of 8 and a number

_____

11. the sum of 4 and a number

_____

12. the product of 2 and a number

_____

13. 3 increased by a number

_____

Define a variable and write an algebraic equation to model each situation.

14. What is the total cost of buying several shirts at $24.95 each?

_____

15. The number of gal of water used to water trees is 30 times the number of trees.

_____

16. What is the number of marbles left in a 48-marble bag after some marbles have been given away?

_____

17. What is the cost of buying several pairs of pants at $32.95 per pair?

_____

Define variables and write an equation to model the relationship in each table.

18.

Number of Tickets	Total Cost
2	$7
4	$14
6	$21

19.

Number of Hours	Distance Traveled
1	55 mi
3	165 mi
5	275 mi

20.

Number of Hours	Total Pay
8	$40
12	$60
16	$80

_____ _____ _____

Algebra 1 Lesson 1-1 **179**

1-1 • Guided Problem Solving

GPS **Student Page 7, Exercise 42**

Multiple Choice Which equation best describes the relationship between the amount of money a in a bag of quarters and the number of quarters q?

A. $a = 0.25q$ **B.** $a = 0.25 + q$ **C.** $q = 0.25a$ **D.** $q = 0.25 + q$

Read and Understand

1. What two quantities are related? _____

Plan and Solve

2. How much money is 1 quarter worth? _____

3. How much money are 2 quarters worth? _____

4. Explain how you would determine the amount of money 5 quarters are worth.

_____

5. How would you express the amount of money q quarters are worth? _____

6. Write an equation that describes the relationship between the amount of money a in a bag of quarters and the number of quarters q. _____

Look Back and Check

7. Check the reasonableness of your answer by explaining why the other answer choices do not make sense.

_____

Solve Another Problem

8. Mark has a pocket full of nickels. Which equation best describes the relationship between the amount of money a in his pocket and the number of nickels n?

   A. $a = n + 0.05$ **B.** $a = 0.05n$ **C.** $n = 0.05 + a$ **D.** $n = 0.05a$

            Guided Problem Solving

Practice 1-2

Exponents and Order of Operations

Simplify each expression.

1. $4 + 6(8)$

_____

2. $\dfrac{4(8 - 2)}{3 + 9}$

_____

3. $4 \times 3^2 + 2$

_____

4. $40 \div 5(2)$

_____

5. $3[4(8 - 2) + 5]$

_____

6. $6 \times (3 + 2) \div 15$

_____

Evaluate each expression.

7. $\dfrac{a + 2b}{5}$ for $a = 1$ and $b = 2$

_____

8. $\dfrac{5m + n}{5}$ for $m = 6$ and $n = 15$

_____

Simplify each expression.

9. $\dfrac{100 - 15}{9 + 8}$

_____

10. $\dfrac{2(3 + 4)}{7}$

_____

11. $\dfrac{3(4 + 12)}{2(7 - 3)}$

_____

12. $14 + 3 \times 4$

_____

13. $8 + 3(4 + 3)$

_____

14. $3 + 4[13 - 2(6 - 3)]$

_____

15. $8(5 + 30 \div 5)$

_____

16. $50 \div 2 + 15 \times 4$

_____

17. $7(9 - 5)$

_____

18. $2(3^2) - 3(2)$

_____

19. $4 + 8 \div 2 + 6 \times 3$

_____

20. $(7 + 8) \div (4 - 1)$

_____

21. $5[2(8 + 5) - 15]$

_____

22. $(6 + 8) \times (8 - 4)$

_____

23. $14 + 6 \times 2^3 - 8 \div 2^2$

_____

Evaluate each expression for $a = 2$ and $b = 6$.

24. $2(7a - b)$

_____

25. $(a^3 + b^2) \div a$

_____

26. $3b \div (2a - 1) + b$

_____

1-2 • Guided Problem Solving

GPS **Student Page 14, Exercise 63**

a. **Geometry** The formula for the volume of a cylinder is $V = \pi r^2 h$. What is the volume of the cylinder? Round your answer to the nearest hundredth of a cubic inch.

b. **Critical Thinking** About how many cubic inches does an ounce of juice fill? Round your answer to the nearest tenth of a cubic inch.

c. The formula for the surface area of a cylinder is $SA = 2\pi r(r + h)$. What is the surface area of the cylinder? Round your answer to the nearest hundredth of a square inch.

Juice
12 fl. oz.
$r = 1.3$ in.
$\leftarrow h = 4.5$ in. $\rightarrow$

Read and Understand

1. What are the two formulas that you will need to use? _____

2. What information is given in the picture? _____

Plan and Solve

3. What is the value you will use for r? _____

4. What is the value you will use for h? _____

5. What is the decimal approximation for π? _____

6. What is the volume of the cylinder? _____

7. What is the surface area of the cylinder? _____

8. About how many cubic inches does an ounce of juice fill? _____

Look Back and Check

9. Round your volume to the nearest cubic inch. Check the reasonableness of your answer by dividing your volume by 2. Your answer should be close to 12, which is the number of ounces of juice in the cylinder.

Solve Another Problem

10. What is the volume of a cylinder if the radius is 2.0 inches and the height is 2.5 inches?

_____

Practice 1-3

Name the set(s) of numbers to which each number belongs.

1. -0.002

2. $12\frac{1}{2}$

3. 8

4. 5π

_____ _____ _____ _____

5. $\sqrt{7}$

6. -22

7. -3.4

8. $\sqrt{36}$

_____ _____ _____ _____

Is each statement *true* or *false*? If the statement is false, give a counterexample.

9. Every whole number is an integer.

10. Every integer is a whole number.

_____ _____

11. Every rational number is a real number.

12. Every multiple of 7 is odd.

_____ _____

Use <, =, or > to compare.

13. $-10.98 \ \blacksquare \ -10.99$

14. $-\frac{1}{3} \ \blacksquare \ -0.3$

15. $-\frac{11}{5} \ \blacksquare \ -\frac{4}{5}$

_____ _____ _____

16. $-\frac{1}{2} \ \blacksquare \ -\frac{5}{10}$

17. $-\frac{3}{8} \ \blacksquare \ -\frac{7}{16}$

18. $\frac{3}{4} \ \blacksquare \ \frac{13}{16}$

_____ _____ _____

Order the numbers in each group from least to greatest.

19. $-\frac{8}{9}, -\frac{7}{8}, -\frac{22}{25}$

20. $-3\frac{4}{9}, -3.45, -3\frac{12}{25}$

21. $-\frac{1}{4}, -\frac{1}{5}, -\frac{1}{3}$

_____ _____ _____

22. $-1.7, -1\frac{3}{4}, -1\frac{7}{9}$

23. $-\frac{3}{4}, -\frac{7}{8}, -\frac{2}{3}$

24. $2\frac{3}{4}, 2\frac{5}{8}, 2.7$

_____ _____ _____

Determine which set of numbers is most reasonable for each situation.

25. the number of dolphins in the ocean

26. the height of a basketball player

_____ _____

27. the number of pets you have

28. the circumference of a compact disk

_____ _____

Find each absolute value.

29. $\left|\frac{3}{10}\right|$

30. $|-327|$

31. $|-3.46|$

32. $\left|-\frac{1}{2}\right|$

_____ _____ _____ _____

1-3 • Guided Problem Solving

GPS **Student Page 21, Exercise 64**

Multiple Choice Use the number line. If R and T are opposites, what is the value of Q?

A. 7   **B.** 0   **C.** −3   **D.** −7

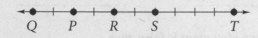

Read and Understand

1. Give an example of two numbers that are opposites. _____

Plan and Solve

2. On the number line above, mark the location of the number 0.

3. On the number line above, label the points R and T with their values.

4. What is the value of Q? _____

Look Back and Check

5. Check that your answer is correct by labeling all the remaining points on the number line.

Solve Another Problem

6. Use the number line. If P and T are opposites, what is the value of R?

    A. 0   **B.** 2   **C.** −2   **D.** −6

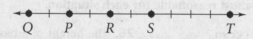

Practice 1-4

The relationships in the tables below are functions. Write a function rule for each.

1.

Number of Baseball Teams	Number of Players Required
1	9
2	18
3	27
4	36

_____

2.

Number of CDs Purchased	Total Cost
1	$13
2	$26
3	$39
4	$52

_____

3.

Number of Homework Questions	Number of Minutes for Homework
1	25
2	30
3	35
4	40

_____

4.

Number of Rides Taken	Cost of Fair
1	$10.00
2	$12.50
3	$15.00
4	$17.50

_____

Identify the independent and dependent quantity in each situation.

5. The amount of money earned babysitting increases with the number of hours spent babysitting.

_____

6. The cost of a skating party increases with the number of people attending the party.

_____

7. The volume of water in a bathtub decreases with the number of minutes it has been draining.

_____

8. The number of people attending the event decreases with the total cost for tickets.

_____

Name _____ Class _____ Date _____

1-4 • Guided Problem Solving

Each side of the first figure is one unit. Find a function rule for the relationship between a figure's number and its perimeter.

Figure 1   Figure 2

Figure 3   Figure 4

Read and Understand

1. How do you find the perimeter of a figure? _____

Plan and Solve

2. Determine the perimeter of each figure above and complete the table.

3. By how much is the perimeter changing each time?

_____

4. Write a function rule for the relationship between the figure's number and its perimeter.

_____

Figure Number	Perimeter
1	■
2	■
3	■
4	■

Look Back and Check

5. Check that your function rule is correct by substituting $n = 3$ to verify that the rule gives the correct perimeter.

_____

Solve Another Problem

6. Each side of the first figure is one unit. Draw and complete a table that shows the figure number and its perimeter. Then find a function rule for the relationship between a figure's number and its perimeter.

Figure 1   Figure 2   Figure 3   Figure 4

Figure Number	1	2	3	4
Perimeter				

Practice 1-5

Make a scatter plot for each set of data below.

1. Height and Hourly Pay of Ten People

Height (inches)	Hourly Pay	Height (inches)	Hourly Pay
62	$6.00	72	$8.00
65	$8.50	72	$6.00
68	$6.50	73	$7.50
70	$6.00	74	$6,25
70	$7.50	74	$8.00

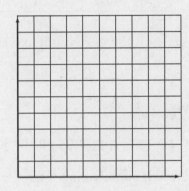

2. Speed of winds in Some U.S. Cites

Station	Average Speed (mi/h)	Highest Speed (mi/h)
Atlanta, GA	9.1	60
Casper, WY	12.9	81
Dallas, TX	10.7	73
Mobile, AL	9.0	63
St. Louis, MO	9.7	60

Source: National Climatic Data Center

Describe the trend in each scatter plot below.

3.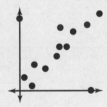

_____

4.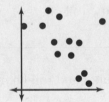

_____

5.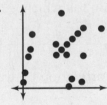

_____

6. In Exercise 1, is there a *positive correlation*, a *negative correlation*, or *no correlation* between height and hourly pay?

_____

7. In Exercise 2, is there a *positive correlation*, a *negative correlation*, or *no correlation* between average wind speed and highest wind speed?

_____

1-5 • Guided Problem Solving

GPS **Student Page 36, Exercise 16**

a. **Transportation** In the scatter plot at the right, what does a point represent?

b. How can you tell if some vehicles traveled the same distance?

c. How can you tell which vehicles paid the same toll charge?

d. Is there a correlation between distance traveled and toll charges? Explain.

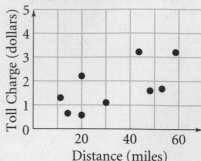

Toll Charges for 9 Vehicles on the Indiana Toll Road

SOURCE: Indiana Department of Highways

Read and Understand

1. What two quantities are related in the scatter plot?

_____

2. What is the scale on the horizontal axis?

_____

Plan and Solve

3. Explain what a point represents on the scatter plot. _____

4. How can you tell if some vehicles traveled the same distance? _____

_____

5. How can you tell which vehicles paid the same toll charge? _____

_____

6. Is there a correlation between distance traveled and toll charges? Explain. _____

_____

_____

Look Back and Check

7. Circle two points that represent two vehicles that paid the same toll charge. Put a square around two vehicles that traveled the same distance. Check the reasonableness of your answer by comparing these pairs of points with your responses above.

Solve Another Problem

8. In the scatter plot above, what are the approximate maximum and minimum toll charges paid by these 9 vehicles?

_____

Name _____ Class _____ Date _____

Practice 1-6

Mean, Median, Mode, and Range

Find the mean, median, and mode. Which measure of central tendency best describes the data?

1. number of cars sold in the past 10 days
1 5 3 2 1 0 4 2 6 1

_____

2. utility bills for the past 6 months
$90 $120 $140 $135 $112 $126

_____

3. prices of a sweater in 5 different stores
$31.25 $27.50 $28.00 $36.95 $32.10

_____

4. scores on a 10-point quiz
7 9 10 8 4 2 6 10 8

_____

Find the range.

5. hourly wages
$7.25 $6.75 $8.10 $9.56 $7.10 $7.75

_____

6. ages of students on the quiz team
15 15 14 16 17 16 16 15

_____

7. a. A bakery collected the following data about the number of loaves of
fresh bread sold on each of 24 business days. Make a stem-and-leaf
plot for the data.

43	39	17	38	50	42	34	28	37	42	40	33
72	36	45	21	29	44	41	37	40	35	51	54

b. Find the mean, median, mode(s), and range of the data.

_____

8. The back-to-back stem-and-leaf plot shows the
number of calls made to each of two police
departments in the last 14 days. Find the mean,
median, mode(s), and range of each side of the
stem-and-leaf plot.

```
    Dept. A        Dept. B
      9 5 2 │3│ 1 4
    8 6 2 1 │4│ 7 9 9
    8 8 8 2 │5│ 0 2 2 2 4
      3 2 1 │6│ 1 1 3
            │7│ 1
```

means 32 ← 2 │ 3 │ 1 → means 31

_____

9. The back-to-back stem-and-leaf plot shows the
average daytime temperature (in °F) at two
different locations for each of the past 15 weeks.
Find the mean, median, mode(s), and range of
each side of the stem-and-leaf plot.

```
     Locn. A          Locn. B
       9 8 7 │6│ 5 6 6 7 9
       7 5 1 0 │7│ 2 4 5 6 8
     9 4 3 3 1 │8│ 0 4 7 9
       1 0 0 │9│ 1
```

means 67 ← 7 │ 6 │ 5 → means 65

_____

1-6 • Guided Problem Solving

GPS **Student Page 44, Exercise 25**

Manufacturing Two manufacturing plants create sheets of steel for medical instruments. The back-to-back stem-and-leaf plot at the right shows data collected from the two plants.

a. Find the mean, median, mode, and range of each set of data.
b. Which measure of central tendency best describes each set of data? Explain.
c. **Reasoning** Which plant has the better quality control? Explain.

Width of Steel (millimeters)

Manufacturing Plant A		Manufacturing Plant B
	4	3 5 9
8 7 4 4 2	5	2 7
4 3 1	6	3 4
	7	2

means 6.1 ← 1 | 6 | 3 → means 6.3

Read and Understand

1. Describe how to determine the mean, median, mode, and range.

_____

Plan and Solve

2. Find the mean, median, mode, and range of each set of data. Record the results in the table.

	Mean	Median	Mode	Range
Plant A				
Plant B				

3. Which measure of central tendency best describes each set of data? Explain.

_____

4. Which plant has the better quality control? Justify your answer.

_____

Look Back and Check

5. Check the reasonableness of your mean values. Are they between the minimum and maximum data values?

Solve Another Problem

6. If 7.5 is added to the data for Plant A, would the same plant have the better quality control? Explain.

1A: Graphic Organizer

For use before Lesson 1-1

Study Skill Always write down your assignments. Do not rely on your memory to recall all assignments from all your classes.

Write your answers.

1. What is the chapter title? _____

2. Find the Table of Contents page for this chapter at the front of the book. Name four topics you will study in this chapter.

   _____   _____

   _____   _____

3. Complete the graphic organizer as you work through the chapter.
   1. Write the title of the chapter in the center oval.
   2. When you begin a lesson, write the name of the lesson in a rectangle.
   3. When you complete that lesson, write a skill or key concept from that lesson in the outer oval linked to that rectangle.

   Continue with steps 2 and 3 clockwise around the graphic organizer.

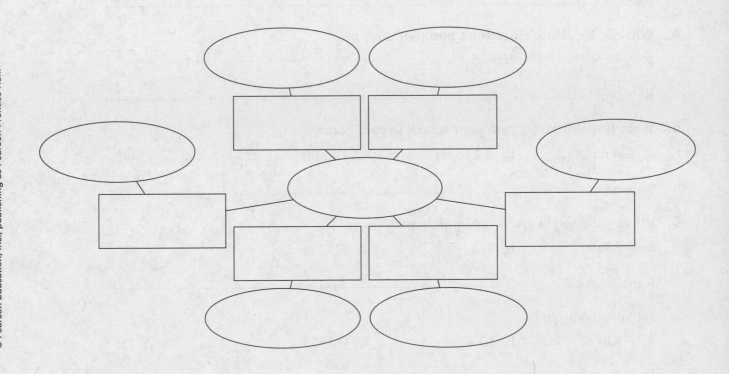

1B: Reading Comprehension

Study Skill When finding the answer to a math problem, be sure your answer makes sense in the context of the problem.

For each exercise, you are given a question with three answer choices. Circle each choice that would be possible in some situation. Some questions may have more than one possible answer. If a choice is not possible, explain.

1. How many buses are needed?

    a. −3   **b.** 2.5   **c.** 3

    Reason: _____

2. What is the temperature?

    a. −5°   **b.** 0°   **c.** 75.5°

    Reason: _____

3. What is the class average on the test?

    a. −15   **b.** 78.4   **c.** 85

    Reason: _____

4. What is the daily change for a group of stock prices?

    a. −10.50   **b.** −5   **c.** 23

    Reason: _____

5. What is the distance from your school to your home?

    a. −6 miles   **b.** 0.25 mile   **c.** 4.4 miles

    Reason: _____

6. What is the total cost of your purchases?

    a. −$30.23   **b.** $13.00   **c.** $23.375

    Reason: _____

7. What is the profit?

    a. −$20.40   **b.** $0   **c.** $125.75

    Reason: _____

8. High-Use Academic Words What does *context* mean in the study skill?

    a. estimation   **b.** situation

1C: Reading/Writing Math Symbols

For use after Lesson 1-2

Study Skill When you take notes in class, keep up with what is being said by using abbreviations. Use abbreviations that you will be able to understand when you review your notes.

Mathematics is a language made up of symbols that represent words and amounts. For example, the mathematical expression 5×2 symbolizes five times two.

Explain the meaning of each mathematical expression using words.

1. $3 \cdot 7$ _____

_____

2. $5n$ _____

_____

3. $3 \div 4$ _____

_____

4. $\frac{7}{12}$ _____

_____

5. 2^x _____

_____

6. $6(7)$ _____

_____

Write each phrase with math symbols.

7. 7 minus 3 _____

8. p divided by 2 _____

9. 4 divided by x _____

10. y equals 9 _____

1D: Visual Vocabulary Practice

For use after Lesson 1-6

Study Skill The Glossary contains the key vocabulary for this course, as well as illustrated examples.

Concept List

absolute value	function rule	inequality
opposites	power	range
scatter plot	variable	whole numbers

Write the concept that best describes each exercise. Choose from the concept list above.

1. m _____	**2.** 5^3 _____	**3.** 12 23 54 81 69 for the data above _____
4. -12 and 12 _____	**5.** 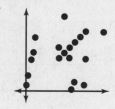 _____	**6.** $\lvert -52 \rvert$ _____
7. $-4 < 10$ _____	**8.** $0, 1, 2, 3, \ldots$ _____	**9.** $P = 5 + 0.02n$ _____

1E: Vocabulary Check

Study Skill Strengthen your vocabulary. Use these pages and add cues and summaries by applying the Cornell Notetaking style.

Write the definition for each word at the right. To check your work, fold the paper back along the dotted line to see the correct answers.

_____ Algebraic Expression

_____

_____

_____ Equation

_____

_____ Natural Numbers

_____

_____ Integers

_____

_____ Absolute Value

_____

1E: Vocabulary Check (continued)

Write the vocabulary word for each definition. To check your work, fold the paper forward along the dotted line to see the correct answers.

A mathematical phrase that can include numbers, variables, and operation symbols.

_____

A mathematical sentence that uses an equal sign.

_____

The counting numbers.

_____

Whole numbers and their opposites.

_____

The distance that a number is from zero on a number line.

_____

1F: Vocabulary Review

Study Skill Many words in English have more than one meaning. Often a word has one meaning in ordinary conversation, and a different specific meaning or exact definition when it is used in math or science or grammar. You can often figure out which meaning to use by looking at the sentence that contains the word. To help you decide what a word means, consider the surroundings, or context, in which you see the word.

Read the mathematical definition in the left column and the sentence in the right column. In the blank in the middle, write the one word from the list below that fits both the definition and the sentence.

base	like	origin	constant
power	function	open	term

Definition		**Sentence**

1. a term that has no variable _____ That noise is _____. It just never seems to stop.

2. a number that is multiplied repeatedly _____ Put this statue on its _____ so it will not fall over.

3. the kind of terms that have exactly the same variable factors _____ I really _____ that kind of food. It is my favorite.

4. the kind of math sentence that has one or more variables _____ The door should be _____ so the customers can come in.

5. the base and exponent of an expression of the form a^n _____ Turn off the _____ before you try to repair those wires.

6. the point where the axes of a coordinate plane intersect _____ What is the _____ of that custom? I wonder how it began.

7. a number, a variable, or the product of a number and one or more variables _____ He will come home from college at the end of the _____.

8. a relation that assigns exactly one value in the range to each value of the domain _____ What is the _____ of that key on the keyboard?

Practice 2-1

Simplify each expression.

1. $6 + (-4)$

_____

2. $-2 + (-13)$

_____

3. $-18 + 4$

_____

4. $15 + (-32)$

_____

5. $-27 + (-14)$

_____

6. $8 + (-3)$

_____

7. $\frac{1}{4} + \left(-\frac{3}{4}\right)$

_____

8. $\frac{2}{3} + \left(-\frac{1}{3}\right)$

_____

9. $|-12| + |-21|$

_____

10. $|-13 + 6|$

_____

11. $-14 + |-7|$

_____

Evaluate each expression for $m = 2.5$.

12. $-m + 1.6$

_____

13. $-3.2 + m$

_____

14. $-2.5 + (-m)$

_____

Simplify.

15. $-3 + (-6) + 14$

_____

16. $4 + (-8) + (-14)$

_____

Simplify.

17. $\begin{bmatrix} 4 & -1 \\ 2 & 5 \end{bmatrix} + \begin{bmatrix} -1 & 2 \\ -2 & -3 \end{bmatrix} = $ _____

18. $\begin{bmatrix} -4.7 \\ 2.3 \\ -1.5 \end{bmatrix} + \begin{bmatrix} 5.1 \\ -2.7 \\ 2.6 \end{bmatrix} = $ _____

19. The temperature at 5:00 A.M. is $-38°F$. The temperature rises $20°F$ by 11:00 A.M. What is the temperature at 11:00 A.M.?

_____

20. A football team has possession of the ball on their own 15-yd line. The next two plays result in a loss of 7 yd and a gain of 3 yd, respectively. On what yard line is the ball after the two plays?

_____

2-1 • Guided Problem Solving

GPS Student Page 62, Exercise 69

Jobs Use the data in the tables.

 a. Write the data in each table as a matrix.
 b. Add the matrices to find the total number of workers in each pay category for each work shift.
 c. How many weekend employees on the evening shift earn $6.50 per hour?
 d. How many weekend employees work the night shift?
 e. **Critical Thinking** Suppose all employees work 8-hour shifts both Saturday and Sunday. How would you use the matrix to find the total wages of the weekend employees?
 f. Find the total wages of the weekend employees.

Number of Employees

Saturday Schedule
Hourly Wage

Shift	$6.25	$6.50	$7.00	$7.50
Day	8	3	5	1
Evening	10	2	2	1
Night	4	1	0	1

Sunday Schedule
Hourly Wage

Shift	$6.25	$6.50	$7.00	$7.50
Day	5	2	1	1
Evening	8	2	0	1
Night	2	1	0	1

Read and Understand

1. What information is given in the tables?

   _____

2. Write a matrix for the Saturday schedule and another for the Sunday schedule.

Plan and Solve

3. Add the matrices to find the total number of workers in each pay category for each work shift.

   _____

4. How many weekend employees on the evening shift earn $6.50 per hour? _____

5. Suppose all employees work 8-hour shifts both Saturday and Sunday. How would you use the matrix to find the total wages of the weekend employees? _____

   _____

6. Find the total wages of the weekend employees. _____

Look Back and Check

7. Explain why a matrix helped to make the information in the table more understandable.

   _____

Solve Another Problem

8. How many weekend night employees are there? _____

Name _____ Class _____ Date _____

Practice 2-2

Subtracting Rational Numbers

Simplify.

1. $13 - 6$

_____

2. $19 - 35$

_____

3. $-4 - 8$

_____

4. $-14 - (-6)$

_____

5. $18 - (-25)$

_____

6. $-32 - 17$

_____

7. $-3 - (-15)$

_____

8. $|-11| - |-29|$

_____

9. $|-4 - 8|$

_____

Evaluate each expression for $c = -3$ and $d = -6$.

10. $c - d$

_____

11. $-c - d$

_____

12. $|c + d|$

_____

13. $-c + d$

_____

Simplify.

14. $8 - (-4) - (-5)$

15. $6 - 10 - 4$

_____

16. $10 - 14 - 15$

_____

Subtract.

17. $\begin{bmatrix} -3 & -1 \\ 2 & 4 \end{bmatrix} - \begin{bmatrix} 5 & -2 \\ -3 & 8 \end{bmatrix}$

_____

18. $\begin{bmatrix} 6.1 & -4 \\ -3.7 & -2.1 \end{bmatrix} - \begin{bmatrix} 7.0 & -2.3 \\ -1.6 & 4.2 \end{bmatrix}$

_____

19. The temperature in the evening was 68°F. The following morning, the temperature was 39°F. What is the difference between the two temperatures?

_____

20. After three plays in which a football team lost 7 yd, gained 3 yd, and lost 1 yd, respectively, the ball was placed on the team's own 30-yd line. Where was the ball before the three plays?

_____

2-2 • Guided Problem Solving

GPS **Student Page 67, Exercise 55**

a. **Sports** Write the data in each table at right as a matrix.

b. Subtract the 2000 matrix from the 2005 matrix to find the changes in participation in sports activities.

c. **Writing** Suppose you invest in sporting goods. In which sport would you invest? Use elements from your matrix to explain.

City-Wide Participation in Sports Activities (thousands)

	Sport	Elementary	High School	College
2000	Basketball	5.5	8.2	4.9
	Tennis	1.4	3.2	3.9
	Soccer	4.2	3.8	1.3
	Volleyball	1.6	5.2	5.1

	Sport	Elementary	High School	College
2005	Basketball	6.8	7.9	4.9
	Tennis	1.0	1.8	1.7
	Soccer	5.6	4.1	1.3
	Volleyball	1.8	4.9	2.9

Read and Understand

1. What information is given in the tables?

_____

2. Write a matrix for each table.

Plan and Solve

3. Subtract the 2000 matrix from the 2005 matrix to find the changes in participation in sports activities.

_____

4. Suppose you invested in sporting goods. In which sport would you invest? Use elements from your matrix to explain.

_____

Look Back and Check

5. Explain how organizing data into a matrix made it easier to learn more about the information in the tables.

_____

Solve Another Problem

6. Use your two original matrices to determine which sport had the highest participation rate in 2000 and in 2005. Explain how you used your matrices to arrive at your answers.

_____

Practice 2-3

Simplify each expression.

1. $(-2)(8)$

_____

2. $(-6)(-9)$

_____

3. $(-3)^4$

_____

4. -2^5

_____

5. $(6)(-8)$

_____

6. $-30 \div (-5)$

_____

Evaluate each expression.

7. x^3 for $x = -5$

_____

8. $s^2 t \div 10$ for $s = -2$ and $t = 10$

_____

9. $-2m + 4n^2$ for $m = -6$ and $n = -5$

_____

10. $(x + 4)^2$ for $x = -11$

_____

Simplify each expression.

11. $2^4 - 3^2 + 5^2$

_____

12. $32 \div (-7 + 5)^3$

_____

13. $18 + 4^2 \div (-8)$

_____

14. $(-8)(-5)(-3)$

_____

15. $(-3)^2 - 4^2$

_____

16. $(-2)^6$

_____

Evaluate each expression.

17. $(a + b)^2$ for $a = 6$ and $b = -8$

_____

18. $d^3 \div e$ for $d = -6$ and $e = -3$

_____

19. $j^5 - 5k$ for $j = -4$ and $k = -1$

_____

20. $4s \div (-3t)$ for $s = -6$ and $t = -2$

_____

2-3 • Guided Problem Solving

GPS **Student Page 75, Exercise 83**

Entertainment As riders plunge down the hill of a roller coaster, you can approximate the height h, in feet, above the ground of their roller coaster car. Use the function $h = 155 - 16t^2$ where t is the number of seconds since the start of the descent.

155 ft

a. How far is a rider from the bottom of the hill after 1 second? 2 seconds?

b. **Critical Thinking** Does it take more than or less than 4 seconds to reach the bottom? Explain.

Read and Understand

1. What do each of the variables in the function represent?

   _____

2. What are the units that would be used for values of h and t? _____

Plan and Solve

3. How far is the rider from the bottom of the hill after 1 second? _____

4. How far is the rider from the bottom of the hill after 2 seconds? _____

5. What value would you use for h if the roller coaster car were at the bottom of the hill? _____

6. Does it take more than or less than 4 seconds to reach the bottom? Explain. _____

   _____

Look Back and Check

7. Explain how you use order of operations when using the roller coaster function.

   _____

Solve Another Problem

8. For a different roller coaster, the height h, in feet, above the ground of the roller coaster car is approximated by the function $h = 200 - 16t^2$. How far is a rider from the bottom of the hill on this roller coaster after 2 seconds?

Name _____ Class _____ Date _____

Practice 2-4

The Distributive Property

Simplify each expression.

1. $2(x + 6)$

2. $-5(8 - b)$

3. $4(-x + 7)$

_____

_____

_____

4. $(5c - 7)(-3)$

5. $-(3k - 12)$

6. $4(x + 7)$

_____

_____

_____

7. $-2(k - 11)$

8. $-(4 - 2b)$

9. $2(3x - 9)$

_____

_____

_____

10. $4(2r + 8)$

11. $-5(b - 5)$

12. $3(f + 2)$

_____

_____

_____

13. $7 + 2(4x - 3)$

14. $2(3h + 2) - 4h$

15. $2(4 + y)$

_____

_____

_____

16. $-w + 4(w + 3)$

17. $2(3a + 2)$

18. $5(t - 3) - 2t$

_____

_____

_____

19. $5(b + 4) - 6b$

20. $2(a - 4) + 15$

21. $5(3x + 12)$

_____

_____

_____

22. $2(m + 1)$

23. $4(2a + 2) - 17$

24. $3(t - 12)$

_____

_____

_____

Write an expression for each phrase.

25. 5 times the quantity x plus 6

_____

26. twice the quantity y minus 8

_____

27. 32 divided by the quantity y plus 12

_____

28. -8 times the quantity 4 decreased by w

_____

L1 Practice

Algebra 1 Lesson 2-4 **205**

2-4 • Guided Problem Solving

GPS Student Page 84, Exercise 78

Shopping Suppose you buy 4 cans of tomatoes at $1.02 each, 3 cans of tuna for $.99 each, and 3 boxes of pasta at $.52 each. Write an expression to model this situation. Then use the Distributive Property to find the total cost.

Read and Understand

1. What is the Distributive Property? _____

2. What type of information is given to you in the problem? _____

Plan and Solve

3. Write an expression that shows how to determine the total amount spent on tomatoes. _____

4. Write an expression that shows how to determine the total amount spent on tuna. _____

5. Write an expression that shows how to determine the total amount spent on pasta. _____

6. Write an expression that models the total amount of money you will spend. _____

7. Use the Distributive Property to find the total cost. _____

Look Back and Check

8. Check the reasonableness of your answer by rounding the cost of each item and estimating the total cost. _____

_____

Solve Another Problem

9. In order to paint your bedroom, you buy 2 gallons of paint that cost $10.50 each, 3 paint brushes that cost $2.99 each, and 2 paint rollers that cost $1.25 each. Write an expression to model this situation. Then use the Distributive Property to find the total cost.

_____

Name_____ Class_____ Date_____

Practice 2-5

Properties of Numbers

Name the property that each equation illustrates.

1. $83 + 6 = 6 + 83$

_____

2. $8 + x = x + 8$

_____

3. $1 \cdot 4y = 4y$

_____

4. $(8 \cdot 7) \cdot 6 = 8 \cdot (7 \cdot 6)$

_____

5. $\frac{2}{3}\left(\frac{3}{2}\right) = 1$

_____

6. $3(a + 2b) = 3a + 6b$

_____

7. $7 + (8 + 15) = (7 + 8) + 15$

_____

8. $x + (-x) = 0$

_____

9. $x + y = y + x$

_____

10. $6 \cdot (x \cdot y) = (6 \cdot x) \cdot y$

_____

11. $16 + 0 = 16$

_____

12. $7(3 + 4y) = 21 + 28y$

_____

13. $0 = 30 \cdot 0$

_____

14. $wr = rw$

_____

Give a reason to justify each step.

15. a. $4c + 3(2 + c) = 4c + 6 + 3c$

    b. _____ $= 4c + 3c + 6$

    c. _____ $= (4c + 3c) + 6$

    d. _____ $= (4 + 3)c + 6$

    e. _____ $= 7c + 6$

16. a. $8w - 4(7 - w) = 8w - 28 + 4w$

    b. _____ $= 8w + (-28) + 4w$

    c. _____ $= 8w + 4w + (-28)$

    d. _____ $= (8 + 4)w + (-28)$

    e. _____ $= 12w + (-28)$

    f. _____ $= 12w - 28$

Use mental math to simplify each expression.

17. $48 + 27 + 2 + 3$

_____

18. $10 \cdot 72 \cdot 5 \cdot 2$

_____

19. $10 \cdot 8 \cdot 3 \cdot 10$

_____

2-5 • Guided Problem Solving

GPS **Student Page 89, Exercise 31**

Shopping Suppose you are buying soccer equipment: a pair of cleats for $31.50, a soccer ball for $14.97, and shin guards for $6.50. Use mental math to find the total cost.

Read and Understand

1. What is the problem asking you to do? _____

2. What two properties of real numbers will
   help you solve this problem using mental math? _____   _____

Plan and Solve

3. Explain what the Commutative Property of Addition states. _____
   _____

4. Explain what the Associative Property of Addition states. _____
   _____

5. How can you use the Commutative Property to rewrite the expression 31.50 + 14.97 + 6.50 in
   order to be able to use mental math? _____

6. How will you use the Associative Property to find the total cost? _____
   _____

7. What is your total cost? _____

Look Back and Check

8. Check the reasonableness of your answer by rounding the cost of each item and estimating the
   total cost. _____
   _____

Solve Another Problem

9. Suppose you are buying new clothes for school: a pair of pants for $24.50, a shirt for $13.99, and
   a pair of shoes for $12.50. Use mental math to find the total cost. _____
   _____

Practice 2-6

Theoretical and Experimental Probability

A driver collected data on how long it takes to drive to work.

Time in minutes	20	25	30
Number of trips	4	8	2

1. Find P(the trip will take 25 min).

_____

2. Find P(the trip will take 20 min).

_____

3. Find P(the trip will take at least 25 min).

_____

Use the data in the line plot to find each probability.

Student Birth Months

```
                        X                           X
X           X           X               X           X
X           X           X     X         X     X     X
X     X     X     X      X     X     X   X     X     X
JAN   FEB   MAR   APR   MAY   JUN   JUL  AUG  SEP  OCT   NOV   DEC
```

4. P(June)   **5.** P(first six months of year)   **6.** P(not December)

_____   _____   _____

A cereal manufacturer selects 100 boxes of cereal at random. Ninety-nine of the boxes are the correct weight. Find each probability.

7. P(the cereal box is the correct weight)

_____

8. P(the cereal box is not the correct weight)

_____

9. There are 24,000 boxes of cereal. Predict how many of the boxes are the correct weight.

_____

10. Patrice has a 40% chance of making a free throw. What is the probability that she will miss the free throw?

_____

11. A box of animal crackers contains five hippos, two lions, three zebras, and four elephants. Find the probability if one animal cracker is chosen at random.

  a. P(a hippo) _____   **b.** P(not an elephant) _____

  c. P(an elephant or a lion) _____

2-6 • Guided Problem Solving

GPS Student Page 97, Exercise 42

Birthdays Each day in the United States, about 753,000 people have a birthday. Each day about 10,700 people celebrate their sixteenth birthday. Find the probability that someone celebrating a birthday today will turn 16. Round to the nearest percent.

Read and Understand

1. What information are you given in the problem? _____

2. What is the problem asking you to figure out? _____

3. How do you compute the probability of an event occurring? _____

_____

Plan and Solve

4. What is the number of favorable events in this situation? _____

5. What is the number of possible outcomes in this situation? _____

6. Find the exact probability that someone celebrating a birthday today will turn 16.

_____

7. Convert your answer to Step 6 to the nearest percent. _____

Look Back and Check

8. The average life expectancy is around 78 years. Check the reasonableness of your answer by assuming that each age from 0 to 78 has same the probability as the probability found in Step 6. Multiply this probability by 79 to account for the probability for each age. Round to the nearest percent. Is your answer near 100%? Did we overestimate or underestimate with our assumption? Explain.

_____

_____

Solve Another Problem

9. What is the probability that someone celebrating a birthday today is *not* turning 16? Round to the nearest percent.

_____

Practice 2-7

1. Suppose you have a dark closet containing seven blue shirts, five yellow shirts, and eight white shirts. You pick two shirts at random from the closet. Find each probability.

   a. P(blue then yellow) with replacing _____

   b. P(blue then yellow) without replacing _____

   c. P(yellow then yellow) with replacing _____

   d. P(yellow then yellow) without replacing _____

A and B are independent events. Find the missing probability.

2. $P(A) = \frac{3}{7}, P(A \text{ and } B) = \frac{1}{3}$. Find $P(B)$.

_____

3. $P(B) = \frac{1}{5}, P(A \text{ and } B) = \frac{2}{13}$. Find $P(A)$.

_____

4. $P(B) = \frac{15}{16}, P(A \text{ and } B) = \frac{3}{4}$. Find $P(A)$.

_____

5. $P(A) = \frac{8}{15}, P(B) = \frac{3}{4}$. Find $P(A \text{ and } B)$.

_____

6. Suppose you draw two tennis balls at random from a bag containing seven pink, four white, three yellow, and two striped balls. Find each probability.

   a. P(yellow then pink) with replacing

   b. P(yellow then pink) without replacing

   _____

   c. P(pink then pink) with replacing

   d. P(pink then pink) without replacing

   _____

Use an equation to solve each problem.

7. A bag contains green and yellow color tiles. You pick two tiles at random without replacing the first one. The probability that the first tile is yellow is $\frac{3}{5}$. The probability of drawing two yellow tiles is $\frac{12}{35}$. Find the probability that the second tile you pick is yellow.

_____

8. A bag contains red and blue marbles. You pick two marbles at random without replacing the first one. The probability of drawing a blue and then a red is $\frac{4}{15}$. The probability that your second marble is red if your first marble is blue is $\frac{2}{3}$. Find the probability that the first marble is blue.

_____

Name _____ Class _____ Date _____

2-7 • Guided Problem Solving

a. Agriculture An acre of land in Indiana is chosen at random. What is the probability that it is cropland?

b. An acre of land is chosen at random from each of the three states listed. What is the probability that all three acres will be cropland?

Percent of Cropland

Alabama	8%
Florida	7%
Indiana	58%

Read and Understand

1. What information is given in the table? _____

2. Are these events independent or dependent? _____

Plan and Solve

3. If an acre of land in Indiana is chosen at random, what is the probability that it is cropland?

   _____

4. If an acre of land in Florida is chosen at random, what is the probability that it is cropland?

   _____

5. If an acre of land in Alabama is chosen at random, what is the probability that it is cropland?

   _____

6. If an acre of land is chosen at random from each of the three states, what is the probability that all three acres will be cropland?

   _____

Look Back and Check

7. Explain why it is reasonable that the probability that all three acres are cropland is much smaller than the probability that the acre of land is crop land in any one state.

   _____

   _____

Solve Another Problem

8. If an acre of land is chosen at random from Alabama and Florida, what is the probability that both acres will be cropland? _____

2A: Graphic Organizer

Study Skill Keep notes as you work through each chapter to help you organize your thinking and to make it easier to review the material when you complete the chapter.

Write your answers.

1. What is the chapter title? _____

2. Find the Table of Contents page for this chapter at the front of the book. Name four topics you will study in this chapter.

   _____   _____

   _____   _____

3. Complete the graphic organizer as you work through the chapter.
   1. Write the title of the chapter in the center oval.
   2. When you begin a lesson, write the name of the lesson in a rectangle.
   3. When you complete that lesson, write a skill or key concept from that lesson in the outer oval linked to that rectangle.
   Continue with steps 2 and 3 clockwise around the graphic organizer.

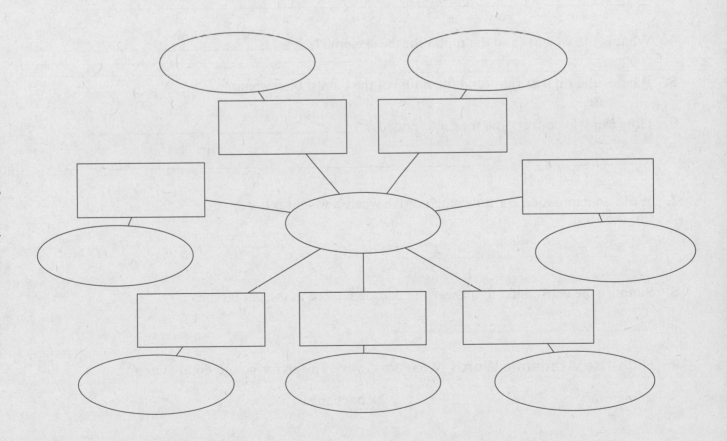

2B: Reading Comprehension

For use after Lesson 2-5

Study Skill When you read a paragraph, it is a good idea to read it twice: once to get an overview, then again to find the essential information.

Read the passage below and answer the following questions.

> The blue whale is the largest animal on earth. A blue whale is about 100 million times larger than the krill, one of the smallest creatures it eats. The skeleton of a blue whale can weigh about 50,000 pounds. The heart of a blue whale can be the size of a small car. The largest recorded blue whale weighed 160 tons. About how much of that weight was *not* the skeleton?

1. What is the subject of this paragraph? _____

2. What are the numbers 50,000 and 160 in the paragraph referring to?

   _____

3. What question are you asked to answer? _____

   _____

4. What is the weight (and the units) for the skeleton? _____

5. What is the total weight (and the units) of the largest blue whale? _____

6. How can you convert 160 tons into pounds? _____

   _____

7. Write an expression for how much of the whale's weight is *not* the skeleton.

   _____

8. Simplify the expression to answer the question asked in the paragraph.

   _____

9. **High-Use Academic Words** What does *convert* mean for you to do in Step 6?

   a. measure   **b.** change

2C: Reading/Writing Math Symbols

For use after Lesson 2-3

Study Skill When you take notes in any subject, it helps if you learn to use abbreviations and symbols such as @ (at); #, #s (number, numbers); w/ (with); w/o (without); s/b (should be).

For Exercises 1–7, match the symbolic expression in Column A with its written expression in Column B by drawing a line between them.

Column A		Column B
1. $2 + x$	**A.**	one-third of x
2. $\dfrac{r}{3}$	**B.**	absolute value of negative 6
3. $-12 \div x$	**C.**	18 decreased by r
4. $18 - r$	**D.**	2 more than x
5. $\dfrac{1}{3}x$	**E.**	the sum of x and y
6. $|-6|$	**F.**	r divided into 3 parts
7. $x + y$	**G.**	negative 12 divided by x

For Exercises 8–14, match the symbolic expression in Column C with its written expression in Column D by drawing a line between them.

Column C		Column D
8. $h - 8$	**H.**	100 minus w
9. $12 + y$	**I.**	twice w
10. $-12x$	**J.**	12 greater than y
11. $2w$	**K.**	quotient of r and 32
12. $k - 14$	**L.**	negative 12 times x
13. $100 - w$	**M.**	14 subtracted from k
14. $\dfrac{r}{32}$	**N.**	8 less than h

2D: Visual Vocabulary Practice

For use after Lesson 2-6

Study Skill If a word is not in the Glossary, use a dictionary to find its meaning.

Concept List

complement of an event	constant	event
like terms	matrix	Multiplication Property of Zero
odds	probability	reciprocals

Write the concept that best describes each exercise.
Choose from the concept list above.

1. $5:6$ _____	**2.** $\frac{3}{5}$ and $\frac{5}{3}$ _____	**3.** $-2x^2y$ and $8x^2y$ _____
4. 27 _____	**5.** $\begin{bmatrix} 4 & -2 & 9 \\ 0 & 6 & -5 \end{bmatrix}$ _____	**6.** tossing a 4 on a number cube _____
7. For every real number n, $n \cdot 0 = 0$ _____	**8.** $\dfrac{\text{number of favorable outcomes}}{\text{number of possible outcomes}}$ _____	**9.** $1 - P(\text{event})$ _____

2E: Vocabulary Check

Study Skill Strengthen your vocabulary. Use these pages and add cues and summaries by applying the Cornell Notetaking style.

Write the definition for each word at the right. To check your work, fold the paper back along the dotted line to see the correct answers.

_____

_____

_____

Multiplicative Inverse

_____

_____

Coefficient

_____

_____

_____

Like Terms

_____

_____

Constant

_____

_____

Matrix

_____

_____

_____

Vocabulary and Study Skills

2E: Vocabulary Check (continued)

Write the vocabulary word for each definition. To check your work, fold the paper forward along the dotted line to see the correct answers.

Given a nonzero rational Number *a/b*, it is *b/a*.

_____

The numerical factor of a term.

_____

These have exactly the same variable factors in a variable expression.

_____

A term that has no variable factor.

_____

A rectangular arrangement of numbers in rows and columns.

_____

2F: Vocabulary Review

For use with Chapter Review

Study Skill It is important to learn the definitions of new terms as soon as they are introduced. Read aloud or recite the new terms as you read them. Reciting a rule, definition, or formula can help you to remember and recall it.

For Exercises 1–7, match each term in Column A with its definition in Column B by drawing a line between them.

Column A		**Column B**	
1.	experimental probability	A.	a process of reasoning logically from given facts to a conclusion
2.	odds	B.	all possible outcomes of an event
3.	dependent events	C.	describes the likelihood of an event by comparing favorale and unfavorable outcomes
4.	deductive reasoning	D.	two events in which the occurrence of one event affects the probability of the second event
5.	like terms	E.	the ratio of the number of times an event actually happens to the number of times the experiment is done
6.	sample space	F.	the ratio of the number of favorable outcomes to the number of possible outcomes if all outcomes have the same chance of happening
7.	theoretical probability	G.	terms with exactly the same variable factors in a variable expression

For Exercises 8–14, match each term in Column C with its definition in Column D by drawing a line between them.

Column C		**Column D**	
8.	coefficient	H.	any group of outcomes in a situation involving probability
9.	independent events	I.	a number, variable, or the product or quotient of a number and one or more variables
10.	term	J.	the result of a single trial in a probability experiment
11.	event	K.	the numerical factor when a term has a variable
12.	constant	L.	two events for which the outcome of one does not affect the other
13.	probability	M.	how likely it is that an event will occur
14.	outcome	N.	a term that has no variable factor

Practice 3-1

Solving Two-Step Equations

Solve each equation. Check your answer.

1. $5a + 2 = 7$

2. $2x + 3 = 7$

3. $3b + 6 = 12$

_____

_____

_____

4. $9 = 5 + 4t$

5. $4a + 1 = 13$

6. $-t + 2 = 12$

_____

_____

_____

Write an equation to model each situation. Then solve.

7. You want to buy a bouquet of yellow roses and baby's breath for $16. The baby's breath costs $3.50 per bunch, and the roses cost $2.50 each. You want one bunch of baby's breath and some roses for your bouquet. How many roses can you buy?

_____

8. Suppose you want to buy one pair of pants and several pairs of socks. The pants cost $24.95, and the socks are $5.95 per pair. How many pairs of socks can you buy if you have $50.00 to spend?

_____

Solve each equation. Check your answer.

9. $67 = -3y + 16$

10. $-d + 7 = 3$

_____

_____

11. $\frac{m}{9} + 7 = 3$

12. $5z + 9 = -21$

_____

_____

13. $3x - 7 = 35$

14. $4s - 13 = 51$

_____

_____

15. $9f + 16 = 70$

16. $-c + 2 = 5$

_____

_____

17. $-67 = -8n + 5$

18. $22 = 7 - 3a$

_____

_____

19. $2x + 23 = 49$

20. $\frac{x}{2} + 8 = -3$

_____

_____

Justify each step.

21. $\quad 24 - x = -16$

22. $\quad \frac{x}{7} + 4 = 15$

a. $24 - x - 24 = -16 - 24$ _____

a. $\frac{x}{7} + 4 - 4 = 15 - 4$ _____

b. $\quad\quad -x = -40$ _____

b. $\quad\quad \frac{x}{7} = 11$ _____

c. $-1(-x) = -1(-40)$ _____

c. $7(\frac{x}{7}) = 7(11)$ _____

d. $\quad\quad\quad x = 40$ _____

d. $\quad\quad\quad x = 77$ _____

3-1 • Guided Problem Solving

GPS **Student Page 123, Exercise 45**

Insurance One health insurance policy pays people for claims by multiplying the claim amount by 0.8 and then subtracting $500. Write a rule that describes the insurance payment as a function of the claim amount. Then find the claim amount for an insurance payment of $4650.

Read and Understand

1. Describe in words how the insurance company determines how to pay people for their insurance claims. _____

2. What two quantities will be related by the function rule? _____

Plan and Solve

3. Define your two variables.

_____   _____

4. Write your rule that describes the insurance payment as a function of the claim amount. _____

5. For which variable will you substitute the value $4650? _____

6. Substitute $4650 in and solve your equation for the claim amount. _____

Look Back and Check

7. Multiplying by 0.8 is equivalent to finding 80% of a number. Check the reasonableness of your answer by finding 80% of your claim amount. Your answer should be $500 more than $4650.

Solve Another Problem

8. What would the insurance payment be for a claim of $3000? _____

Practice 3-2

Solving Multi-Step Equations

Solve each equation. Check your answer.

1. $2n + 3n + 7 = -41$

2. $3h - 5h + 11 = 17$

3. $2t + 8 - t = -3$

_____

_____

_____

4. $6a - 2a = -36$

5. $3c - 8c + 7 = -18$

6. $7g + 14 - 5g = -8$

_____

_____

_____

7. $2b - 6 + 3b = 14$

8. $2(a - 4) + 15 = 13$

9. $7 + 2(a - 3) = -9$

_____

_____

_____

10. $13 + 2(5c - 2) = 29$

11. $5(3x + 12) = -15$

12. $4(2a + 2) - 17 = 15$

_____

_____

_____

13. $2(m + 1) = 16$

14. $-4x + 3(2x - 5) = 31$

15. $3(t - 12) = 27$

_____

_____

_____

16. $-w + 4(w + 3) = -12$

17. $2(3a + 2) = -8$

18. $5(b + 4) - 6b = -24$

_____

_____

_____

Write an equation to model each situation. Then solve.

19. The attendance at a baseball game was 400 people. Student tickets cost
$2 and adult tickets cost $3. Total ticket sales were $1050. How many
tickets of each type were sold?

_____

20. The perimeter of a pool table is 30 ft. The table is twice as long as it is
wide. What is the length of the pool table?

_____

3-2 • Guided Problem Solving

GPS **Student Page 130, Exercise 58**

Cell Phones Jane's cell phone plan is $40 per month plus $.15 per minute for each minute over 200 minutes of call time. If Jane's cell phone bill is $58.00, for how many extra calling minutes was she billed?

Read and Understand

1. Explain how the amount of Jane's phone bill is determined? _____

2. What is the problem asking you to determine? _____

Plan and Solve

3. What would Jane's phone bill be if she talked for exactly 200 minutes? _____

4. What would Jane's phone bill be if she talked for 10 extra minutes? _____

5. Write an equation to model this situation. _____

6. Use your equation to determine how many extra calling minutes Jane was billed for if her phone bill was $58.00. _____

Look Back and Check

7. Is this a reasonable plan? How many minutes do you talk on the telephone each month? Is it reasonable to allow 200 minutes before charging extra? _____

_____

Solve Another Problem

8. Janet's cable company charges her a basic fee of $59. For each premium channel, she is charged an extra $12. How many premium channels does she have if her total bill is $107 each month?

_____

Practice 3-3

Equations With Variables on Both Sides

Solve each equation. Check your answer. If appropriate, write *identity* or *no solution*.

1. $7 - 2n = n - 14$ **2.** $2(4 - 2r) = -2(r + 5)$ **3.** $3d + 8 = 2d - 7$

_____   _____   _____

4. $6t = 3(t + 4) - t$ **5.** $8z - 7 = 3z - 7 + 5z$ **6.** $7x - 8 = 3x + 12$

_____   _____   _____

7. $3(n - 1) = 5n + 3 - 2n$ **8.** $6k - 25 = 7 - 2k$ **9.** $3v - 9 = 7 + 2v - v$

_____   _____   _____

10. $6 - 4d = 16 - 9d$ **11.** $2s - 12 + 2s = 4s - 12$ **12.** $4b - 1 = -4 + 4b + 3$

_____   _____   _____

13. $6y + 9 = 3(2y + 3)$ **14.** $4g + 7 = 5g - 1 - g$ **15.** $2(n + 2) = 5n - 5$

_____   _____   _____

16. $6 - 3d = 5(2 - d)$ **17.** $3v + 8 = 8 + 2v + v$ **18.** $5(r + 3) = 2r + 6$

_____   _____   _____

Write an equation to model each situation. Then solve. Check your answer.

19. Hans needs to rent a moving truck. Suppose Company A charges a rate of $40 per day and Company B charges a $60 fee plus $20 per day. For what number of days is the cost the same?

_____

20. Suppose your club is selling candles to raise money. It costs $100 to rent a booth from which to sell the candles. If the candles cost your club $1 each and are sold for $5 each, how many candles must be sold to equal your expenses?

_____

3-3 • Guided Problem Solving

GPS **Student Page 138, Exercise 40**

Spreadsheet Don set up a spreadsheet to solve
$5(x - 3) = 4 - 3(x + 1)$.

a. Does Don's spreadsheet show a solution to the equation?

b. Between which two values of x is the solution to the equation? How do you know?

c. For what values of x is $4 - 3(x + 1)$ less than $5(x - 3)$?

	A	B	C
1	x	$5(x - 3)$	$4 - 3(x + 1)$
2	−5	−40	16
3	−3	−30	10
4	−1	−20	4
5	1	−10	−2
6	3	0	−8

Read and Understand

1. Describe what the values in each column represent. _____

_____

2. What is Don trying to use the spreadsheet for? _____

Plan and Solve

3. Explain what a solution to an equation is. _____

_____

4. Does Don's spreadsheet show a solution to the equation? _____

5. Between what two values of x is the solution to the equation? _____

   How do you know? _____

6. For what values of x is $4 - 3(x + 1)$ less than $5(x - 3)$? _____

Look Back and Check

7. Check the reasonableness of your answer by substituting a value between 1 and 3 into your equation to see if the sides are approximately equal to each other.

Solve Another Problem

8. Describe how Don could set up a spreadsheet to solve $2(x + 5) - 2 = 4(x - 7)$.

Name _____ Class _____ Date _____

Practice 3-4   Ratio and Proportion

Find each unit rate.

1. $\dfrac{\$3}{4\text{ lb}}$

_____

2. $\dfrac{861\text{ bagels}}{3\text{ d}}$

_____

3. $\dfrac{850\text{ cal}}{1.25\text{ h}}$

_____

4. An 8-ounce bottle of lotion costs $4.50. What is the cost per ounce? _____

Which pairs of ratios could form a proportion? Justify your answer.

5. $\dfrac{6}{9}, \dfrac{10}{15}$

_____

6. $\dfrac{3}{4}, \dfrac{18}{24}$

_____

7. $\dfrac{16}{2}, \dfrac{8}{1}$

_____

Solve each proportion.

8. $\dfrac{g}{5} = \dfrac{6}{10}$

_____

9. $\dfrac{z}{4} = \dfrac{7}{8}$

_____

10. $-\dfrac{m}{5} = -\dfrac{2}{5}$

_____

11. $\dfrac{4}{6} = \dfrac{x}{24}$

_____

12. $\dfrac{s}{3} = \dfrac{7}{10}$

_____

13. $\dfrac{4}{9} = \dfrac{10}{r}$

_____

14. $\dfrac{5}{4} = \dfrac{c}{12}$

_____

15. $\dfrac{2}{6} = \dfrac{p}{9}$

_____

16. $\dfrac{f}{6} = \dfrac{3}{4}$

_____

17. $\dfrac{15}{a} = \dfrac{3}{8}$

_____

18. $\dfrac{3}{4} = \dfrac{k}{24}$

_____

19. $\dfrac{a}{6} = \dfrac{3}{9}$

_____

20. $\dfrac{4}{5} = \dfrac{k}{9}$

_____

21. $\dfrac{3}{y} = \dfrac{5}{8}$

_____

22. $\dfrac{t}{7} = \dfrac{9}{21}$

_____

23. $\dfrac{2}{9} = \dfrac{10}{x}$

_____

24. $\dfrac{x}{15} = \dfrac{3}{4}$

_____

25. $\dfrac{3}{6} = \dfrac{x-3}{8}$

_____

26. You are riding your bicycle. It takes you 28 min to go 8 mi. If you
continue traveling at the same rate, how long will it take you to go 15 mi? _____

27. A canary's heart beats 130 times in 12 s. Use a
proportion to find how many times its heart beats in 50 s. _____

3-4 • Guided Problem Solving

GPS **Student Page 147, Exercise 56**

Bonnie and Tim do some yardwork for their neighbor. The ratio comparing the amount of time each one works is 7 : 4. The neighbor pays them $88. If Bonnie worked more, how much should each of them receive?

Read and Understand

1. What does the ratio 7 : 4 describe? _____

2. If an equation were used to solve this problem, what would x represent? _____

Plan and Solve

3. Write a verbal model for this problem. _____

4. Let b represent the amount of money Bonnie earns. Write an expression that represents how much money Tim will make. _____

5. Write an equation to model this situation. _____

6. Solve the equation to find b. _____

7. How much money did each person receive? _____

Look Back and Check

8. Check the amount each person earned to make sure Bonnie made more money than Tim. Why is this reasonable?

Solve Another Problem

9. If 2 tons of rock costs $15.50, then how many tons of rock can you buy for $45?

_____

Name_____ Class_____ Date_____

Practice 3-5

Proportions and Similar Figures

Each pair of figures is similar. Find the length of *x*.

1.
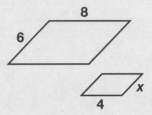

_____

2.
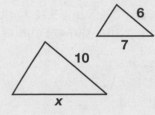

_____

3.
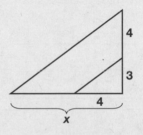

_____

4.
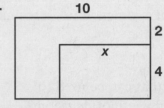

_____

5.
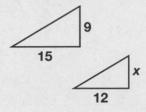

_____

6.
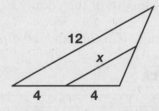

_____

Use a proportion to solve.

7. $\triangle ABC$ is similar to $\triangle XYZ$. The length AB is 10. The length BC is 7. Find the length XY if the length YZ is 14.

_____

8. Marty has a scale model of a car. The scale is 1 in. : 32 in. If the model is 6.75 in. long, how long is the actual car?

_____

9. Angie is using similar triangles to find the height of a tree. A stick that is 5 ft tall casts a shadow that is 4 ft long. The tree casts a shadow that is 22 ft long. How tall is the tree?

_____

3-5 • Guided Problem Solving

GPS **Student Page 153, Exercise 23**

Architecture A blueprint scale is 1 in. : 9 ft. On the plan, the room measures 2.5 in. by 3 in. What are the actual dimensions of the room?

Read and Understand

1. What is the blueprint scale? _____

2. How large is the room on the plans? _____

3. What is the problem asking you to determine? _____

Plan and Solve

4. Write a proportion that can be used to determine the actual width of the room. _____

5. Write a proportion that can be used to determine the actual length of the room. _____

6. Solve your proportions to find the actual dimensions of the room. _____

Look Back and Check

7. The blueprint scale written as a ratio is $\frac{1}{9}$, and as a decimal is approximately 0.11. Check the reasonableness of your answers by checking to see if the ratios of each dimension reduce to $\frac{1}{9}$ or 0.11.

Solve Another Problem

8. What are the actual dimensions of the room if the scale is 1 in. : 6 ft?

Practice 3-6

Write and solve an equation for each situation.

1. A passenger train's speed is 60 mi/h, and a freight train's speed is 40 mi/h. The passenger train travels the same distance in 1.5 h less time than the freight train. How long does each train take to make the trip?

   _____

2. Lois rode her bike to visit a friend. She traveled at 10 mi/h. While she was there, it began to rain. Her friend drove her home in a car traveling at 25 mi/h. Lois took 1.5 h longer to go to her friend's than to return home. How many hours did it take Lois to ride to her friend's house?

   _____

3. The length of a rectangle is 4 in. greater than the width. The perimeter of the rectangle is 24 in. Find the dimensions of the rectangle.

   _____

4. The length of a rectangle is twice the width. The perimeter is 48 in. Find the dimensions of the rectangle.

   _____

5. At 10:00 A.M., a car leaves a house at a rate of 60 mi/h. At the same time, another car leaves the same house at a rate of 50 mi/h in the opposite direction. At what time will the cars be 330 miles apart?

   _____

6. Fred begins walking toward John's house at 3 mi/h. John leaves his house at the same time and walks toward Fred's house on the same path at a rate of 2 mi/h. How long will it be before they meet if the distance between the houses is 4 miles?

   _____

7. Find three consecutive integers whose sum is 126.

   _____

8. The sum of four consecutive odd integers is 216. Find the four integers.

   _____

9. A rectangular picture frame is to be 8 in. longer than it is wide. Dennis uses 84 in. of oak to frame the picture. What is the width of the frame?

   _____

10. Each of two congruent sides of an isosceles triangle is 8 in. less than twice the base. The perimeter of the triangle is 74 in. What is the length of the base?

   _____

3-6 • Guided Problem Solving

GPS **Student Page 164, Exercise 22**

At 12:00 P.M. a truck leaves Centerville traveling 45 mi/h. One
hour later a train leaves Centerville traveling 60 mi/h. They arrive
in Smithfield at the same time.

Time	Truck 45t	Train 60(t − 1)
1 P.M.	45 mi	0 mi
2 P.M.	90 mi	60 mi
3 P.M.	135 mi	120 mi
4 P.M.	180 mi	180 mi
5 P.M.	225 mi	240 mi

a. Use the table to find when the train and truck arrive in
Smithfield.

b. **Critical Thinking** What piece of information can you get
from the table that you would NOT get by solving the
equation $45t = 60(t − 1)$?

Read and Understand

1. What information are you given in the problem? _____

2. What is the problem asking you to figure out? _____

Plan and Solve

3. Explain how you can use the table to determine
   when the train and truck arrive in Smithfield. _____

   _____

4. At what time did the train and truck arrive in Smithfield? _____

5. What information would you have if you solved the equation for t? _____

6. What piece of information can you get from the
   table that you would *not* get by solving the equation? _____

Look Back and Check

7. The truck traveled for 4 hours, and the train traveled for 3 hours.
   Check the reasonableness of your answer by evaluating the appropriate
   expressions for each time to see if the distances are equal.

Solve Another Problem

8. A delivery van drives due east toward its destination at 55 mph.
   Another van drives due west at 60 mph. After 3 hours they are
   345 miles apart. How far did each van travel?

_____

Practice 3-7

Find each percent of change. Describe the percent of change as an increase or decrease. Round to the nearest whole number.

1. 36 g to 27 g

2. 40 cm to 100 cm

3. 90 in. to 45 in.

4. 500 lb to 1500 lb

_____

_____

_____

_____

5. $100 to $140

6. 100 mi to 175 mi

7. 280 m to 320 m

8. 58 to 76

_____

_____

_____

_____

9. 60 to 150

10. 600 mi to 480 mi

11. 18 to 27

12. 290 yd to 261 yd

_____

_____

_____

_____

Find each percent of change. Describe the percent of change as an increase or decrease. Round to the nearest whole number.

13. In 1980, Texas had 27 U.S. Representatives. That number increased to 30 in 2000. Find the percent of change.

_____

14. In 1980, the average annual tuition charge for a four-year public university was $840. The average annual tuition charge in 2000 was $3356. What is the percent of change?

_____

15. In 1990, Atlanta, GA, failed to meet air quality standards on 42 days. In 1999, Atlanta failed to meet air quality standards on 61 days. What is the percent of change?

_____

Find the greatest possible error and the percent error for each measurement.

16. 3 cm

17. 0.5 cm

18. 16 in.

19. 36.85 g

_____

_____

_____

_____

Find the minimum and maximum possible areas for rectangles with the following measurements.

20. 8 cm × 10 cm

21. 3 in. × 5 in.

22. 8 m × 12 m

_____

_____

_____

3-7 • Guided Problem Solving

GPS **Student Page 172, Exercise 50**

Sales Suppose that you are selling sweatshirts for a class fundraiser.
The wholesaler charges you $8 for each sweatshirt.

a. You charge $16 for each sweatshirt. Find the percent of increase.

b. Generalize your answer to part (a). Doubling a price is the same as a
____?____ of increase.

c. After the fundraiser is over, you reduce the price on the remaining
sweatshirts to $8. Find the percent of decrease.

d. Generalize your answer to part (c). Cutting a price in half is the same
as a ____?____ of decrease.

Read and Understand

1. What information is given in the problem? _____

2. Explain how to determine the percent of increase and the percent of decrease. _____

_____

Plan and Solve

3. You charge $16 for each sweatshirt. What is the percent of increase? _____

4. Generalize your answer. Doubling a price is the same as a _____ %
increase.

5. After the fundraiser is over, you reduce the price on the
remaining sweatshirts to $8. Find the percent of decrease. _____

6. Generalize your answer. Cutting a price in half is the same as a _____ %
decrease.

Look Back and Check

7. Explain why it is reasonable that doubling a price is the same as a 100%
of increase and cutting a price in half is the same as a 50% of decrease. _____

_____

Solve Another Problem

8. Ticket prices for the school yearbook have been
raised from $15 to $30. What is the percent of increase? _____

Practice 3-8

Finding and Estimating Square Roots

Tell whether each expression is *rational* or *irrational*.

1. $-\sqrt{64}$ **2.** $\sqrt{1600}$ **3.** $\pm\sqrt{160}$ **4.** $\sqrt{144}$

_____   _____   _____   _____

Use a calculator to find each square root to the nearest hundredth.

5. $\sqrt{20}$ **6.** $\sqrt{73}$ **7.** $-\sqrt{38}$ **8.** $\sqrt{130}$

_____   _____   _____   _____

9. $\sqrt{149.3}$ **10.** $-\sqrt{8.7}$ **11.** $\sqrt{213.8}$ **12.** $-\sqrt{320.7}$

_____   _____   _____   _____

Simplify each expression.

13. $\sqrt{49}$ **14.** $-\sqrt{2.25}$ **15.** $\sqrt{\dfrac{1}{16}}$ **16.** $\sqrt{400}$

_____   _____   _____   _____

17. $\sqrt{6.25}$ **18.** $\pm\sqrt{\dfrac{36}{25}}$ **19.** $\sqrt{196}$ **20.** $\sqrt{2.56}$

_____   _____   _____   _____

Between what two consecutive integers is each square root?

21. $\sqrt{40}$ **22.** $\sqrt{139}$ **23.** $-\sqrt{75}$ **24.** $\sqrt{93}$

_____   _____   _____   _____

Solve the following problems. Round to the nearest tenth if necessary.

25. You are to put a metal brace inside a square shipping container. The
formula $d = \sqrt{2x^2}$ gives the length of the metal brace, where x is the
length of the side of the container. Find the length of the brace for
each container side length.

a. $x = 3$ ft   **b.** $x = 4.5$ ft   **c.** $x = 5$ ft   **d.** $x = 8$ ft

_____   _____   _____   _____

3-8 • Guided Problem Solving

GPS **Student Page 179, Exercise 52**

Physics If you drop an object, the time t in seconds that it takes to fall d feet

is given by the formula $t = \sqrt{\dfrac{d}{16}}$.

a. Find the time it takes an object to fall 400 ft.
b. Find the time it takes an object to fall 1600 ft.
c. **Critical Thinking** In part (b), the object falls four times as far as in part (a). Does it take four times as long to fall? Explain.

Read and Understand

1. What information is given in the problem? _____

2. Explain what each variable represents. _____

Plan and Solve

3. Find the time it takes an object to fall 400 ft. _____

4. Find the time it takes an object to fall 1600 ft. _____

5. Does it take four times as long for an object to fall four times as far? _____

Look Back and Check

6. Explain why it is reasonable that the time does not increase at the same rate as the distance.

   _____

   _____

Solve Another Problem

7. Find the time it takes an object to fall 800 ft. _____

Practice 3-9

The Pythagorean Theorem

Use the triangle at the right. Find the length of the missing side to the nearest tenth.

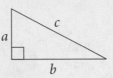

1. $a = 12, b = 35, c = \blacksquare$

2. $a = 10, b = \blacksquare, c = 26$

3. $a = 11, b = \blacksquare, c = 61$

_____

_____

_____

4. $a = 36, b = 15, c = \blacksquare$

5. $a = 8, b = 15, c = \blacksquare$

6. $a = \blacksquare, b = 24, c = 40$

_____

_____

_____

7. $a = 18, b = \blacksquare, c = 35$

8. $a = 17, b = \blacksquare, c = 49$

9. $a = \blacksquare, b = 80, c = 90$

_____

_____

_____

10. $a = 8, b = 8, c = \blacksquare$

11. $a = \blacksquare, b = 27, c = 33$

12. $a = \blacksquare, b = 13, c = 24$

_____

_____

_____

Determine whether the given lengths are sides of a right triangle.

13. 20, 21, 29

14. 16, 30, 34

15. 24, 60, 66

16. 23, 18, 14

_____

_____

_____

_____

17. 10, 24, 28

18. 45, 28, 53

19. $\frac{4}{5}, \frac{3}{5}, 1$

20. 24, 70, 74

_____

_____

_____

_____

Find the missing length to the nearest tenth.

21. A ladder is 25 ft long. The ladder needs to reach to a window that is 24 ft above the ground. How far away from the building should the bottom of the ladder be placed?

_____

22. Suppose you are making a sail in the shape of a right triangle for a sailboat. The length of the longest side of the sail is 65 ft. The sail is to be 63 ft high. What is the length of the third side of the sail?

_____

23. Suppose you leave your house and travel 13 mi due west. Then you travel 3 mi due south. How far are you from your house?

_____

3-9 • Guided Problem Solving

GPS **Student Page 185, Exercise 40**

Solar Power Solar cars use panels built out of photovoltaic cells, which convert sunlight into electricity. Consider a car like the one shown. Not counting the driver's "bubble," the panels form a rectangle.

a. The length of the rectangle is 13 ft and the diagonal is 14.7 ft. Find the width. Round to the nearest tenth of a foot.

b. Find the area of the rectangle.

c. The panels produce a maximum power of about 11 watts/ft^2. Find the maximum power produced by the panels on the car. Round to the nearest watt.

Read and Understand

1. Make a sketch and label it with the known information.

Plan and Solve

2. What relationship can be used to determine the width of the rectangle? _____

3. What is the width of the rectangle rounded to the nearest tenth of a foot? _____

4. Find the area of the rectangle. _____

5. The panels produce a maximum power of about 11 watts/ft^2. Find the maximum power produced by the panels on the car, rounded to the nearest watt. _____

Look Back and Check

6. Check the reasonableness of your answer by verifying that your numbers for the rectangle's dimensions satisfy the Pythagorean Theorem.

Solve Another Problem

7. If the maximum power of the panels is increased to 15 watts/ft^2, what will be the maximum power produced by the panels on the car? _____

3A: Graphic Organizer

For use before Lesson 3-1

Study Skill Keep notes as you work through each chapter to help you organize your thinking and to make it easier to review the material when you complete the chapter.

Write your answers.

1. What is the chapter title? _____

2. Find the Table of Contents page for this chapter at the front of the book. Name four topics you will study in this chapter.

   _____ _____

   _____ _____

3. Complete the graphic organizer as you work through the chapter.
   1. Write the title of the chapter in the center oval.
   2. When you begin a lesson, write the name of the lesson in a rectangle.
   3. When you complete that lesson, write a skill or key concept from that lesson in the outer oval linked to that rectangle.
   Continue with steps 2 and 3 clockwise around the graphic organizer.

3B: Reading Comprehension

Study Skill Some math problems have many steps and can be confusing. Sometimes, if you hurry through a problem, you leave out important steps. Think carefully about what the next step to solving a problem might be.

The equations and justification statements given below are the correct ones to find the length of b in the right triangle.

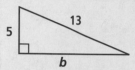

Steps	Justifications	Thoughts for Organizing Steps
$a^2 + b^2 = c^2$		Use the Pythagorean Theorem.
$5^2 + b^2 = 13^2$	Substitute 5 for a and 13 for c.	Replace variables with any known values.
$25 + b^2 = 169$	Simplify by squaring each number.	Perform existing calculations.
$b^2 = 144$	Simplify.	
$\sqrt{b^2} = \sqrt{144}$	Find the principal square root of each side.	More work is needed to isolate the variable.
$b = 12$	Simplify.	

Find the length of the missing side of each right triangle shown.

1.

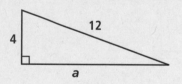

2.

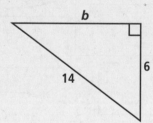

3. **High-Use Academic Words** What does it mean to *isolate*, as mentioned in the last sentence in the thoughts for organizing steps?
   a. rewrite the equation so that the variable is by itself
   b. replace the variable with a known value

3C: Reading/Writing Math Symbols For use after Lesson 3-4

Study Skill There are many symbols that are abbreviations for longer words. Using these symbols when taking notes helps you keep up with the person giving the notes. Learn these symbols for quicker note taking.

Write what each abbreviated math symbol means.

1. ¢/oz _____

2. mi/h _____

3. ft/min _____

4. km/h _____

5. ft/mi _____

6. $/yr _____

7. $/lb _____

8. ft/wk _____

9. gal/wk _____

10. mi/gal _____

11. lb/in^2 _____

12. ft/s^2 _____

13. m/s^2 _____

14. $/oz _____

Write each phrase in symbol form.

15. miles per gallon _____

16. dollars per pound _____

17. kilometers per hour _____

18. feet per minute _____

3D: Visual Vocabulary Practice
High-Use Academic Words

For use after Lesson 3-4

Study Skills If a word is not in the Glossary, use a dictionary to find its meaning.

Concept List

approximate	compare	convert
define	describe	evaluate
explain	identify	model

Write the concept that best describes each exercise. Choose from the concept list above.

1. Let n = number of CDs. _____	**2.** $a = -5$ $3 \cdot a + 4 = 3 \cdot (-5) + 4$ $\qquad = -15 + 4$ $\qquad = -11$ _____	**3.** $\pi \approx \frac{22}{7}$ _____
4. x-coordinate $\downarrow$ $(-2, 4)$ $\uparrow$ y-coordinate _____	**5.** $2 + (-5)$  -3 $2 + (-5) = -3$ _____	**6.** The graph is a function because there is exactly one range value for each domain value. _____
7. $-6 < 5$ _____	**8.** To plot $(-2, 3)$, move 2 units to the left of the origin. Then move 3 units up. _____	**9.** $10 \text{ gal} \cdot \frac{4 \text{ qt}}{1 \text{ gal}} = 40 \text{ qt}$ _____

3E: Vocabulary Check

Study Skill Strengthen your vocabulary. Use these pages and add cues and summaries by applying the Cornell Notetaking style.

Write the definition for each word at the right. To check your work, fold the paper back along the dotted line to see the correct answers.

_____

_____

_____   Identity

_____

_____   Ratio

_____

_____   Unit Analysis

_____

_____   Proportion

_____

_____   Cross Products

_____

Vocabulary and Study Skills

3E: Vocabulary Check (continued)

Write the vocabulary word for each definition. To check your work, fold the paper forward along the dotted line to see the correct answers.

An equation that is true for every value of the variable.

_____

A comparison of two numbers by division.

_____

The process of selecting conversion factors to produce appropriate units.

_____

An equation that states that two ratios are equal.

_____

In a proportion, $\frac{a}{b} = \frac{c}{d}$, the products ad and bc. These products are equal.

_____

3F: Vocabulary Review Puzzle

For use with Chapter Review

Study Skill When you complete a puzzle such as a word search, read the list of words carefully and completely. As you identify each word in the word search, circle it and then cross off the word from the list. Pay special attention to the spelling of each word.

Complete the word search.

rate	proportion	leg	hypotenuse
theorem	dilation	percent	identity
scale drawing	square root	similar figures	Pythagorean
equation	conditional	ratio	equivalent

```
L  E  E  G  Z  X  D  I  L  A  T  I  O  N  M  P
A  N  E  P  Y  T  H  A  G  O  R  E  A  N  T
N  P  E  R  C  E  N  T  D  Y  C  S  P  A  H
O  D  E  O  M  Z  G  I  N  E  K  C  Q  H  E
I  O  S  P  O  D  E  N  R  T  Y  A  U  Y  O
T  E  I  O  N  J  K  L  E  A  R  L  D  P  R
I  W  D  R  A  T  I  O  N  R  O  E  U  O  E
D  H  T  T  F  Y  L  O  M  F  D  D  M  T  M
N  V  D  I  L  A  I  I  O  N  K  R  A  E  J
O  T  R  O  S  T  C  F  U  N  B  A  T  N  S
C  F  Y  N  A  W  O  R  D  S  X  W  H  U  T
E  E  Q  U  I  V  A  L  E  N  T  I  W  S  F
C  S  Q  U  A  R  E  R  O  O  T  N  B  E  L
X  E  I  D  E  N  T  I  T  Y  D  G  S  T  U
S  I  M  I  L  A  R  F  I  G  U  R  E  S  C
```

Practice 4-1

Inequalities and Their Graphs

Determine whether each number is a solution of the given inequality.

1. $x \le -8$ a. -10 b. 6 c. -8

2. $-1 > x$ a. 0 b. -3 c. -6

3. $2y + 1 > -5$ a. -4 b. -2 c. 4

4. $7x - 14 \le 6x - 16$ a. 0 b. -4 c. 2

5. $n(n - 6) \ge -4$ a. 3 b. -2 c. 5

Write an inequality for each graph.

6.

7.

Graph each inequality.

8. $x > 6$

9. $y \le -10$

10. $8 \ge b$

Define a variable and write an inequality to model each situation.

11. The temperature in a refrigerated truck must be kept at or below 38°F. _____

12. The maximum weight on an elevator is 2000 pounds. _____

13. A least 20 students were sick with the flu. _____

14. The maximum occupancy in an auditorium is 250 people. _____

Match the inequality with its graph.

15. $6 < x$ 16. $-6 \ge x$ 17. $4 > x$ 18. $x \le -4$

A.

B.

C.

D.

Name_____ Class_____ Date_____

4-1 • Guided Problem Solving

GPS **Student Page 204, Exercise 65**

Air Travel Your travel agent is making plans for you to go from Chicago to New Orleans. A direct flight costs too much. Option A consists of flights from Chicago to Dallas to New Orleans. Option B consists of flights from Chicago to Orlando to New Orleans. Write an inequality comparing the mileage of these two options.

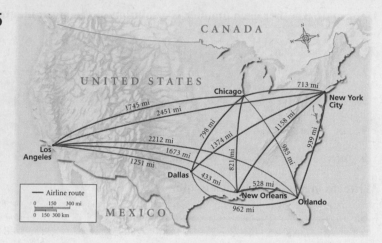

Read and Understand

1. Describe option A._____

2. Describe option B._____

3. The problem asks you to write an inequality for what? _____

Plan and Solve

4. What is the mileage between each of the cities in option A?

   Chicago to Dallas _____   Dallas to New Orleans _____

5. What is the total mileage for option A? _____

6. What is the mileage between each of the cities in option B?

   Chicago to Orlando _____   Orlando to New Orleans _____

7. What is the total mileage for option B? _____

8. Write an inequality comparing the mileage for option A and option B. _____

Look Back and Check

9. Write a sentence to describe the relationship between the mileage for option A and option B. Check that this sentence matches your inequality written above.

   _____

Solve Another Problem

10. An office supply store sells a pack of pencils for $.99, a notebook for $1.29, and scissors for $1.39. A discount store sells the same pack of pencils for $1.09, the notebook for $1.25, and the scissors for $1.19. Write an inequality comparing the total costs of school supplies at each store. _____

Guided Problem Solving

Practice 4-2

Solving Inequalities Using Addition and Subtraction

Solve each inequality. Graph and Check the solution.

1. $n - 7 \geq 2$

$\longleftrightarrow$

2. $10 + y > 12$

$\longleftrightarrow$

3. $7 + b > 13$

$\longleftrightarrow$

4. $0 > d - 2.7$

$\longleftrightarrow$

5. $f + 4 \geq 14$

$\longleftrightarrow$

6. $x + 1 \leq -3$

$\longleftrightarrow$

7. $d - 13 \leq -8$

$\longleftrightarrow$

8. $m - 7 \geq -8$

$\longleftrightarrow$

9. $12 + v < 19$

$\longleftrightarrow$

10. $-4 \leq t + 9$

$\longleftrightarrow$

11. $6 < y - 3$

$\longleftrightarrow$

12. $a + 15 > 19$

$\longleftrightarrow$

13. $8 + d < 9$

$\longleftrightarrow$

14. $s + 3 \leq 3$

$\longleftrightarrow$

15. $9 + h \leq 5$

$\longleftrightarrow$

16. $12 + d + 3 \leq 10$

$\longleftrightarrow$

Write and solve an inequality that models each situation.

17. It will take at least 360 points for Kiko's team to win the math contest. The scores for Kiko's teammates were 94, 82, and 87, but one of Kiko's teammates lost 2 of those points for an incomplete answer. How many points must Kiko earn for her team to win the contest?

18. This season, Nora has 125 at-bats in softball. By the end of the season she wants to have at least 140 at-bats. How many more at-bats does Nora need to reach her goal?

19. The average wind speed increased 19 mi/h from 8 A.M. to noon. The average wind speed decreased 5 mi/h from noon to 4 P.M. At 4 P.M., the average wind speed was at least 32 mi/h. What is the minimum value of the average wind speed at 8 A.M.?

20. Suppose it takes no more than 25 min for you to get to school. If you have traveled for 13.5 min already, how much longer, at most, might you take to get to school?

4-2 • Guided Problem Solving

GPS Student Page 209, Exercise 62

Gymnastics Suppose your sister wants to qualify for a regional gymnastics competition. At today's competition she must score at least 34.0 points. She scored 8.8 on the vault, 7.9 on the balance beam, and 8.2 on the uneven parallel bars. The event that remains is the floor exercise.

a. Write and solve an inequality that models the information.
b. Explain what the solution means in terms of the original situation.
c. **Open-Ended** Write three scores your sister could make that would allow her to qualify for the regional gymnastics competition.

Read and Understand

1. How many points must your sister score at today's competition? _____

2. How many points did
she score on the vault? _____ balance beam? _____ uneven parallel bars? _____

Plan and Solve

3. How many total points has your sister scored at the competition so far? _____

4. Write an inequality that models the information. _____

5. What is the solution to the inequality? _____

6. Explain what the solution means in terms of the original situation. _____

_____

7. Write three scores that your sister could make that would allow her to qualify for the regional gymnastics competition. _____

Look Back and Check

8. Check each of your scores by adding 24.9 to each one. Your answers should all be at least 34.0.

_____

Solve Another Problem

9. Samuel's mother has set a limit of 8 hours per week of Internet use. On Monday Samuel used the Internet for 0.75 hours, on Tuesday for 1.5 hours, and on Wednesday for 0.5 hours. Write and solve an inequality in order to determine the maximum amount of Internet time Samuel has for the remaining days of the week.

_____

Name _____ Class _____ Date _____

Practice 4-3
Solving Inequalities Using Multiplication and Division

Solve each inequality. Graph and check the solution.

1. $\frac{15}{8} \le \frac{5}{2}s$

2. $60 \le 12b$

3. $-\frac{4}{5}r < 8$

4. $\frac{5}{2} < \frac{n}{8}$

5. $-9n \ge -36$

6. $\frac{n}{7} \ge -6$

7. $-7c < 28$

8. $16d > -64$

9. $-\frac{t}{3} < -5$

10 $54 < -6k$

11. $\frac{w}{7} > 0$

12. $2.6v > 6.5$

13. $-4 < -\frac{2}{5}m$

14. $17 < \frac{p}{2}$

15. $0.9 \le -1.8v$

16. $-5 \le -\frac{x}{9}$

17. $-1 \ge \frac{d}{7}$

18. $-3x \ge 21$

19. $\frac{c}{12} < \frac{3}{4}$

20. $\frac{a}{4} \le -1$

Write and solve an inequality that models each situation.

21. Suppose you and a friend are working for a nursery planting trees. Together you can plant 8 trees per hour. What is the greatest number of hours that you and your friend would need to plant at most 40 trees?

22. Suppose the physics club is going on a field trip. Members will be riding in vans that will hold 7 people each including the driver. At least 28 people will be going on the field trip. What is the least number of vans needed to make the trip?

23. The Garcias are putting a brick border along one edge of their flower garden. The flower garden is no more than 31 ft long. If each brick is 6 in. long, what is the greatest number of bricks needed?

4-3 • Guided Problem Solving

GPS **Student Page 216, Exercise 76**

A friend calls you and asks you to meet at a location 3 miles from your home in 20 minutes. You set off on your bicycle after the telephone call. Write and solve an inequality to find the average rate in miles per minute you could ride to be at your meeting place within 20 minutes.

Read and Understand

1. How far away is the meeting location? _____

2. How much time do you have to get there? _____

3. What unit should be used to represent rate? _____

Plan and Solve

4. Let r represent your rate. Write and solve an inequality to find the average rate you could ride to be at your meeting place *within* 20 minutes.

   _____

5. Express your minimum rate as miles/hour. _____

Look Back and Check

6. Give one rate that would allow you to meet your friend within 20 minutes. Check your answer by multiplying your rate by 20. Your answer is the distance you will travel at that rate for 20 minutes. Is your answer more than 5 miles?

Solve Another Problem

7. The student council is planning the next school dance. The total expenses for the dance will be $2500 and they expect 200 students to attend. Write and solve an inequality to find the minimum ticket price per student that should be charged in order to cover expenses.

   _____

Practice 4-4

Solve each inequality. Check the solution.

1. $2z + 7 < z + 10$

2. $4(k - 1) > 4$

3. $h + 2(3h + 4) \geq 1$

4. $r + 4 > 13 - 2r$

5. $6u - 18 - 4u < 22$

6. $2(3 + 3g) \geq 2g + 14$

7. $2h - 13 < -3$

8. $-4p + 28 > 8$

9. $8m - 8 \geq 12 + 4m$

10. $5 + 6a > -1$

11. $-5x + 12 < -18$

12. $13t - 8t > -45$

Write and solve an inequality that models each situation.

13. Ernest works in the shipping department loading shipping crates with boxes. Each empty crate weighs 150 lb. How many boxes, each weighing 35 lb, can Ernest put in the crate if the total weight is to be no more than 850 lb?

14. Beatriz is in charge of setting up a banquet hall. She has five tables that will seat six people each. If no more than 62 people will attend, how many more tables seating four people each will she need?

15. The student council is sponsoring a concert as a fund raiser. Tickets are $3 for students and $5 for adults. The student council wants to raise at least $1000. If 200 students attend, how many adults must attend?

Solve each inequality. Check the solution.

16. $-18 < 2(12 - 3b)$

17. $5n + 3 - 4n < -5 - 3n$

18. $36 > 4(2d + 10)$

19. $3j + 2 - 2j < -10$

20. $7(2z + 3) > 35$

4-4 • Guided Problem Solving

GPS Student Page 223, Exercise 43

Expenses The sophomore class is planning a picnic. The cost of a permit to use a city park is $250. To pay for the permit, there is a fee of $.75 for each sophomore and $1.25 for each guest who is not a sophomore. Two hundred sophomores plan to attend. Write and solve an inequality to find out how many guests must attend for the sophomores to pay for the permit.

Read and Understand

1. What is the cost of a permit? _____

2. How many sophomores are expected to attend? _____

3. What is the cost for each guest that attends? _____

Plan and Solve

4. How much money will the class earn from sophomores? _____

5. Write and solve an inequality to find out how many guests must attend for the sophomores to pay for the permit. _____

Look Back and Check

6. Use your original inequality to check if the sophomores would be able to pay for the permit if 90 guests attended. _____

Solve Another Problem

7. Mark and Anthony are going to a movie tonight. They know that each ticket will cost $9. Together they have $30 to spend on tickets and a large popcorn for each of them. Write and solve an inequality to determine how much the popcorn can cost in order for Mark and Anthony to have enough money.

_____

Practice 4-5

Compound Inequalities

Solve each compound inequality and graph the solution.

1. $-5 < s + 5 < 5$

2. $1 < 3x + 4 < 10$

3. $k - 3 > 1$ or $k - 3 < -1$

4. $b - 2 > 18$ or $3b < 54$

5. $-4d > 8$ and $2d > -6$

6. $-4 < t + 2 < 4$

7. $-3 < 3 + s < 7$

8. $3j \geq 6$ or $3j \leq -6$

9. $-1 < \frac{1}{2}x < 1$

10. $g + 2 > -1$ or $g - 6 < -9$

11. $-6 < 9 + 3y < 6$

12. $3f > 15$ or $2f < -4$

13. $d - 3 > 4$ or $d - 3 < -4$

14. $1 > 2h + 3 > -1$

15. $7 + 2a > 9$ or $-4a > 8$

16. $2z > 2.1$ or $3z < -5.85$

17. $c - 1 \geq 2$ or $c - 1 \leq -2$

18. $h + 2.8 < 1.8$ or $h + 2.8 > 4.8$

Write and solve a compound inequality that represents each situation. Graph your solution.

19. The crowd that heard the President speak was estimated to be 10,000 people. The actual crowd could be 750 people more or less than this. What are the possible values for the actual crowd size?

20. Susie has designed an exercise program for herself. One part of the program requires her to walk between 25 and 30 miles each week. She plans to walk the same distance each day five days a week. What is the range of miles that she should walk each day?

4-5 • Guided Problem Solving

GPS **Student Page 231, Exercise 46**

Meteorology The graph below shows the average monthly high and low temperatures for Detroit, Michigan, and Charlotte, North Carolina. Write a compound inequality for Charlotte's average temperature in June.

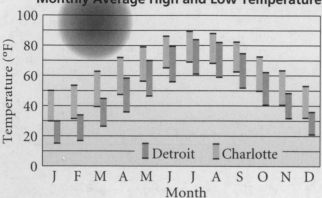

SOURCE: Statistical Abstract of the United States

Read and Understand

1. What is the high temperature in June for Charlotte? _____

2. What is the low temperature in June for Charlotte? _____

Plan and Solve

3. Will this compound inequality be formed by the word *and* or the word *or*? _____

   Explain. _____

   _____

4. Write a compound inequality for Charlotte's average temperature in June. _____

Look Back and Check

5. Explain why your inequality makes sense. _____

   _____

Solve Another Problem

6. Write a compound inequality for Detroit's average temperature
   in the winter months of December, January, February, and March. _____

Practice 4-6

Absolute Value Equations and Inequalities

Solve each inequality. Graph the solution.

1. $|d| > 2$

2. $|h| > 6$

3. $|2k| > 8$

4. $|s + 4| > 2$

5. $|3c - 6| \geq 3$

6. $|2n + 3| \leq 5$

7. $\left|\dfrac{2}{3}x\right| \leq 4$

8. $9 > |6 + 3t|$

9. $|j| - 2 \geq 6$

10. $5 > |v + 2| + 3$

11. $|4y + 11| < 7$

12. $|2n - 1| \geq 1$

13. $-2|h - 2| > -2$

14. $3|2x| \leq 12$

15. $3|s - 4| + 21 \leq 27$

16. $-6|w - 3| < -24$

Solve each equation. If there is no solution, write *no solution*.

17. $|a| = 9.5$ **18.** $|b| = -2$ **19.** $|d| - 25 = -13$ **20.** $-4|7 + d| = -44$

Write and solve an absolute value equation or inequality that represents each situation.

21. The average number of cucumber seeds in a package is 25. The number of seeds in the package can vary by three. Find the range of acceptable numbers of seeds in each package.

22. Leona was in a golf tournament last week. All four of her rounds of golf were within 2 strokes of par. If par was 72, find the range of scores that Leona could have shot for each round of the golf tournament.

23. Victor's goal is to earn $75 per week at his after-school job. Last month he was within $6.50 of his goal. Find the range of amounts that Victor might have earned last month.

24. The ideal length of a particular metal rod is 25.5 cm. The measured length may vary from the ideal length by at most 0.025 cm. Find the range of acceptable lengths for the rod.

4-6 • Guided Problem Solving

GPS **Student Page 238, Exercise 57**

Elections In a poll for the upcoming mayoral election, 42% of likely voters said they planned to vote for Lucy Jones. This poll has a margin of error of ± 3 percentage points. Use the inequality $|v - 42| \leq 3$ to find the least and greatest percent of voters v likely to vote for Lucy Jones according to this poll.

Read and Understand

1. What percentage of voters said they planned to vote for Lucy Jones? _____

2. What is the margin of error for this poll? _____

Plan and Solve

3. Write an inequality to determine the greatest percent of voters. _____

4. Solve the inequality in Step 3. _____

5. What is the greatest percent of voters? _____

6. Write an inequality to determine the least percent of voters. _____

7. Solve the inequality in Step 6. _____

8. What is the least percent of voters? _____

Look Back and Check

9. Show that your answers fall within the margin of error for this poll. _____
_____

Solve Another Problem

10. On average a household of 4 people uses 241 gallons of water each day. A 30-gallon change from the previous months could indicate a problem. More than a 30-gallon increase in water use could indicate a leak in a pipe. More than a 30-gallon decrease in water use could indicate a faulty water meter. Solve the inequality $|g - 242| \leq 30$ to determine the upper and lower limits of normal water usage.

    upper limit: _____

    lower limit: _____

4A: Graphic Organizer

Study Skill Before you start your new chapter, read the major headings and summaries. This will give you a good overview of the chapter.

Write your answers.

1. What is the chapter title? _____

2. Find the Table of Contents page for this chapter at the front of the book.
   Name four topics you will study in this chapter.

   _____   _____

   _____   _____

3. Complete the graphic organizer as you work through the chapter.
   1. Write the title of the chapter in the center oval.
   2. When you begin a lesson, write the name of the lesson in a rectangle.
   3. When you complete that lesson, write a skill or key concept from that lesson in the outer oval linked to that rectangle.

   Continue with steps 2 and 3 clockwise around the graphic organizer.

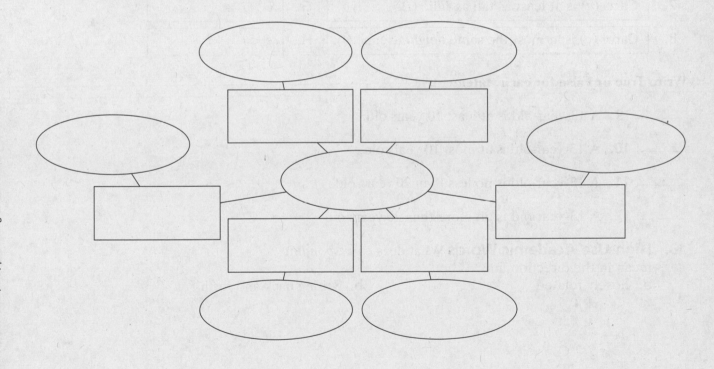

4B: Reading Comprehension

For use after Lesson 4-4

Study Skill When reading a word problem, it is sometimes difficult to determine which inequality sign should be used.

For Exercises 1–8 match each expression in Column A with its corresponding inequality symbol or expression in Column B by drawing a line between them.

	Column A		Column B
1.	is less than	**A.**	$\geq$
2.	is greater than	**B.**	$\leq$
3.	is less than or equal to	**C.**	$>$
4.	is greater than or equal to	**D.**	$<$
5.	Connie (c) is not as tall as Jose (j).	**E.**	$c \geq j$
6.	Cory (c) is older than Janishia (j).	**F.**	$c \leq j$
7.	Chris (c) is at least as tall as Julie (j).	**G.**	$c > j$
8.	Carol (c) is at most the same height as Jane (j).	**H.**	$c < j$

Write True or False for each statement.

_____ **9.** A 13-year-old is at least 10 years old.

_____ **10.** A 13-year-old is at most 10 years old.

_____ **11.** A 13-year-old is no less than 20 years old.

_____ **12.** A 13-year-old is no more than 20 years old.

13. High-Use Academic Words What does *corresponding* mean in the direction line?
    a. closely related   **b.** writing back and forth

4C: Reading/Writing Math Symbols

For use after Lesson 4-2

Vocabulary and Study Skills

Study Skill Keep your homework in a special notebook or section in a loose-leaf binder. This way you will always be able to find it quickly.

Write how to read each symbol.

1. $<$ _____

2. $>$ _____

3. $\leq$ _____

4. $\geq$ _____

5. $=$ _____

Write how to read each expression.

6. $8 > 4$ _____

7. $12 < 25$ _____

8. $3x \leq 15$ _____

9. $4x + 2 \geq 12$ _____

10. $12x = 36$ _____

Write each phrase in symbols.

11. 8 is less than 12 _____

12. 17 is greater than 2 _____

13. $12x$ is more than 36 _____

14. $15x$ minus 8 is less than 32 _____

15. $10x$ plus 4 is greater than or equal to 15 _____

16. $3x$ take away 12 is less than or equal to 21 _____

17. $32x$ equals $4x$ more than 12 _____

4D: Visual Vocabulary Practice

For use after Lesson 4-6

Study Skills When a math exercise is difficult, try to determine what makes it difficult. Is it a word that you don't understand? Are the numbers difficult to use?

Concept List

absolute value	absolute value inequality	Addition Property of Inequality
compound inequality	graph of a compound inequality	graph of an inequality
equivalent inequalities	identity	inequality

Write the concept that best describes each exercise.
Choose from the concept list above.

1. $\lvert -10 \rvert$ _____	**2.** 3 4 5 6 7 _____	**3.** $-2 < x < 10$ _____
4. $2m - 6 \geq 2(m - 3)$ _____	**5.** $\begin{aligned} x - 5 &> 2 \\ x &> 7 \end{aligned}$ _____	**6.** $p \leq -12$ _____
7. If $a < b$, then $a + c < b + c$. _____	**8.** −4 −3 −2 −1 0 1 _____	**9.** $\lvert -6r + 7 \rvert > 12$ _____

4E: Vocabulary Check

Study Skill Strengthen your vocabulary. Use these pages and add cues and summaries by applying the Cornell Notetaking style.

Write the definition for each word at the right. To check your work, fold the paper back along the dotted line to see the correct answers.

_____

_____

_____

_____

Inequality

_____

Solution of an inequality

_____

_____

Variable

_____

_____

Identity

_____

_____

Evaluate an expression

_____

_____

Vocabulary and Study Skills

4E: Vocabulary Check (continued)

**Write the vocabulary word for each definition. To check your work,
fold the paper forward along the dotted line to see the correct answers.**

An mathematical sentence
that compares the value
of two expression using a
less-than or greater-than
symbol.

_____

The value or values of a
variable in an inequality
that makes the inequality
true.

_____

A symbol, usually a letter,
that represents one or
more numbers.

_____

An equation that is true
for every value.

_____

Substitute a given number
for each variable, and then
simplify.

_____

4F: Vocabulary Review Puzzle

For use with Chapter Review

Study Skill You will encounter many new terms as you read a mathematics textbook. Read aloud or recite the new terms as you read them. This will help you remember and recall rules, definitions, and formulas for future use.

Unscramble the UPPERCASE letters to form a math word or phrase that completes each sentence.

1. The multiplicative inverse of a number is always its RLREIPACCO.

2. An XENNPTEO shows repeated multiplication.

3. LOHWE SURBEMN are the nonnegative integers.

4. A EVBALRAI is a symbol, usually a letter, that represents one or more numbers.

5. The numerical factor when a term has a variable is a CINCEFFITOE.

6. A coordinate plane is divided by its axes into four TANQAUSRD.

7. An TEITINYD is an equation that is true for every value.

8. COOPDUNM EUNIISAQELTI are joined by *and* or *or*.

Practice 5-1

The graph shows the relationship between time and speed for a bus.

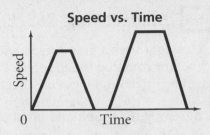

Speed vs. Time

1. Label the sections of the graph that show the speed increasing.

2. Label the section of the graph that shows the bus not moving.

3. Label the sections of the graph that show the bus moving at a constant speed.

The graph shows the relationship between time and distance from home.

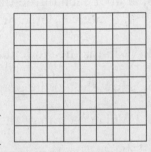

Your Trip to See Friends

4. What do the flat parts of the graph represent?

   _____

5. What do the sections from 3 P.M. to 4 P.M. and from 5 P.M. to 6 P.M. represent?

   _____

6. What does the section from 12 P.M. to 1 P.M. represent?

   _____

Sketch a graph to describe the following. Explain the activity in each section of the graph.

7. the speed of a person driving to the mall and having to stop at two stoplights

   _____

   _____

   _____

5-1 • Guided Problem Solving

GPS Student Page 255, Exercise 15

A student uses a graphing calculator, a data collector, and a motion detector to make the graph at the right, which shows a classmate's distance from the motion detector.

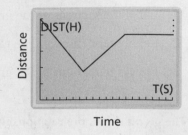

a. Copy the graph and label each section.
b. During which section was the student walking toward the motion detector?
c. During which section(s) was the student walking at constant speed?

Read and Understand

1. What variables do the horizontal and vertical axes on the graph represent? _____

2. What are you asked to do? _____

Plan and Solve

3. Label each of the three segments of the graph in terms of whether the student's distance from the motion detector is increasing, decreasing, or remaining constant over that interval.

4. What is the student doing when the graph is horizontal? _____

5. How should the graph look when the student is walking toward the detector? _____

6. Which section of the graph matches the answer to Step 5? _____

7. Constant speed means distance changing steadily over time. What should the graph look like when this is happening? _____

8. Which sections does the answer to Step 7 describe? _____

Look Back and Check

9. Give a verbal description of the student's behavior from start to finish. Is this description consistent with your earlier answers?

_____

Solve Another Problem

10. Suppose the graph were rotated 180 degrees, putting the flat portion on the left. (You can rotate the page to visualize the result.) Give a verbal description of the student's behavior as described by the resulting graph.

_____

Practice 5-2

Relations and Functions

Determine whether each of the following relations is a function.

1. $\left\{(-1, 0), (1, 1), (3, 2), \left(4, 2\frac{1}{2}\right)\right\}$

2. $\{(2, 2), (3, 3), (6, 5), (3, 1)\}$

3.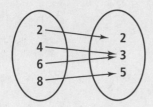

4.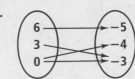

5.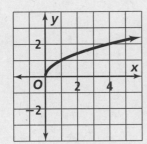

6.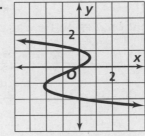

Evaluate each function rule for $x = 2$.

7. $f(x) = 3x - 4$

8. $f(x) = -x + 2$

Find the range of each function for the given domain.

9. $f(x) = -2x + 1; \{3, -1, 0, 1\}$

10. $f(x) = x^2 + x; \{-1, 0, 2\}$

11. $h(x) = -x^2; \{-2, -1, 3\}$

12. $g(x) = -\frac{1}{2}|x| + 1; \{-2, -1, 1\}$

5-2 • Guided Problem Solving

GPS Student Page 261, Exercise 42

Travel Suppose your family is driving home from vacation. The car averages 25 miles per gallon, and you are 180 miles from home. The function $d = 180 - 25g$ relates the number of gallons of gas g the car will use to your distance from home d.

a. Make a table for $d = 180 - 25g$. Use 2, 4, 6, and 8 as domain values.

b. Estimation Based on the table, how many gallons of gasoline are needed to get home?

c. The gas tank holds 15 gallons when it is full. Describe a reasonable domain and range for this situation. Explain your answer.

Read and Understand

1. Explain where the equation $d = 180 - 25g$ comes from.

_____

2. What are you asked to do? _____

Plan and Solve

3. Using $d = 180 - 25g$, fill in the value of d for each value of g.

g	2	4	6	8
d				

4. Home is reached when $d = 0$. Based on the table, approximately what value of g would lead to $d = 0$? _____

5. Since the gas tank can hold up to 15 gallons, what is a reasonable domain for d as a function of g? In other words, what values of g are possible? _____

6. Use the answers to Step 5, together with $d = 180 - 25g$, to find the range for d as a function of g—that is, what values of d are possible. _____

Look Back and Check

7. Check that your answer to Step 4 is reasonable by finding how far the car will travel on this many gallons. Is this distance close to 180 miles? _____

Solve Another Problem

8. A double cheeseburger contains 520 calories. A 150-lb adult, jogging, burns about 115 calories per mile. Write a function that describes how many calories still remain to be burned off after the adult has eaten the burger and then run a certain number of miles.

_____

Practice 5-3

Model the rule $f(x) = x + 1$ with a table of values and a graph.

1.

x	f(x) = x + 1
−3	
−1	
0	
1	
3	

2. The admission to the school festival is $3.00 per vehicle plus $.50 per passenger. The total admission is a function of the number of passengers.

   a. Make a table showing the total admission for vehicles with 1, 2, 3, and 4 passengers.

n	T(n) = 3 + 0.50n

   b. Should the points of the graph be connected by a line? Explain.

_____

_____

Graph each function.

3. $y = 4x + 2$

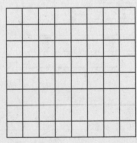

4. $f(x) = |-2x|$

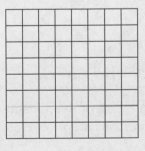

Make a table of values for the points indicated on each graph.

5.

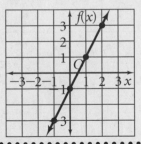

x	f(x)

6.

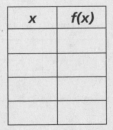

x	f(x)

Name _____ Class _____ Date _____

5-3 • Guided Problem Solving

GPS **Student Page 267, Exercise 38**

a. Make a table for the perimeters of the rectangles formed by each set of darkened tiles.

b. The perimeter $P(t)$ is a function of the number of tiles t. Write a rule for the data in your table and graph the function.

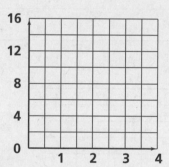
Fig. 1 Fig. 2   Fig. 3   Fig. 4

Read and Understand

1. How many darkened tiles are there in each figure? _____

2. What are you asked to find? _____

Plan and Solve

3. Counting each darkened tile as a 1-by-1 square, find the perimeter of each block of tiles. Enter the answers in the table.

Number of tiles (*t*)	1	2	3	4
Perimeter (*P*)				

4. Find two numbers *a* and *b* that allow you to write a rule for the data in the form $P(t) = at + b$. _____

5. Graph the function found in Step 4.

```
16
12
 8
 4
 0
    1   2   3   4
```

Look Back and Check

6. Draw a block of five tiles in a row, and verify that the function from Step 4 correctly predicts the perimeter. _____

Solve Another Problem

7. Write a function rule based on the following table. _____

x	1	2	3	4
y	4	1	−2	−5

Practice 5-4

Write a function rule for each table.

1.

x	f(x)
1	4
3	6
5	8
7	10

_____

2.

x	f(x)
0	0
1	3
2	6
3	9

_____

3.

x	f(x)
0	−5
2	−3
4	−1
6	1

_____

Write a function rule.

4. the total cost $t(c)$ of c pounds of apples, if each pound of apples costs $.90

_____

5. the height $f(h)$ of an object in feet when you know the height h in yards

_____

6. a. Write a function rule to determine the change you would get from
$10 when purchasing items that cost $1.50 each.

_____

b. Calculate the change when 4 of these items are purchased.

_____

c. Can you purchase 7 of these items with $10?

_____

7. You invest $500 to buy jackets and then sell them for $25.00 each.

a. Write a function rule to determine your profit.

_____

b. Use your rule to find your profit after selling 50 jackets.

_____

c. How many jackets do you need to sell to get back your investment?

_____

5-4 • Guided Problem Solving

GPS Student Page 273, Exercise 24

Water Usage Use the function in the table at the right.

a. Identify the dependent and independent variables.
b. Write a rule to describe the function.
c. How many gallons of water would you use for 7 loads of laundry?
d. **Critical Thinking** In one month, you used 442 gallons of water for laundry. How many loads did you wash?

Water Used for Laundry	
1 load	34 gallons
2 loads	68 gallons
3 loads	102 gallons
4 loads	136 gallons

Read and Understand

1. What are the dependent and independent variables? _____

2. After you have identified the dependent and independent variables, what else are you asked to do? _____

Plan and Solve

3. Subtract 34 from 68, then subtract 68 from 102, and then subtract 102 from 136. The answer should be the same each time. What is it? _____

4. Complete the sentence: "Each load of laundry requires _____."

5. Use the answer to Step 4 to write a function rule. _____

6. Use the function found in Step 5 to find the number of gallons of water required for 7 loads of laundry. _____

7. Set the function found in Step 5 equal to 442 gallons, then solve the resulting equation to find the number of loads. _____

Look Back and Check

8. No loads of laundry should require zero gallons of water. Check that the function you wrote supports this conclusion. _____

Solve Another Problem

9. A motorcycle on the freeway gets 45 miles per gallon. Write a rule that describes miles covered as a function of gallons used. _____

Practice 5-5

Direct Variation

Is each equation a direct variation? If it is, find the constant of variation.

1. $y = 3x$

2. $6x + 2y = 0$

3. $y = 3x + 7$

_____

_____

_____

4. $6x - y = 0$

5. $8x - 4y = 0$

6. $x - 4y = 5$

_____

_____

_____

The ordered pairs in each exercise are for the same direct variation. Find each missing value.

7. $(2, 1)$ and $(8, y)$

8. $(-2, 8)$ and $(x, 12)$

9. $(2, y)$ and $(10, 15)$

_____

_____

_____

10. $(3, y)$ and $(6, 10)$

11. $(2, y)$ and $(12, 18)$

12. $(-4, 3)$ and $(x, 6)$

_____

_____

_____

For the data in each table, tell whether y varies directly with x. If it does, write an equation for the direct variation.

13.

x	y
3	6
6	12
9	18

_____

14.

x	y
2	8
4	16
6	24

_____

15.

x	y
8	6
10	9
22	27

_____

16. Your percent grade varies directly with the number of correct answers. You got a grade of 80 when you had 20 correct answers.

a. Write an equation for the relationship between percent grade and number of correct answers.

_____

b. What would your percent grade be with 24 correct answers?

_____

5-5 • Guided Problem Solving

GPS Student Page 281, Exercise 45

Biology The amount of blood in a person's body varies directly with body weight. A person who weighs 160 lb has about 5 qt of blood.

- **a.** Find the constant of variation.
- **b.** Write an equation relating quarts of blood to weight.
- **c.** **Open-Ended** Estimate the number of quarts of blood in your body.

Read and Understand

1. What is another way of saying "y varies directly with x"? _____

2. What are you being asked to do? _____

Plan and Solve

3. What is the general form of a direct variation? _____

4. When $x = 160$, $y = 5$. Use this information to find k, the constant of variation. _____

5. Use the answer to Step 4 to write an equation
   relating quarts of blood to weight in pounds. _____

6. Use the equation found in Step 5 to estimate
   the volume of blood in your own body. _____

Look Back and Check

7. If blood volume varies directly with body weight, and
   a 160-lb person has 5 quarts of blood, then a person
   twice as big ought to have twice as much blood.
   Verify that your equation supports this conclusion. _____

Solve Another Problem

8. "A pint is a pound the whole world round." That's not exactly
   true, but it's pretty close for a liquid such as water or blood.
   Since 1 quart = 2 pints, a quart of blood weighs about 2 pounds.
   Write an equation relating *pounds* of blood to pounds of overall
   body weight. What fraction of your body weight consists of blood? _____

Practice 5-6

Inverse Variation

Suppose _y_ varies inversely with _x_. Write an equation for each inverse variation.

1. $x = 3$ when $y = 2$

_____

2. $x = 4$ when $y = 5$

_____

3. $x = 7$ when $y = 3$

_____

4. $x = 6$ when $y = 3$

_____

5. $x = 11$ when $y = 4$

_____

6. $y = 5$ when $x = 3$

_____

Each pair of points is on the graph of an inverse variation. Find the missing value.

7. $(5, 8)$ and $(4, m)$

_____

8. $(16, 5)$ and $(10, h)$

_____

9. $(14, 8)$ and $(c, 7)$

_____

10. $(3, 18)$ and $(a, 27)$

_____

11. $(4, 28)$ and $(3, p)$

_____

12. $(16, 3)$ and $(g, 24)$

_____

State whether each situation represents a direct variation or an inverse variation.

13. The cost of a $25 pizza is split among some friends.

_____

14. You purchase some strawberries at $1.29/lb.

_____

Tell whether the data in each table is a _direct variation_, or an _inverse variation_. Write an equation to model the data.

15.

x	2	5	10
y	25	10	5

_____

16.

x	3	6	12
y	16	8	4

_____

17.

x	3	4	7
y	33	44	77

_____

18.

x	2	4	6
y	4	8	12

_____

19.

x	2	4	5
y	10	5	4

_____

20.

x	4	6	24
y	3	2	0.5

_____

5-6 • Guided Problem Solving

GPS Student Page 289, Exercise 45

a. **Earnings** Suppose you want to earn $80. How long will it take you if you are paid $5/h; $8/h; $10/h; $20/h?

b. What are the two variable quantities in part (a)?

c. Write an equation to represent this situation.

Read and Understand

1. What are you asked to find?

_____

Plan and Solve

2. How are the quantities "pay," "hours worked," and "hourly rate of pay" related?

_____

3. Use division to fill in the table with the number of hours needed to earn $80 for each pay rate.

Rate of Pay	$5/hr	$8/hr	$10/hr	$20/hr
Hours Worked				

4. Of the three quantities in Step 2, which one is given as a fixed quantity in this problem? At what value is it fixed? _____

5. What are the variable quantities in the problem? _____

6. Use your answer to Step 2 to write an equation relating the fixed and variable quantities in this problem. _____

Look Back and Check

7. Use the table to confirm that you have written the correct equation.

Solve Another Problem

8. A shopper has $200 to spend and plans to spend all the money to buy a single type of item. Write an equation relating the price of each item and the number of items being purchased to the total amount being spent, which is $200. _____

Practice 5-7

Find the common difference of each arithmetic sequence.

1. $2, 8, 14, 20, \ldots$

_____

2. $7, 4, 1, -2, \ldots$

_____

3. $-20, -15, -10, -5, \ldots$

_____

4. $-11, -8, -5, -2, \ldots$

_____

5. $6\frac{1}{2}, 7, 7\frac{1}{2}, 8, \ldots$

_____

6. $9\frac{1}{2}, 9, 8\frac{1}{2}, 8, \ldots$

_____

Find the fifth and tenth terms of each sequence.

7. $2, 4, 6, 8, \ldots$

_____

8. $16, 12, 8, 4, \ldots$

_____

9. $3, 6, 9, 12, \ldots$

_____

10. $-19, -22, -25, -28, \ldots$

_____

11. $5, 10, 15, 20, \ldots$

_____

12. $-1.3, -0.3, 0.7, 1.7, \ldots$

_____

Find the next two terms in each sequence.

13. $1, 3, 5, 7, \ldots$

_____

14. $-4, 0, 4, 8, \ldots$

_____

15. $1, -4, -9, -14, \ldots$

_____

16. $9.8, 0.7, -8.4, -17.5, \ldots$

_____

Determine whether each sequence is arithmetic. Justify your answer.

17. $2.3, 2.1, 1.9, 1.7, \ldots$

_____

18. $5, -5, 5, -5, \ldots$

_____

19. $4, 8, 16, 32, \ldots$

_____

20. $100, 81, 64, 49, \ldots$

_____

5-7 • Guided Problem Solving

GPS Student Page 295, Exercise 55

The first five rows of Pascal's Triangle are at the right.

a. Predict the numbers in the sixth row.
b. Find the sum of the numbers in each of the first five rows.
c. Predict the sum of the numbers in the sixth row.

```
            1
          1   1
        1   2   1
      1   3   3   1
    1   4   6   4   1
```

Read and Understand

1. What are you asked to do? _____

Plan and Solve

2. Except for the 1's, every number in a row is based
   on two other nearby numbers. What is the relationship? _____

3. Predict the numbers in the sixth row. _____

4. What is the sum of the numbers in each of the first five rows? _____

5. What is the pattern for the sequence of numbers in your answer to Step 4?

   _____

6. Based on the pattern in Step 5, what should be the sum for row six? _____

Look Back and Check

7. Check your answer to Step 6 by adding up the numbers predicted in Step 3.

   _____

Solve Another Problem

8. The first five rows of another triangle of numbers are at the
   right. Predict the numbers in the sixth row.

```
            1
          1   1
        1   3   1
      1   5   5   1
    1   7  13   7   1
```

5A: Graphic Organizer

For use before Lesson 5-1

Study Skill Develop a method of note taking, including punctuation and abbreviations. Take your notes in a large notebook. A large notebook will allow you to jot down information without running out of paper or space.

Write your answers.

1. What is the chapter title? _____

2. Find the Table of Contents page for this chapter at the front of the book. Name four topics you will study in this chapter.

   _____   _____

   _____   _____

3. Complete the graphic organizer as you work through the chapter.
   1. Write the title of the chapter in the center oval.
   2. When you begin a lesson, write the name of the lesson in a rectangle.
   3. When you complete that lesson, write a skill or key concept from that lesson in the outer oval linked to that rectangle.
   Continue with steps 2 and 3 clockwise around the graphic organizer.

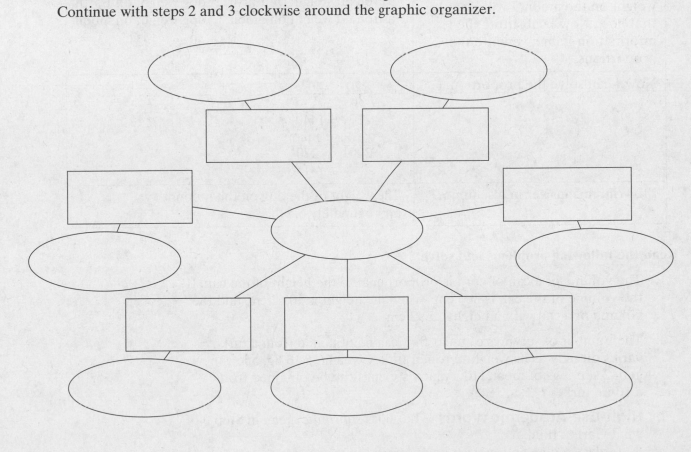

5B: Reading Comprehension

For use after Lesson 5-6

Study Skill After reading a section, try and recall the information. Ask yourself questions. If you cannot remember enough information re-read parts you forgot.

Read the problem and follow along with Carlita as she solves the problem.

> The weight of an object on Earth is directly proportional to the weight of the same object on the moon. A 220-lb astronaut would weigh 36 lb on the moon. How much would a 40-lb dog weigh on the moon?

What Carlita Thinks	What Carlita Writes
I read the problem and write down the important information.	220 lb astronaut = 36 lb on moon 40 lb dog = ?
Where should I start? It says the object is directly proportional, so I set up a proportion.	$\dfrac{\text{astronaut weight on Earth}}{\text{astronaut weight on moon}} = \dfrac{\text{dog weight on Earth}}{\text{dog weight on moon}}$
Since I am looking for the dog weight on the moon, I will let that be x. Now I substitute the information I am given into the proportions.	$\dfrac{\text{astronaut weight on Earth}}{\text{astronaut weight on moon}} = \dfrac{\text{dog weight on Earth}}{\text{dog weight on moon}}$ $\dfrac{220}{36} = \dfrac{40}{x}$
Now I can solve the proportion.	$\dfrac{220}{36} = \dfrac{40}{x}$ $220x = 1440$ $\dfrac{220x}{220} = \dfrac{1440}{220}$ $x \approx 6.5$
I'll write my answer in a sentence.	The weight of the dog on the moon is approximately 6.5 lb.

Read the following problems and solve.

1. The volume of a can of corn is proportional to the height of the can. If the volume of the can is 300 cm³ when the height is 10.62 cm, find the volume of a can with a height 15.92 cm.

2. The number of servings of meat that can be obtained from a turkey varies directly as its weight. From a turkey weighing 16 kg, one can get 42 servings of meat. How many servings can be obtained from a 10-kg turkey?

3. **High-Use Academic Words** What does *substitute* mean in Step 3 of what Carlita thinks?

   a. replace a description with its numerical value

   b. guess a value for x and see if it makes the proportion true

5C: Reading/Writing Math Symbols

For use after Lesson 5-2

Study Skill When you take notes, it helps if you learn to use abbreviations and symbols that represent words. You should also use math symbols whenever possible.

For Exercises 1–8, match the symbolic expression in Column A with its written expression in Column B by drawing a line between them.

Column A	**Column B**
1. $k - 14 < 12$	**A.** 15 times x equals 12 more than x
2. $12 + y$	**B.** twelve times x
3. $|-4|$	**C.** kilometers per hour
4. $15x = 12 + x$	**D.** a number take away 14 is less than 12
5. km/h	**E.** twelve plus y
6. \$/gal	**F.** 21 decreased by w
7. $12x$	**G.** dollars per gallon
8. $21 - w$	**H.** absolute value of negative four

For Exercises 9–16, match the symbolic expression in Column C with its written expression in Column D by drawing a line between them.

Column C	**Column D**
9. $12 \geq 12x$	**A.** miles per gallon
10. 25%	**B.** dollars per pound
11. $12 < x$	**C.** 12 is greater than or equal to twelve times x
12. \$/lb	**D.** twenty-five percent
13. mi/gal	**E.** 5 times a number x is less than or equal to 25
14. $\frac{1}{4}x$	**F.** 12 is less than a number x
15. $5x \leq 25$	**G.** 4 divided into w parts
16. $4 \div w$	**H.** one-fourth of x

Vocabulary and Study Skills

5D: Visual Vocabulary Practice

For use after Lesson 5-7

Study Skill When you come across something you don't understand, view it as an opportunity to increase your brain power.

Concept List

arithmetic sequence	common difference	conjecture
continuous data	direct variation	discrete data
function notation	inverse variation	relation

Write the concept that best describes each exercise. Choose from the concept list above.

1. an infant's weight over time	**2.** The pattern is "divide the previous term by 5."	**3.** $\{(-2, 1), (3, 0), (5, -9)\}$
_____	_____	_____
4. $y = \dfrac{9}{x}$	**5.** $-4, \;\; 5, \;\; 14, \;\; 23$ $\quad +9 \quad +9 \quad +9$	**6.** the number of children in each family in a neighborhood
_____	_____	_____
7. $-7, -4, -1, 2, 5, 8, \ldots$	**8.** $f(x) = 3x - 11$	**9.** $y = 14x$
_____	_____	_____

Vocabulary and Study Skills

5E: Vocabulary Check

Study Skill Strengthen your vocabulary. Use these pages and add cues and summaries by applying the Cornell Notetaking style.

Write the definition for each word at the right. To check your work, fold the paper back along the dotted line to see the correct answers.

_____

_____   Relation

_____

_____

_____   Vertical-line test

_____

_____

_____   Function notation

_____

_____

_____   Continuous data

_____

_____

_____   Direct variation

_____

_____

5E: Vocabulary Check (continued)

Write the vocabulary word for each definition. To check your work,
fold the paper forward along the dotted line to see the correct answers.

A set of ordered pairs.

_____

If any vertical line passes
through more than one
point of the graph, then for
some value of x there is
more than one value of y.

_____

Using $f(x)$ to indicate the
outputs of a function.

_____

Data where numbers
between any two data
values have meaning.

_____

A function of the form
$y = kx$, where $k \neq 0$.

_____

Name _____ Class _____ Date _____

5F: Vocabulary Review Puzzle   For use with Chapter Review

Study Skill When you read, your eyes make small stops along a line of words. Good readers make fewer stops when they read. The more stops you make when you read, the harder it is for you to comprehend what you've read. Try to concentrate and free yourself of distractions as you read.

Complete the crossword puzzle.

ACROSS	
7. the result of a single trial	**3.** type of reasoning where conclusions are based on patterns you observe
8. a number pattern	**4.** set of second coordinates in an ordered pair
10. an equation involving two or more variables	**5.** a term that has no variable
15. an equation that describes a function	**6.** rational numbers and irrational numbers
	9. each item in a matrix
	11. a comparison of two numbers by division
DOWN	**12.** multiplicative inverse
1. a conclusion you reach by inductive reasoning	**13.** a data value that is much higher or lower than any other data values in the set
2. has two parts, a base and an exponent	**14.** a relation that assigns exactly one value in the range to each value in the domain

Practice 6-1

Rate of Change and Slope

· ·

Find the slope of each line.

1.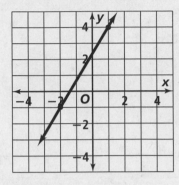

2.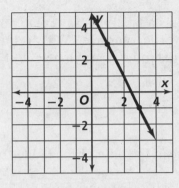

3.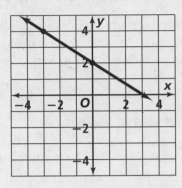

_____   _____   _____

Find the slope of the line that passes through each pair of points.

4. $(4, 4), (7, 5)$

5. $(8, 3), (4, 6)$

6. $(2, 5), (4, 7)$

_____   _____   _____

7. $(-1, 7), (4, -2)$

8. $(1, 6), (5, 9)$

9. $(-3, -6), (3, 4)$

_____   _____   _____

Find the rate of change.

10.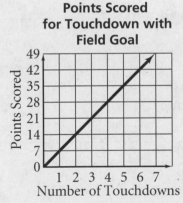

Points Scored for Touchdown with Field Goal

11.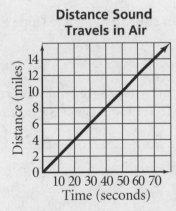

Distance Sound Travels in Air

12.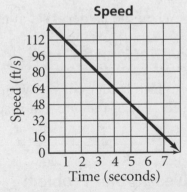

Speed

_____   _____   _____

Name_____ Class_____ Date_____

6-1 • Guided Problem Solving

GPS **Student Page 314, Exercise 42**

Construction An extension ladder has a label that says, "Do not place base of ladder less than 5 ft from the vertical surface." What is the greatest slope possible if the ladder can safely extend to reach a height of 12 ft? Of 18 ft?

Read and Understand

1. How close to the vertical surface can the base of the ladder be placed? _____

2. How high can the ladder safely reach? (Two answers) _____

3. What are you asked to find? _____

Plan and Solve

4. How does the slope of the ladder relate to the height it reaches and to the placement of its base?

_____

5. What placement of the base makes the slope as great as possible? _____

6. When the ladder is set at maximum slope, how high does it reach? (Two answers) _____

7. When the ladder is set at maximum slope, what is the slope? (Two answers) _____

Look Back and Check

8. Which ladder ends up with the greater slope—the one that reaches to 12 ft or the one that reaches to 18 ft? Does the answer make sense?

_____

Solve Another Problem

9. For safety, an extension ladder should not be set at a slope greater than 3. If the ladder is placed against a wall at this slope and reaches a height of 12 ft, how far is the base from the wall?

_____

Guided Problem Solving

Practice 6-2

Slope-Intercept Form

Find the slope and *y*-intercept of each equation. Then graph.

1. $y = x + 4$ _____

2. $y = 2x - 2$ _____

3. $y = \frac{1}{2}x - 4$ _____

4. $y = \frac{2}{5}x + 3$ _____

5. $y = -x - 4$ _____

6. $y = -5x - 6$ _____

Write an equation of a line with the given slope and *y*-intercept.

7. $m = 2, b = 4$ _____

8. $m = -3, b = -5$ _____

9. $m = -\frac{3}{4}, b = -2$ _____

10. $m = -1, b = 3$ _____

11. $m = -\frac{2}{3}, b = -5$ _____

12. $m = 4, b = 0$ _____

Write the slope-intercept form of the equation for each line.

13.

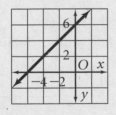

_____

14.

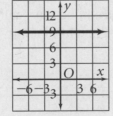

_____

15.

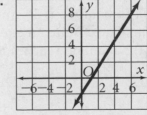

_____

L1 Practice

Algebra 1 Lesson 6-2

6-2 • Guided Problem Solving

GPS **Student Page 321, Exercise 57**

a. A candle begins burning at time $t = 0$. Its original height is 12 in. After 30 min the height of the candle is 8 in. Draw a graph showing the change in the height of the candle.

b. Write an equation that relates the height of the candle to the time it has been burning.

c. How many minutes after the candle has been lit will it burn out?

Read and Understand

1. What is the candle's starting height at time $t = 0$? _____

2. What is the candle's height at time $t = 30$ min? _____

3. What are you asked to do? _____

Plan and Solve

4. Plot two points to represent the candle heights at different times. Graph the changing candle height by drawing a ray from the first point through the second one.

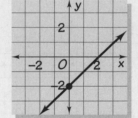

5. What is the *y*-intercept of the graph? _____

6. What is the slope of the graph? _____

7. Use the *y*-intercept and the slope to write the slope-intercept form of the equation relating candle height h to time t. _____

8. Use the equation from Question 7 to find t when the candle height h equals zero. _____

Look Back and Check

9. Check that the time it takes the candle to burn down its full length of 12 in. is three times the time it takes to burn down a third of that distance, namely 4 in. _____

Solve Another Problem

10. A stalk of bamboo is 30 cm tall when measured one day (call this $t = 0$) and is 42 cm tall 24 hours later. Write an equation that relates height in cm to time in hours. Then predict the time when the bamboo reaches a height of 90 cm.

Guided Problem Solving

Name _____ Class _____ Date _____

Practice 6-3

Model each situation with a linear function and graph. Is it reasonable to include negative numbers in the range?

1. A gas station charges $2.50 per gallon for diesel.

   _____

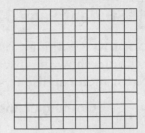

2. It costs a craftsperson $110 to bring 150 picture frames to market, and the picture frames sell for $2. The difference between the cost and the income from sales is the craftsperson's profit.

   _____

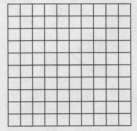

3. Temperature on the Fahrenheit scale is a linear function of temperature on the Celsius scale. Ten degrees Celsius equals 50 degrees Fahrenheit, and 25 degrees Celsius equals 77 degrees Fahrenheit.

   _____

Write a linear function for the graph then state and interpret the slope and the _y_-intercept.

4. A rental cabin charges a flat fee per week, plus a per-person cost based on how many guests are staying.

   _____

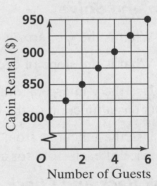

6-3 • Guided Problem Solving

GPS **Student Page 326, Exercise 7**

Shopping Clothing Connection and Teen World are having sales.
The graphs show the discounted price as a function of the original
price for merchandise from each shop.

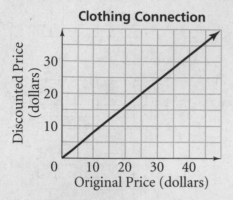

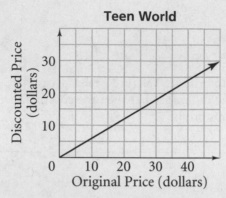

a. Which store has a greater discount? Explain.

b. Write a linear function to model the situation in each store.

c. A customer buys merchandise originally priced at $16 from each
store. What is the discounted price at each store?

Read and Understand

1. What do each of the two graphs show? _____

2. What are you asked to do? _____

_____

Plan and Solve

3. What is the y-intercept of each graph? _____

4. What is the slope of each graph? _____

5. Use the y-intercept and the slope to write the discount price
(y) as a function of the original price (x) for each store. _____

6. Use the functions from Step 5 to find the discount
price at each store for an original price of $16. _____

Look Back and Check

7. Do the answers from Step 6 match the graphs
for Clothing Connection and Teen World? Explain. _____

Solve Another Problem

8. Suppose a third store has a graph similar to the ones for
Clothing Connection and Teen World, but it passes through
the point (40, 30). Write a linear function for this store,
and find the discount price when the original price is $16. _____

Practice 6-4

Standard Form

•••

Graph each equation using *x*- and *y*-intercepts.

1. $x + y = 6$

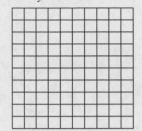

2. $-2x + 3y = 6$

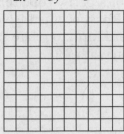

3. $3x + 4y = 12$

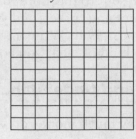

4. $y = -5$

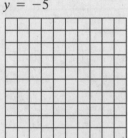

5. $x = 6$

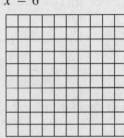

6. $5x + 2y = 5$

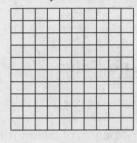

Write each equation in standard form using integers.

7. $y = 2x - 7$

_____

8. $y = 3x - 7$

_____

9. $y = -5x - 8$

_____

10. $y = 6x - 24$

_____

11. $y = \frac{7}{2}x - 11$

_____

12. $y = \frac{5}{2}x + \frac{25}{2}$

_____

13. $y = -\frac{x}{5} + \frac{2}{5}$

_____

14. $y = -4x - 20$

_____

15. The drama club is performing a musical. Tickets cost $5 for adults and $3 for students. The drama club wants to raise $450.

a. Write an equation to find the number of each type of ticket they should sell.

_____

b. Graph your equation.

c. Use your graph to find two different combinations of tickets sold.

_____

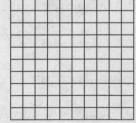

16. A baker buys $70 worth of flour and sugar for the bakery. A bag of flour costs $5, and a bag of sugar costs $7.

a. Write an equation to find the number of bags of each type the baker can buy.

_____

b. Graph your equation.

•••

6-4 • Guided Problem Solving

GPS **Student Page 334, Exercise 48**

You are sent to the store to buy sliced meat for a party. You are told to get roast beef and turkey, and you are given $30. Roast beef is $4.29/lb and turkey is $3.99/lb. Write an equation in standard form to relate the pounds of each kind of meat you could buy at the store with $30.

Read and Understand

1. How much money do you have to spend? _____

2. What is the cost per pound for roast beef? For turkey? _____

3. What are you asked to do? _____

Plan and Solve

4. What will the variables x and y represent in this situation? _____

5. Write an expression for how much money is spent on roast beef, and another expression for how much money is spent on turkey. _____

6. Write an expression for how much money is spent altogether. _____

7. Write an equation which says that the total amount spent equals the amount you have to spend. _____

Look Back and Check

8. Suppose you bought all beef and no turkey. How much beef would you bring back to the party? Does this seem like a reasonable real-world amount? _____

_____

Solve Another Problem

9. A street vendor who sells hot dogs and sodas makes $0.75 of profit on every soda but loses $0.10 on every hot dog. Using x for sodas and y for hot dogs, write an equation in standard form to describe a morning on which the vendor made a profit of exactly $81.

_____

Practice 6-5

Point-Slope Form and Writing Linear Equations

Write an equation in point-slope form for the line through the given points or through the given point with the given slope.

1. $(4, 6), (5, 7)$

_____

2. $(-3, 4); m = -2$

_____

3. $(-3, 5); m = 6$

_____

4. $(2, -5); m = \frac{1}{2}$

_____

5. $(5, -1); m = -\frac{2}{3}$

_____

6. $(-3, 4), (1, 6)$

_____

7. $(2, 1), (-2, -1)$

_____

8. $(-3, 4); m = -\frac{1}{4}$

_____

9. $(3, 7); m = 0$

_____

10. $(3, 1); m$ undefined

_____

11. $(5, 6), (3, 10)$

_____

12. $(2, 3); m = \frac{4}{9}$

_____

Is the relationship shown by the data linear? If it is, model the data with an equation.

13.

x	y
1	-1
2	3
3	7
4	11

_____

14.

x	y
-2	5
0	7
2	8
4	11

_____

15.

x	y
-2	5
3	-5
7	-13
11	-21

_____

Write an equation of each line in point-slope form.

16.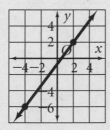

_____

17.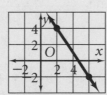

_____

18.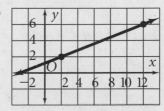

_____

6-5 • Guided Problem Solving

GPS **Student Page 340, Exercises 55**

Environment Worldwide carbon monoxide emissions are decreasing about 2.6 million metric tons each year. In 1991, carbon monoxide emissions were 79 million metric tons. Use a linear equation to model the relationship between carbon monoxide emissions and time. Let $x = 91$ correspond to 1991.

Read and Understand

1. What is the annual rate of decrease of worldwide carbon monoxide emissions?

   _____

2. What was the total of worldwide carbon monoxide emissions in 1991? _____

3. What are you being asked to do? _____

Plan and Solve

4. Write the information about worldwide emissions in 1991 as an ordered pair representing a data point. _____

5. How does the rate of emission describe the graph of the relation between time and emissions? What form of linear equation is easiest to write, given the information in the problem?

   _____

6. Write the appropriate linear equation. _____

7. Convert the equation to slope-intercept form. _____

Look Back and Check

8. Substitute 91 for x in the final equation and verify that the corresponding value of y is 79.

Solve Another Problem

9. An accountant at a manufacturing company assumes that a particular piece of company-owned machinery declines in value by $1800 per year. When the machine is 3 years old, it is valued at $21,600. Use a linear equation to model the relation between the machine's age and its accounting value. _____

Practice 6-6

Parallel and Perpendicular Lines

Find the slope of a line parallel to the graph of each equation.

1. $y = 3x + 5$

2. $y = \frac{2}{3}x + 4$

3. $y = -7x - 8$

_____

_____

_____

4. $-x + 4y = 8$

5. $y - 9 = 0$

6. $x = -2$

_____

_____

_____

Write an equation for the line that is perpendicular to the given line and that passes through the given point.

7. $(6, 4); y = 3x - 2$

8. $(-5, 5); y = -5x + 9$

9. $(-1, -4); y = \frac{1}{6}x + 1$

_____

_____

_____

10.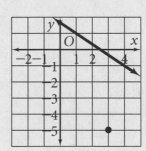

11.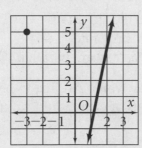

12.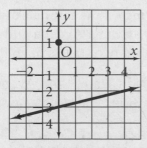

_____

_____

_____

Write an equation for the line that is parallel to the given line and that passes through the given point.

13. $(3, 2); y = 2x - 1$

14. $(3, 3); y = 3x - 2$

15. $(2, -4); y = x - 5$

_____

_____

_____

16.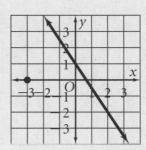

17.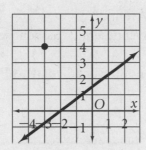

18.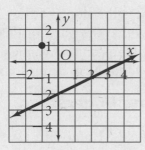

_____

_____

_____

Tell whether the lines for each pair of equations are *parallel*, *perpendicular*, or *neither*.

19. $3x + y = 2$
$x + 3y = 2$

20. $y = -3$
$y = 3$

21. $x = 4$
$y = -3$

_____

_____

_____

6-6 • Guided Problem Solving

GPS **Student Page 347, Exercises 47–49**

Use the map below to answer the questions that follow.

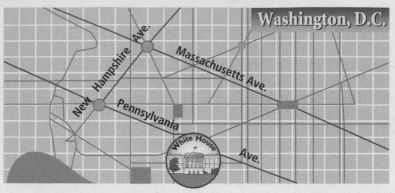

a. What is the slope of New Hampshire Avenue?

b. Show that the parts of Pennsylvania Avenue and Massachusetts Avenue near New Hampshire Avenue are parallel.

c. Show that New Hampshire Avenue is not perpendicular to Pennsylvania Avenue.

Read and Understand

1. Find New Hampshire Avenue, Pennsylvania Avenue, and Massachusetts Avenue on the map. What is the white grid for? _____

Plan and Solve

2. Find the slope of New Hampshire Avenue by examining the segment that runs from Pennsylvania Avenue to a little more than one grid square past Massachusetts Avenue.

_____

3. Staying on the left half of the map, find the slopes of Pennsylvania Avenue and Massachusetts Avenue. If those two streets have the same slope, they are parallel. _____

4. For New Hampshire Avenue and Pennsylvania Avenue to be perpendicular, their slopes must be negative reciprocals of each other. Are they? _____

Look Back and Check

5. On the left half of the map, draw a line with a slope of 2 through Pennsylvania Avenue and Massachusetts Avenue, and verify by inspection that the line is perpendicular to those two streets and not parallel to New Hampshire Avenue.

Solve Another Problem

6. What slope would a street have to have to be perpendicular to New Hampshire Avenue? Draw a line on the map to verify your result. _____

Practice 6-7

Scatter Plots and Equations of Lines

Decide whether the data in each scatter plot follow a linear pattern. If they do, find the equation of a trend line.

1.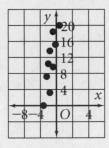

2.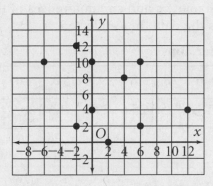

3.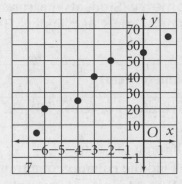

Use a graphing calculator to find the equation of the line of best fit for the following data. Find the value of the correlation coefficient r and determine if there is a strong correlation between the data.

4.

x	y
1	7
2	5
3	−1
4	3
5	−5

5.

x	y
1	6
2	15
3	−5
4	1
5	−2

6.

x	y
1	5
4	8
8	3
13	10
19	13

Draw a scatter plot. Write the equation of the trend line.

7.

x	y
1	17
2	20
3	22
4	26
5	28
6	31

8.

x	y
1	18
2	20
3	24
4	30
5	28
6	33

6-7 • Guided Problem Solving

GPS **Student Page 354, Exercise 12**

Geometry Students measured the diameters and circumferences of the tops of a variety of cylinders. Below is the data they collected.

Cylinder Tops

Diameter (cm)	3	3	5	6	8	8	9.5	10	10	12
Circumference (cm)	9.3	9.5	16	18.8	25	25.6	29.5	31.5	30.9	39.5

a. Graph the data.
b. Find the equation of a trend line.
c. What does the slope of the equation mean?
d. Find the diameter of a cylinder with a circumference of 45 cm.

Read and Understand

1. What are the lower and upper limits on the range of diameter? Of circumferences?

_____

2. In simple, nonquantitative terms, what is the relation between diameter and circumference?

_____

Plan and Solve

3. Select graph ranges and plot each pair of diameter and circumference values as a data point.

_____

4. Using visual inspection, add a trend line to the graph.

5. Using two convenient points on the trend line, write a point-slope equation for the line.

_____

6. Convert the equation from Question 5 to slope-intercept form. _____

7. What does the slope of the equation mean? (*Hint:* Treat the *y*-intercept as approximately 0.)

_____

Look Back and Check

8. Compare your results with what you know about the relation between the ratio of a circle's circumference to its diameter. _____

Solve Another Problem

9. Choose two other data points and repeat Questions 5–8. _____

Practice 6-8

Graphing Absolute Value Equations

Graph each equation by translating $y = |x|$.

1. $y = |x| - 6$

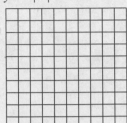

2. $y = |x + 3|$

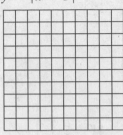

3. $y = |x + 3| - 2$

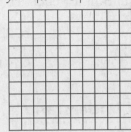

Graph each equation by translating $y = -|x|$.

4. $y = -|x| + 2$

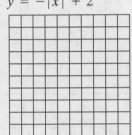

5. $y = -|x - 2| + 1$

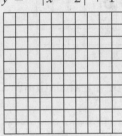

6. $y = -|x - 5| + 2$

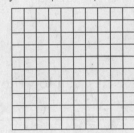

Write an equation for each translation of $y = |x|$.

7. up 3 units, right 1 unit

8. down 2 units, left 4 units

9. down 5 units, right 3 units

_____

_____

_____

Write an equation for each translation of $y = -|x|$.

10. right 7 units, up 4 units

11. down 2 units, left 1 unit

12. up 3 units, right 4 units

_____

_____

_____

Write an equation for the given graphs.

13.

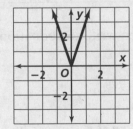

_____

14.

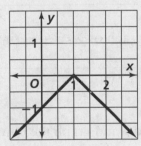

_____

15.

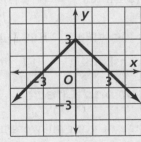

_____

6-8 • Guided Problem Solving

GPS **Student Page 362, Exercises 32–35**

Write an equation for each translation of $y = -|x|$.

a. 2 units up

b. 2.25 units left

c. $\frac{3}{2}$ units down

c. 4 units right

Read and Understand

1. Draw the graph of $y = -|x|$.

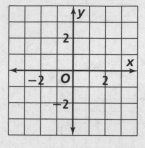

2. What does it mean to write an equation for a translation? _____

_____

Plan and Solve

3. How does one shift the graph of the equation $y = -|x|$ up or down? _____

_____

4. How does one shift the graph of the equation $y = -|x|$ left or right? _____

_____

5. Write the equation that translates the graph of $y = -|x|$ up 2 units. Then write the equation that translates $y = -|x|$ down $\frac{3}{2}$ units. _____

6. Write the equation that translates the graph of $y = -|x|$ right 4 units. Then write the equation that translates $y = -|x|$ left 2.25 units. _____

Look Back and Check

7. Pick one of your answers in Steps 5 and 6 and graph the equation. Verify that it is shifted the way it is supposed to be.

Solve Another Problem

8. Write an equation for the translation of $y = |x| + 5$ down 5 units,

then simplify the right side. Why does the result make sense? _____

Practice

6A: Graphic Organizer

For use before Lesson 6-1

Study Skill When taking notes, do not try and write down everything that the teacher is saying. Spend more time listening and write down the main points and examples. If you are writing as fast as you can, you cannot be listening as well.

Write your answers.

1. What is the chapter title? _____

2. Find the Table of Contents page for this chapter at the front of the book. Name four topics you will study in this chapter.

   _____   _____

   _____   _____

3. Complete the graphic organizer as you work through the chapter.
   1. Write the title of the chapter in the center oval.
   2. When you begin a lesson, write the name of the lesson in a rectangle.
   3. When you complete that lesson, write a skill or key concept from that lesson in the outer oval linked to that rectangle.
   Continue with steps 2 and 3 clockwise around the graphic organizer.

6B: Reading Comprehension

For use after Lesson 6-2

Study Skill Reading and interpreting diagrams, graphs, and charts is an important skill in algebra and in everyday life. When you read diagrams, graphs, and charts, pay close attention to the details they contain.

Interpret each graph. Then match the graph to the sentence that describes the relationship shown.

1.

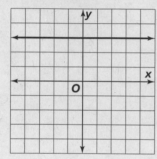

A. As *x* increases, *y* increases.

2.

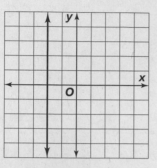

B. As *x* increases, *y* decreases.

3.

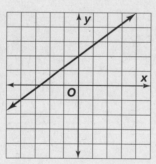

C. As *x* increases, *y* is constant.

4.

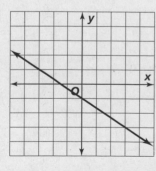

D. As *y* increases, *x* is constant.

5. High-Use Academic Words In the direction line, what does *interpret* mean for you to do?

    a. identify the slope and *y*-intercept   **b.** understand what is being conveyed

Vocabulary and Study Skills

6C: Reading/Writing Math Symbols   For use after Lesson 6-6

Study Skill Many times you need to refer to concepts taught in previous lessons. Use the Table of Contents or Index to locate these concepts.

Write what each of the symbols, variables, or equations represents. The first one is done for you.

1. $(x, 0)$ <u> x-intercept   </u>

2. $|x|$ _____

3. $\geq$ _____

4. $y = mx + b$ _____

5. $<$ _____

6. $Ax + By = C$ _____

7. $=$ _____

8. m, in $y = mx + b$ _____

9. b, in $y = mx + b$ _____

10. $-x$ _____

11. $(0, y)$ _____

12. $\times$ _____

6D: Visual Vocabulary Practice
High-Use Academic Words

For use after Lesson 6-8

Study Skills Use Venn Diagrams to understand the relationship between words whose meanings overlap such as squares, rectangles, and quadrilaterals or real number, integers, and counting numbers.

Concept List

analyze	common	equivalent
graph	order	pattern
property	rule	table

Write the concept that best describes each exercise. Choose from the concept list above.

1. To solve an inequality in the form $|A| < b$, where A is a variable expression and $b > 0$, solve $-b < A < b$. _____	**2.** $y = -\frac{3}{2}$ and $4y = -6$	**3.** <table><tr><td>x</td><td>y</td></tr><tr><td>1</td><td>12</td></tr><tr><td>2</td><td>13</td></tr><tr><td>3</td><td>14</td></tr><tr><td>4</td><td>15</td></tr></table> _____
4. $-8, 16, -32, 64, \ldots$ _____	**5.** 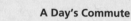 **A Day's Commute** 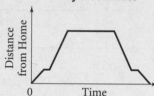 _____	**6.** $-5, -2, 0, \frac{1}{2}, 7$ _____
7. The difference between terms in the sequence $17, 13, 9, 5, \ldots$ _____	**8.** $-4 \cdot 3 = 3 \cdot -4$ _____	**9.** Jorge found the percent of change from \$15 to \$10 to be 50%. What error did he make? _____

6E: Vocabulary Check

For use after Lesson 6-3

Study Skill Strengthen your vocabulary. Use these pages and add cues and summaries by applying the Cornell Notetaking style.

Write the definition for each word at the right. To check your work, fold the paper back along the dotted line to see the correct answers.

_____

_____

_____

_____

Rate of change

_____

_____

Slope

_____

_____

_____

Linear equation

_____

_____

_____

Parent function

_____

_____

Slope-intercept form

_____

_____

6E: Vocabulary Check (continued)

For use after Lesson 6-3

Write the vocabulary word for each definition. To check your work,
fold the paper forward along the dotted line to see the correct answers.

Change in the dependent
variable, divided by
change in the independent
variable.

_____

The rate of change
of a line on a graph.

_____

An equation whose
graph is a line.

_____

The simplest equation
of a function.

_____

$y = mx + b$.

_____

6F: Vocabulary Review

Study Skill Always read direction lines before doing any exercises. What you think you are supposed to do may be different from what the directions call for.

Circle the word that best completes the sentence.

1. (*Parallel lines, Perpendicular lines*) are lines in the same plane that never intersect.

2. The point where a line crosses the *y*-axis is known as the (*x-intercept, y-intercept*).

3. The linear equation $y = mx + b$ is in (*slope-intercept, point-slope*) form.

4. The (*slope, equation*) of a line is its rate of vertical change over horizontal change.

5. The (*domain, range*) of a relation is the set of second coordinates in the ordered pairs.

6. (*Dependent, Independent*) events are events that do not influence one another.

7. The (*mean, median*) is the middle value in a set of numbers when arranged in numerical order.

8. A(n) (*exponent, variable*) is a symbol, usually a letter, that represents one or more numbers.

9. The (*absolute value, reciprocal*) of a number is its multiplicative inverse.

10. The equation $3 + 4 = 4 + 3$ illustrates the (*Identity Property of Addition, Commutative Property of Addition*).

11. When a value is less than its original amount, the percent of (*increase, decrease*) can be found.

12. A V-shaped graph that points upwards or downwards is the graph of a(n) (*linear, absolute value*) equation.

Practice 7-1

Solving Systems by Graphing

Solve by graphing. Write *no solution* or *infinitely many solutions* where appropriate.

1. $y = 4x - 2$

$y = -3x + 5$

_____

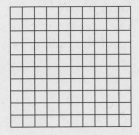

2. $y = \frac{1}{4}x + 3$

$\frac{1}{4}x - y = 5$

_____

3. $y = x - 5$

$y = \frac{1}{5}x + 4$

_____

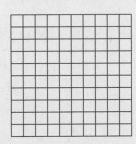

4. $y = -x - 2$

$y = -3x - 4$

_____

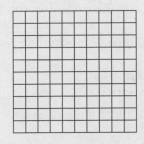

5. $y = x$

$y = 2x + 1$

_____

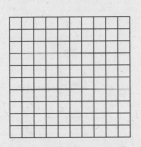

6. $y = \frac{2}{3}x - 2$

$y = x - 3$

_____

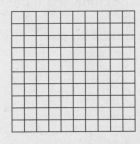

7. $x = y + 7$

$y = x + 7$

_____

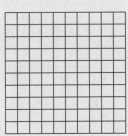

8. $2x + y = -5$

$y = -2x + 5$

_____

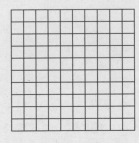

9. $x - y = 1$

$y = \frac{3}{4}x + 1$

_____

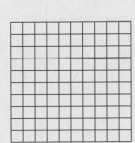

10. $3x - 3y = 9$

$y = x - 3$

_____

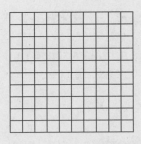

7-1 • Guided Problem Solving

$\boxed{\text{GPS}}$ **Student Page 378, Exercise 25**

Soccer Jim and Tony are on opposing teams in a soccer match. They are running after the same ball. Jim's path is the line $y = 3x$. Tony's path is the line $y = -2x + 100$. Solve by graphing to find the coordinates of the ball.

Read and Understand

1. What is the equation for Jim's path to the ball? _____

2. What is the equation for Tony's path to the ball? _____

3. What are you asked to find? _____

Plan and Solve

4. Find the slope and y-intercept for $y = 3x$. _____

5. Find the slope and y-intercept for $y = -2x + 100$. _____

6. Graph the two equations on the same set of axes.

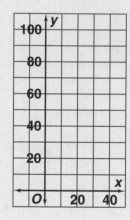

7. What are the coordinates of the point where the two lines cross? _____

Look Back and Check

8. Does it makes sense that the paths of two opposing players would cross at the ball? Would it make sense for two players on the same team?

_____

Solve Another Problem

9. Suppose Tony's path were instead given by $y = -x + 40$. Where would you locate the ball?

_____

Practice 7-2

Solving Systems Using Substitution

Solve each system using substitution. Write *no solution* or *infinitely many solutions* where appropriate.

1. $y = x$
$2y = -2x + 4$

_____

2. $y = x + 8$
$y = 5x$

_____

3. $y = 3x - 9$
$y = 2x - 4$

_____

4. $y = x - 7$
$3x + y = 9$

_____

5. $y = 2x - 5$
$-2x + y = -5$

_____

6. $4x - 2y = 0$
$x + y = -6$

_____

7. $4x + y = 12$
$y = -4x + 5$

_____

8. $y = 2x + 7$
$y = 5x + 4$

_____

9. $2x + 4y = -8$
$-3x + y = 2$

_____

10. $6x + 2y = 10$
$y = -3x + 5$

_____

11. $4x - 2y = 8$
$y = 2x + 9$

_____

12. $5x + 1y = 10$
$\frac{1}{5}y = 2 - x$

_____

13. $2x + y = -1$
$x + y = -2$

_____

14. $y = -\frac{1}{4}x + 5$
$x + 4y = -8$

_____

15. $y = -\frac{1}{3}x + 1$
$2x + 6y = 6$

_____

16. $3x + 6y = -7$
$5x + y = -10$

_____

17. $3x - y = -9$
$x + 1 = -y$

_____

18. $y = \frac{1}{3}x + 5$
$x = 3y + 9$

_____

19. At a concession stand, popcorn costs $1.10 and nachos cost $2.35. One day, the receipts for a total of 172 popcorn and nachos were $294.20. How many popcorns were sold?

7-2 • Guided Problem Solving

GPS **Student Page 384, Exercise 24**

Buying a Car Suppose you are thinking about buying one of two cars. Car A will cost $17,655. You can expect to pay an average of $1230 per year for fuel, maintenance, and repairs. Car B will cost about $15,900. Fuel, maintenance, and repairs for it will average about $1425 per year. After how many years are the total costs for the cars the same?

Read and Understand

1. What are the costs involved in owning car A? _____

2. What are the costs involved in owning car B? _____

3. What are you asked to find? _____

Plan and Solve

4. Write an equation for car A that describes total cost as a function of time. _____

5. Write another equation that does the same for car B. _____

6. Why will solving the two equations as a system give the answer to the problem?

   _____

7. To solve the system of two equations, does it make more sense to replace c with an expression containing t, or vice versa? Explain. _____

8. Make the appropriate replacement, then solve for the remaining variable. _____

9. Use your answer to Step 8 to give the solution to the problem as stated. _____

Look Back and Check

10. Explain why it makes sense that the total costs would be the same after several years of ownership. _____

Solve Another Problem

11. Suppose car C costs $16,815 to buy and $1350 per year to operate. At what time are the total costs the same as for car A? At what time are they the same as for car B?

Practice 7-3

Solve by elimination. Show your work.

1. $2x + y = 16$
$3x - y = 4$

_____

2. $x + y = 0$
$x - y = 4$

_____

3. $5x + 3y = -4$
$x + y = -4$

_____

4. $-3x + 2y = -6$
$-2x + y = 6$

_____

5. $4x + 3y = -3$
$2x + y = -1$

_____

6. $x + 2y = 1$
$x - y = -5$

_____

7. $3x - y = 10$
$2x - y = 5$

_____

8. $x - y = 3$
$3x + y = 25$

_____

9. $3x + 5y = 10$
$x - 5y = -10$

_____

10. $-2x + y = -9$
$x - 3y = 3$

_____

11. $4x - 3y = 11$
$3x - 5y = -11$

_____

12. $2x - y = 8$
$3x - 2y = 0$

_____

13. $2x - y = 7$
$-x + y = 6$

_____

14. $x + 2y = 2$
$3x + 4y = 22$

_____

15. $10x - 4y = 6$
$10x + 3y = 13$

_____

16. $4x - 7y = -15$
$-4x - 3y = -15$

_____

17. $x + y = -34$
$-2x - y = -20$

_____

18. $-2x + y = 7$
$-5x + y = 4$

_____

19. Andrea buys four shirts and three pairs of pants for $85.50. She returns the next day and buys three shirts and five pairs of pants for $115.00. What is the price of each shirt and each pair of pants?

_____

Name _____ Class _____ Date _____

7-3 • Guided Problem Solving

GPS **Student Page 392, Exercise 30**

a. **Business** A company sells brass and steel machine parts. One shipment contains 3 brass and 10 steel parts and costs $48. A second shipment contains 7 brass and 4 steel parts and costs $54. Find the cost of each machine part.

b. How much would a shipment containing 10 brass and 13 steel machine parts cost?

Read and Understand

1. What kind of information are you given about each of the two shipments?

_____

2. What are you asked to find? _____

Plan and Solve

3. Write an equation relating the known cost of the first shipment to the unknown cost of each type of part. Use b for brass and s for steel. _____

4. Write another equation that does the same for the second shipment. _____

5. What will be the first step in solving the pair of equations by the elimination method?

_____

6. Eliminate the variable s to obtain an equation in b only. _____

7. Solve the equation from Step 6 for b, then substitute the value for b back into one of the original equations and find the value for s. Interpret the results.

_____

_____

8. Use the cost of each part to predict the cost of a shipment containing 10 brass and 13 steel parts.

_____

Look Back and Check

9. Does it seem right that one type of part costs significantly more than the other? Explain.

_____

Solve Another Problem

10. You have $10,000 to divide between two investments. One investment will yield a profit of 3%, while the other will yield 5%. How much would you put into each investment for a profit of $445?

_____

Practice 7-4

Use a system of linear equations to solve each problem.

1. Your science test is worth 100 points and contains 38 questions. There are two-point and five-point questions on the test. How many of each type of question are on the test?

_____

2. Suppose you are starting a cleaning service. You have spent $315 on supplies. To clean a house, you use $4 worth of supplies. You charge $25 per house. How many houses must you clean to break even?

_____

3. The baseball team and the softball team had fundraisers to buy supplies for their trip to the championship game. The baseball team spent $135 buying six cases of juice and one case of bottled water. The softball team spent $110 buying four cases of juice and two cases of bottled water. How much did a case of juice cost? How much did a case of bottled water cost?

_____

4. Rachelle spends 330 min/wk exercising. Her ratio of time spent on aerobics to time spent on weight training is 6 to 5. How many minutes per week does she spend on aerobics? How many minutes per week does she spend on weight training?

_____

5. Suppose you invest $1530 in equipment to put your school logo on T-shirts. You buy each T-shirt for $3. After you have placed the logo on a shirt, you sell the shirt for $20. How many T-shirts must you sell to break even?

_____

6. Suppose you bought supplies for a party. Three rolls of streamers and 15 balloons cost $30. Later, you bought 2 rolls of streamers and 4 balloons for $11. How much did each roll of streamers cost? How much did each balloon cost?

_____

7-4 • Guided Problem Solving

GPS **Student Page 401, Exercise 21**

Consumer Decisions Suppose you are trying to decide whether to buy ski equipment. Typically, it costs you $60 a day to rent ski equipment and buy a lift ticket. You can buy ski equipment for about $400. A lift ticket alone costs $35 for one day.

a. Find the break-even point.

b. **Critical Thinking** If you expect to ski 5 days a year, should you buy the ski equipment? Explain.

Read and Understand

1. What are your total costs if you buy the equipment? If you don't? _____

2. What are you asked to find out? _____

Plan and Solve

3. Write an equation relating your total cost to the number of days you ski, assuming you buy the equipment. _____

4. Write another equation relating costs to days, assuming you don't buy the equipment.

   _____

5. Which method of solving the system is best? Explain why. _____

6. Solve the system to find the break-even point. Interpret the answer. _____

7. If you expect to ski 5 days a year, does it make sense to buy the ski equipment? Give your reasons.

   _____

   _____

Look Back and Check

8. Does the break-even point seem realistic? _____

   _____

Solve Another Problem

9. Suppose you cannot afford the new equipment but have an opportunity to buy used equipment for $275. If the used equipment can be expected to last two seasons, what should you do?

   _____

Practice 7-5

Linear Inequalities

● ●

Graph each linear inequality.

1. $y \geq -8$

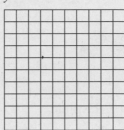

2. $x + y < -6$

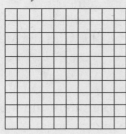

3. $y < x$

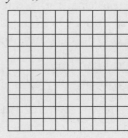

4. $y < 3x - 1$

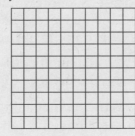

5. $y \geq \frac{1}{2}x + 3$

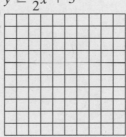

6. $y > x + 4$

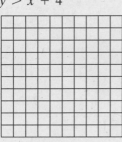

7. $x \geq -3$

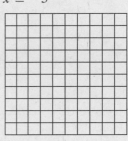

8. $y \leq \frac{1}{2}x + 4$

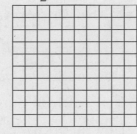

9. Suppose your school is raising money for the Red Cross. You make $5 on each T-shirt and $3 on each sweatshirt that you sell. How many of each must you sell to raise more than $150?

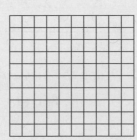

   a. Write a linear inequality that describes the situation.

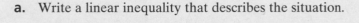

   b. Graph the inequality.

   c. Write two possible solutions to the problem.

_____

10. Suppose you intend to spend no more than $60 on music CDs. New CDs cost $12 and used CDs cost $5. How many CDs of each type can you buy?

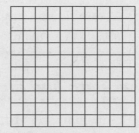

   a. Write a linear inequality that describes the situation.

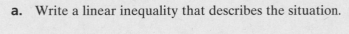

   b. Graph the inequality.

   c. Write two possible solutions to the problem.

_____

● ●

7-5 • Guided Problem Solving

GPS **Student Page 408, Exercise 37**

Budget Suppose you work at a local radio station. You are in charge
of a $180 budget for new tapes and CDs. Record companies will give
you 21 promotional (free) CDs. You can buy tapes for $8 and CDs for $12.

Let x = the number of CDs you can buy.
Let y = the number of tapes you can buy.

a. Write an inequality that shows
   the number of tapes and CDs
   you can buy.

b. Graph the inequality.

c. Is (8, 9) a solution of the inequality? Explain
   what the solution means.

d. If you buy only tapes and you buy as many as
   possible, how many new recordings will the station get?

Read and Understand

1. How much do tapes cost? _____

2. How much do CDs cost? _____

3. How much do you have to spend? _____

4. How many CDs can you get for free? _____

Plan and Solve

5. Write an inequality which says that the amount spent on tapes and
   CDs has to be less than or equal to $180, using x for CDs and y for tapes. _____

6. Graph the inequality.

7. Does the point (8, 9) lie inside the solution region? If yes, what does does that mean?

   _____

   _____

   _____

8. Assuming you buy only tapes (which are cheaper), how many can
   you buy? Consult the graph. Then add the free CDs to find the
   maximum number of recordings you can obtain on your budget. _____

Look Back and Check

9. How many recordings could you obtain if you bought only CDs? Does it make sense that the
   answer is less than for Step 8?

Solve Another Problem

10. How many tapes and CDs should you buy to end up with twicc as many CDs as tapes (including
    the free CDs), while having as little money left over as possible? _____

Practice 7-6

Systems of Linear Inequalities

Solve each system by graphing. Show your work.

1. $y < 4$
$y > 2$

2. $x < 4$
$y > 2$

3. $x + y > -3$
$-x + y < -2$

4. $x + y < 2$
$x + y > 5$

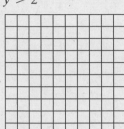

5. $y < 2x - 3$
$-2x + y > 5$

6. $-x + y < -5$
$y \geq -x + 1$

7. $y \geq \frac{1}{4}x + 1$
$y \geq \frac{3}{4}x - 1$

8. $2x - y < 5$
$-\frac{1}{2}x + y > 5$

  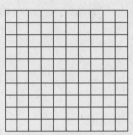 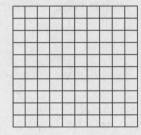

9. $-4x + 2y < -2$
$-2x + y > 3$

10. $x < 1$
$x > 4$

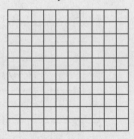 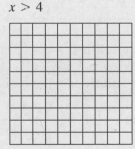

11. In basketball you score 2 points for a field goal and 1 point for a free throw. Suppose that you have scored at least 3 points in every game this season, and have a season high score of 15 points in one game. How many field goals and free throws could you have made in any one game?

a. Write a system of two inequalities that describes this situation.

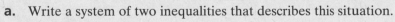

b. Graph the system to show all possible solutions.

c. Write one possible solution to the problem.

 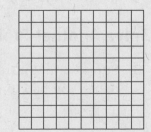

7-6 • Guided Problem Solving

GPS **Student Page 416, Exercise 35**

a. **Business** A clothing store has a going-out-of-business sale. They are selling pants for $10.99 and shirts for $4.99. You can spend as much as $45 and want to buy at least one pair of pants. Write and graph a system of inequalities that describes this situation.

b. Suppose you need to buy at least three pairs of pants. From your graph, find all the ordered pairs that are possible solutions.

Read and Understand

1. What is the cost of one pair of pants, and of two shirts, and how much can you spend?

   _____

2. What other restrictions are there on how many pants and shirts you buy?

   _____

3. What are you asked to do? _____

Plan and Solve

4. Write an inequality which says that the amount spent on pants and shirts has to be less than or equal to $45, using x for pants and y for shirts. Write another inequality stating that you buy at least 1 pair of pants. _____

5. Graph the system of inequalities.

6. List all the ordered pair solutions where x is greater than or equal to 3.

   _____

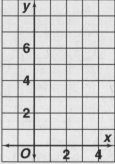

Look Back and Check

7. Suppose you were to buy just pants, as many as you could. How many would you buy? Is this one of the solutions found in Step 6? _____

Solve Another Problem

8. Suppose that instead of having to buy some minimum number of pants, you had to buy at least 6 shirts. List all the ordered pair solutions. _____

7A: Graphic Organizer

For use before Lesson 7-1

Study Skill When taking notes, write as clearly as possible.
Use abbreviations of your own invention when possible.
The amount of time needed to recopy messy notes would
be better spent rereading and thinking about them.

Write your answers.

1. What is the chapter title? _____

2. Find the Table of Contents page for this chapter at the front of the book.
   Name four topics you will study in this chapter.

   _____   _____

   _____   _____

3. Complete the graphic organizer as you work through the chapter.
   1. Write the title of the chapter in the center oval.
   2. When you begin a lesson, write the name of the lesson in a
      rectangle.
   3. When you complete that lesson, write a skill or key concept from
      that lesson in the outer oval linked to that rectangle.
   Continue with steps 2 and 3 clockwise around the graphic organizer.

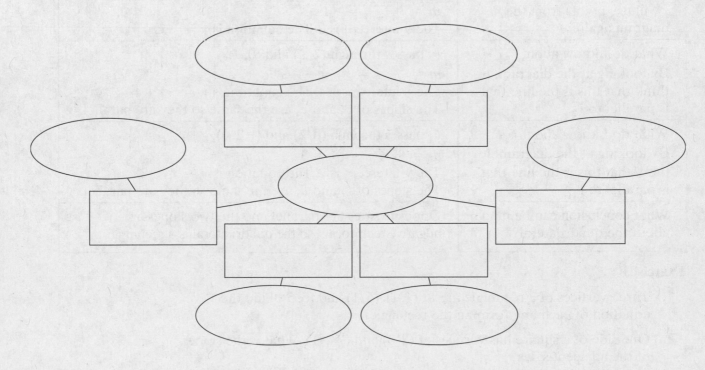

7B: Reading Comprehension

For use after Lesson 7-5

Study Skill Reading a math textbook requires being able to extract information from a graph, figure, diagram, or picture. Take time to look for relationships between lines, points, etc.

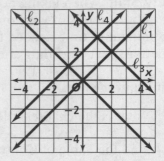

Follow the thought process that Matthew thinks and writes.

In the graph, a quadrilateral is formed by four intersecting lines denoted $\ell_1, \ell_2, \ell_3,$ and ℓ_4. Find the equation of each line. Use this information to draw a conclusion about the quadrilateral.

What Matthew Thinks	What Matthew Writes
I have to find the equations of four lines. What information appears to be true about the lines?	There appear to be two pairs of parallel lines. If that is true, there will only be two slopes. The shape also appears to be a rectangle. If that is true, the two slopes will be negative reciprocals of each other since the lines are perpendicular.
What do I know about ℓ_1? I must look at the diagram to find points that the line passes through.	ℓ_1 passes through $(0, 0)$ and $(2, 2)$. $m = \frac{2 - 0}{2 - 0} = 1$ The y-intercept is 0. The equation of ℓ_1 is $y = x$.
What do I know about ℓ_2? I will use points from the diagram again.	ℓ_2 passes through $(0, 0)$ and $(-1, 1)$. $m = \frac{1 - 0}{-1 - 0} = -1$ The y-intercept is 0. The equation is $y = -x$.
What do I know about ℓ_3? By looking at the diagram, I think that this is the line that is parallel to ℓ_2.	ℓ_3 passes through $(2, 2)$ and $(0, 4)$. $m = \frac{4 - 2}{0 - 2} = \frac{2}{-2} = -1$ The y-intercept is 4. The equation is $y = -x + 4$. The slopes of ℓ_2 and ℓ_3 are the same so they are parallel.
What do I know about ℓ_4? By looking at the diagram, I think that this is the line that is parallel to ℓ_1.	ℓ_4 passes through $(0, 2)$ and $(-2, 0)$. $m = \frac{0 - 2}{-2 - 0} = \frac{-2}{-2} = 1$ The y-intercept is 2. The equation is $y = x + 2$. The slopes of ℓ_1 and ℓ_4 are the same so they are parallel.
What conclusion can be made about the quadrilateral?	Opposite sides are parallel and the two slopes are negative reciprocals, so the quadrilateral is a rectangle.

Exercises

1. Three vertices of a rectangle are at $(1, 1)$, $(5, 1)$ and $(5, 5)$. Find the equation of each line forming the rectangle.

2. One side of a square has vertices at $(2, 3)$ and $(-2, 1)$. What is the slope of the adjacent sides?

3. **High-Use Academic Words** In the direction box at the top of the page, what does *draw a conclusion* mean for you to do?
   a. identify special characteristics
   b. identify general characteristics

Vocabulary and Study Skills

7C: Reading/Writing Math Symbols

For use after Lesson 7-2

Study Skill Many graphs look very similar. You must look for details in the graphs and their equations, and decide what those details symbolize.

Look at each inequality, and then choose its correct graph.

1. $y \geq 3$

A. 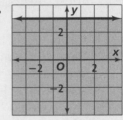 B. 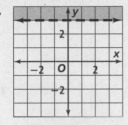 C.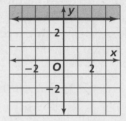

2. $x < 2$

A. 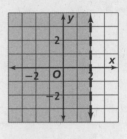 B. 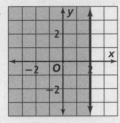 C.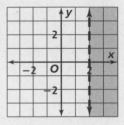

3. $y \leq x + 2$

A. 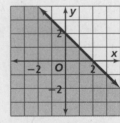 B. 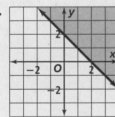 C.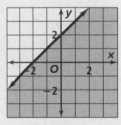

4. $y > 2x + 5$

A. 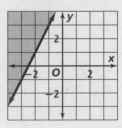 B. 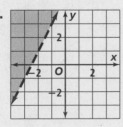 C.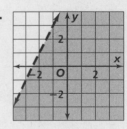

7D: Visual Vocabulary Practice

For use after Lesson 7-6

Study Skill Making sense of mathematical symbols is like reading a foreign language that uses different letters.

Concept List

elimination method	infinitely many solutions	solution of a system of equations
no solution	linear inequality	solution of a system of linear inequalities
solutions of an inequality	substitution method	system of linear inequalities

Write the concept that best describes each exercise.
Choose from the concept list above.

1. $\quad y = 4 - 3x$ $\quad\quad x + 2y = -1$ $x + 2(4 - 3x) = -1$ _____	**2.** 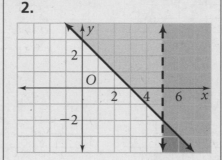 _____	**3.** $\quad y > 9x + 8$ _____
4. 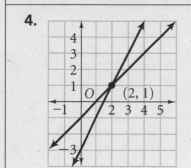 _____	**5.** $\quad 5x + 9y = 11$ $\quad -5x + 3y = -5$ $\quad\quad\quad 12y = 6$ _____	**6.** $\quad 4x - y = 10$ $\quad 8x - 2y = 20$ _____
7. $\quad y \geq 3x - 1$ $\quad 6x + y < 5$ _____	**8.** $\quad 3x + 5y = 10$ $\quad 3x + 5y = -2$ _____	**9.** 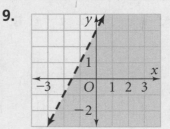 _____

Vocabulary and Study Skills

7E: Vocabulary Check

Study Skill Strengthen your vocabulary. Use these pages and add cues and summaries by applying the Cornell Notetaking style.

Write the definition for each word at the right. To check your work, fold the paper back along the dotted line to see the correct answers.

_____

_____

_____

System of linear
equations

_____

_____

Solution of a system

_____

_____

_____

No solution

_____

_____

_____

Substitution method

_____

_____

_____

Elimination method

_____

Vocabulary and Study Skills

7E: Vocabulary Check (continued)

Write the vocabulary word for each definition. To check your work, fold the paper forward along the dotted line to see the correct answers.

Two or more linear equations together.

_____

Any ordered pair in a system that makes *all* the equations true.

_____

A system of equations whose graphs do not intersect.

_____

Solving a system by replacing one variable with an equivalent expression containing the other variable.

_____

Using the Addition and Subtraction Properties of Equality to solve a system.

_____

Vocabulary and Study Skills

7F: Vocabulary Review

For use with Chapter Review

Study Skill To be successful in math you need to understand meanings of words. Learn one term at a time, moving on to the next when you are confident of your knowledge of the first.

For Exercises 1–7 match each term in Column A with its definition in Column B by drawing a line between them.

Column A

1. system of linear equations
2. solutions of an inequality
3. constant
4. linear inequality
5. parallel lines
6. variable
7. ratio

Column B

A. a comparison of two numbers by division

B. two or more linear equations using the same variables

C. a term that has no variable

D. lines in the same plane that never intersect

E. a statement representing a region of the coordinate plane

F. a symbol that represents one or more numbers

G. the coordinates of the points that make the inequality true

For Exercises 8–14 match each term in Column C with its definition in Column D by drawing a line between them.

Column C

8. outcome
9. substitution method
10. power
11. solution of the system
12. sequence
13. reciprocal
14. slope

Column D

A. any ordered pair that makes all of the equations in the system true

B. multiplicative inverse

C. a method of solving systems of equations by replacing one variable with an equivalent expression

D. a number pattern

E. has 2 parts, a base and an exponent

F. the rate of vertical change to horizontal change of a line

G. the result of a single trial

Practice 8-1

Simplify each expression.

1. 23^0

_____

2. 2^{-2}

_____

3. 3^{-3}

_____

4. $12 \cdot 5^0$

_____

5. 7^0

_____

6. $\dfrac{3}{5^{-1}}$

_____

7. $\dfrac{6^{-2}}{6^0}$

_____

8. $(13.6)^0$

_____

9. 9^{-1}

_____

Evaluate each expression for $x = -2$ and $y = 6$.

10. y^{-2}

_____

11. x^{-3}

_____

12. $(-x)^{-4}$

_____

13. $4x^{-3}$

_____

14. $2y^{-2}$

_____

15. $(3x)^{-2}$

_____

Simplify each expression.

16. x^{-4}

_____

17. xy^{-5}

_____

18. $a^{-2}b$

_____

19. $\dfrac{1}{x^{-3}}$

_____

20. $\dfrac{3}{a^{-8}}$

_____

21. $\dfrac{5}{d^{-7}}$

_____

Write each number as a power of 10 using a negative exponent.

22. $\dfrac{1}{10,000}$

_____

23. $\dfrac{1}{1,000,000}$

_____

24. $\dfrac{1}{10,000,000}$

_____

Write each expression as a decimal.

25. 10^{-3}

_____

26. 10^{-5}

_____

27. $9 \cdot 10^{-1}$

_____

8-1 • Guided Problem Solving

GPS Student Page 434, Exercise 79

Probability Suppose your history teacher gives you a multiple-choice quiz. There are four questions, each with five answer choices. The probability p of guessing the answer to a question correctly is $\frac{1}{5}$. The probability q of guessing the answer to each question incorrectly is $\frac{4}{5}$.

a. The table has expressions to find the probability of correctly guessing a certain number of answers on this quiz. Complete the table.

Multiple-Choice Quiz

Number Correct	Expression	Probability
0	$p^0 q^4$	$\left(\frac{1}{5}\right)^0\left(\frac{4}{5}\right)^4 = 0.4096$
1	$4p^1 q^3$	
2	$6p^2 q^2$	
3	$4p^3 q^1$	
4	$p^4 q^0$	

b. Which number of correct answers is most likely?

Read and Understand

1. How many questions are there on the quiz, and how many choices for each question? _____

2. For any one question, what is the chance of getting a right answer? A wrong answer? _____

Plan and Solve

3. Using the answer to Step 2, evaluate $4p^1 q^3$. In the table, fill in the probability for 1 correct.

4. Fill in the rest of the Probability column in the same way.

5. Which number(s) of correct answers have the highest probability? _____

Look Back and Check

6. Since the number of correct answers is sure to be either 0, 1, 2, 3 or 4, the sum of all the probabilities should equal 1. Does it? _____

Solve Another Problem

7. Suppose that each quiz question has 4 answer choices instead of 5, so that $p = \frac{1}{4}$ and $q = \frac{3}{4}$. Repeat Steps 3 through 5.

Practice 8-2

Scientific Notation

Write each number in standard notation.

1. 3×10^4

2. 6×10^{-2}

3. 4.7×10^5

4. 2.34×10^{-5}

5. 8.155×10^7

6. 5.0307×10^2

7. 42.4×10^6

8. 7.502×10^8

9. 0.018×10^{-1}

Write each number in scientific notation.

10. 24,000,000

11. 525,000,000,000

12. 0.00000063

13. 385×10^3

14. 426×10^{-3}

15. 0.07×10^6

Simplify. Write each answer using scientific notation.

16. $4(4 \times 10^5)$

17. $5(6 \times 10^{-2})$

18. $7(9 \times 10^9)$

19. $8(9 \times 10^6)$

20. $3(1.2 \times 10^{-4})$

21. $2(6.1 \times 10^{-8})$

22. $3(1.2 \times 10^{-4})$

23. $3(4.3 \times 10^{-4})$

24. $3(3.2 \times 10^{-2})$

8-2 • Guided Problem Solving

GPS **Student Page 439, Exercise 43**

Computers A computer can perform 4.66×10^8 instructions per second. How many instructions is that per minute? Per hour? Use scientific notation.

Read and Understand

1. How many instructions can the computer perform in one second? _____

2. What are you asked to do? _____

Plan and Solve

3. What conversion factor do you multiply by to convert instructions per second into instructions per minute? _____

4. Perform the multiplication to find the number of instructions per minute. Do not yet worry about proper scientific notation form. _____

5. Now put the answer from Step 4 in proper scientific notation form, by moving the decimal point and adjusting the exponent on the 10. _____

6. Repeat Steps 3 through 5 for the conversion from instructions per minute to instructions per hour. _____

Look Back and Check

7. You should be able to get the answer to Step 6 by converting directly from instructionsper second to instructions per hour. Verify that this works. _____

Solve Another Problem

8. Light travels at a speed of 3×10^8 meters per second. Use the number of seconds in a minute, the number of minutes in an hour, the number of hours in a day, and the number of days in a year to write the speed of light in meters per year. Then convert to kilometers per year. Use scientific notation.

_____

Practice 8-3

Multiplication Properties of Exponents

Simplify each expression.

1. $(5a^{-2})(5a^6)$

_____

2. $(-6x^6)(4x^6)$

_____

3. $t^{-5} \cdot t^{-10}$

_____

4. $r^3 \cdot r$

_____

5. $3^7 \cdot 3^6$

_____

6. $(3p^{-15})(6p^{11})$

_____

7. $\dfrac{1}{y^{-7} \cdot y^5}$

_____

8. $b^6 \cdot q^2 \cdot b^3$

_____

9. $\dfrac{1}{x^5 \cdot x^{-3}}$

_____

10. $r^6 \cdot a^4 \cdot a \cdot r^4$

_____

11. $\dfrac{1}{h^7 \cdot h^3}$

_____

12. $2^3 \cdot 2^2$

_____

13. $f^5 \cdot f^2 \cdot f^0$

_____

14. $r^6 \cdot r^{-13}$

_____

15. $5^{-6} \cdot 5^4$

_____

Simplify each expression. Write each answer in scientific notation.

16. $(5 \times 10^6)(5 \times 10^{-4})$

_____

17. $(3 \times 10^8)(2 \times 10^4)$

_____

18. $(9.5 \times 10^{-4})(2 \times 10^{-5})$

_____

19. $(4 \times 10^9)(4.1 \times 10^8)$

_____

20. $(7.2 \times 10^{-7})(2 \times 10^{-5})$

_____

21. $(5 \times 10^7)(6 \times 10^3)$

_____

22. $(6 \times 10^{-6})(5.2 \times 10^4)$

_____

23. $(6 \times 10^6)(6 \times 10^8)$

_____

24. $(6.1 \times 10^9)(8 \times 10^{14})$

_____

8-3 • Guided Problem Solving

GPS **Student Page 445, Exercise 56**

Medicine Medical X-rays, with a wavelength of about 10^{-10} meter, can penetrate your skin.

a. Ultraviolet rays, which cause sunburn by penetrating only the top layers of skin, have a wavelength about 1000 times the wavelength of an X-ray. Find the wavelength of ultraviolet rays.

b. Critical Thinking The wavelengths of visible light are between 4×10^{-7} meters and 7.5×10^{-7} meters. Are these wavelengths longer or shorter than those of ultraviolet rays? Explain.

Read and Understand

1. What is given as the wavelength of medical X-rays? _____

2. What is the conversion factor relating the wavelengths of medical X-rays and ultraviolet rays?

_____

3. What are you asked to do? _____

_____

Plan and Solve

4. Multiply the wavelength of medical X-rays by the appropriate conversion factor to find the approximate wavelength of ultraviolet rays. _____

5. Compare the wavelengths of ultraviolet rays to the wavelengths for visible light. Which is longer? Explain. _____

Look Back and Check

6. If ultraviolet rays can burn the skin more than visible light rays can, what would you expect for X-rays, given how all the wavelengths compare? Explain. Does your conclusion fit with what you know to be true?

_____

_____

Solve Another Problem

7. Infrared rays have wavelengths in the neighborhood of 10^{-5} meter. Is this longer or shorter than X-rays? Than ultraviolet rays? Than visible light?

_____

_____

Practice 8-4

Simplify each expression.

1. $(4a^5)^2$

2. $(2^{-2})^6$

3. $(5^2)^2$

_____

_____

_____

4. $(x^5)^2$

5. $2^7 \cdot (2^3)^2$

6. $d^2 \cdot (d^4)^4$

_____

_____

_____

7. $c^4 \cdot (c^6)^2$

8. $(z^{-4})^{-3}$

9. $(a^2b)^4$

_____

_____

_____

10. $(d^2)^{-4}$

11. $(b^{-3})^6$

12. $(y^5)^3$

_____

_____

_____

13. $(s^2)^8$

14. $(x^4y)^3$

15. $d^5 \cdot (d^2)^4$

_____

_____

_____

Simplify. Write each answer in scientific notation.

16. $10^{-9} \cdot (2 \times 10^2)^2$

17. $(3 \times 10^{-6})^3$

18. $10^4 \cdot (4 \times 10^6)^3$

_____

_____

_____

19. $(7 \times 10^7)^2$

20. $10^{-3} \cdot (2 \times 10^3)^5$

21. $(6 \times 10^5)^3$

_____

_____

_____

22. $(5 \times 10^5)^4$

23. $(2 \times 10^{-3})^3$

24. $(5 \times 10^2)^{-3}$

_____

_____

_____

8-4 • Guided Problem Solving

GPS **Student Page 450, Exercise 51**

a. **Geometry** Write an expression for the surface area of each cube.
b. How many times greater than the surface area of the small cube is the surface area of the large cube?
c. Write an expression for the volume of each cube.
d. How many times greater than the volume of the small cube is the volume of the large cube?

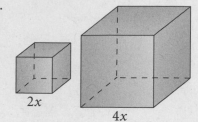

2x

4x

Read and Understand

1. What are you asked to do? _____

Plan and Solve

2. How many faces (sides) does a cube have? _____

3. For a cube whose edges have length s, what expression represents the area of each face?

_____

4. Write an expression for the surface area of a cube with edges of length s. Then write an expression for the surface area of each cube pictured above. _____

5. Use division to find the ratio of the large cube's surface area to the small cube's surface area.

_____

6. Write an expression for the volume of a cube with edges of length s. _____

7. Write an expression for the volume of each cube pictured above. _____

8. Use division to find the ratio of the large cube's volume to the small cube's volume. _____

Look Back and Check

9. If the side length s of a cube is doubled, by what factor should the quantity s^2 increase? What about the quantity s^3? Check that your answer agrees with your earlier findings. _____

Solve Another Problem

10. Suppose the larger cube had a side length of $6x$ instead of $4x$. Write expressions for its surface area and volume, and compare those to the surface area and volume of the small cube.

_____

Name_____ Class_____ Date_____

Practice 8-5

Division Properties of Exponents

Simplify each expression.

1. $\dfrac{c^{13}}{c^7}$

2. $\left(\dfrac{a^3}{b^2}\right)^4$

3. $\left(\dfrac{2}{3}\right)^{-2}$

4. $\dfrac{3^7}{3^4}$

5. $\dfrac{7^{-4}}{7^{-7}}$

6. $\dfrac{a^6b^3}{a^4b}$

7. $\left(-\dfrac{3}{2^3}\right)^{-2}$

8. $\dfrac{z^6}{z^{-4}}$

9. $\left(\dfrac{s^{-4}}{t^{-1}}\right)^{-2}$

10. $\dfrac{m^4}{m^8}$

11. $\left(\dfrac{2^2m^5n^{-3}}{p^4}\right)^0$

12. $\dfrac{4^6}{4^8}$

13. $\dfrac{x^5y^3}{x^2y^9}$

14. $\dfrac{h^{-12}}{h^{-7}}$

15. $\dfrac{4^{-1}}{4^2}$

16. $\dfrac{n^8}{n^{14}}$

17. $\left(\dfrac{r^3s^{-1}}{r^2s^6}\right)^{-1}$

18. $\dfrac{n^{-7}}{n^5}$

Simplify each quotient. Write each answer in scientific notation.

19. $\dfrac{2.16\times10^{-9}}{4.36\times10^{-5}}$

20. $\dfrac{8.43\times10^{-4}}{2.64\times10^{-6}}$

21. $\dfrac{6\times10^8}{3\times10^4}$

22. $\dfrac{7.5\times10^7}{3\times10^{10}}$

23. $\dfrac{8.19\times10^5}{4.76\times10^{-4}}$

24. $\dfrac{4\times10^{-6}}{2\times10^5}$

25. $\dfrac{3.6\times10^6}{9\times10^{-3}}$

26. $\dfrac{3.9\times10^4}{1.3\times10^9}$

27. $\dfrac{4.9\times10^{12}}{7\times10^3}$

8-5 • Guided Problem Solving

GPS **Student Page 457, Exercise 50**

Telecommunications In 2000, there were 97.4 million households with telephones. The people in these households made 544 billion local calls and 97 billion long distance calls.

  a. Write each number in scientific notation.
  b. What was the average number of local calls placed per household? Round to the nearest whole number.
  c. What was the average number of long distance calls placed per household? Round to the nearest whole number.

Read and Understand

1. How many households had telephones in the year 2000? _____

2. How many local and long distance calls did these households make? _____

3. What are you being asked to find? _____

Plan and Solve

4. What are 1 million and 1 billion written as powers of 10? _____

5. Write 97.4 million households, 544 billion local calls, and 97 billion long distance calls using the powers of 10 from Step 4, then convert to scientific notation.

   _____

6. Use division to find the average number of local calls per household to the nearest whole number.

   _____

7. Use division to find the average number of long distance calls per household to the nearest whole number. _____

Look Back and Check

8. The ratio of your answers in Steps 6 and 7 should equal the ratio of total local calls to total long distance calls. What is that ratio? _____

Solve Another Problem

9. In 2000, Los Angeles County, with an area of 4061 square miles, was home to 6.1 million motor vehicles. Write each number in scientific notation and find the average number of vehicles per square mile to the nearest whole number. _____

Practice 8-6

Geometric Sequences

Find the next three terms of each sequence.

1. $3, 9, 27, 81, \ldots$

_____

2. $\frac{3}{4}, -\frac{1}{4}, \frac{1}{12}, -\frac{1}{36}, \ldots$

_____

3. $16, 8, \frac{8}{2}, \frac{8}{4}, \ldots$

_____

4. $30, -10, \frac{10}{3}, -\frac{10}{9}, \ldots$

_____

5. $\frac{1}{3}, 1\frac{1}{3}, 5\frac{1}{3}, 21\frac{1}{3}, \ldots$

_____

6. $60, 30, 15, 7.5, \ldots$

_____

Determine whether each sequence is arithmetic or geometric.

7. $1, \frac{2}{5}, \frac{4}{25}, \frac{8}{125}, \ldots$

_____

8. $6, 2, -2, -6, \ldots$

_____

9. $-25, -20, -15, -10, \ldots$

_____

10. $6, -3, \frac{3}{2}, -\frac{3}{4}, \ldots$

_____

Write a rule for each sequence.

11. $3, 9, 27, 81, \ldots$

_____

12. $\frac{3}{4}, -\frac{1}{4}, \frac{1}{12}, -\frac{1}{36}, \ldots$

_____

13. $16, 8, \frac{8}{2}, \frac{8}{4}, \ldots$

_____

14. $30, -10, \frac{10}{3}, -\frac{10}{9}, \ldots$

_____

15. $1, 4, 16, 64, \ldots$

_____

16. $6, 12, 24, 48, \ldots$

_____

17. $125, 25, 5, 1, \ldots$

_____

18. $50, 25, 12.5, 6.25, \ldots$

_____

Find the first, fourth, and eighth terms of each sequence.

19. $A(n) = -1 \cdot 5^{n-1}$

20. $A(n) = 4 \cdot 2^{n-1}$

21. $A(n) = \frac{1}{2} \cdot 2^{n-1}$

Write a rule and find the given term in each geometric sequence described below.

22. What is the sixth term when the first term is 4 and the common ratio is 3?

_____

23. What is the fifth term when the first term is -2 and the common ratio is $-\frac{1}{2}$?

8-6 • Guided Problem Solving

GPS **Student Page 464, Exercise 41**

Physics On the first swing, a pendulum swings through an arc of length 36 centimeters. On each successive swing, the length of the arc is 90% of the length of the previous swing.

a. Write a rule to model this situation.
b. **Critical Thinking** What value of n would you use to find the length of the arc on the sixth swing? Explain.
c. Find the length of the arc on the sixth swing, to the nearest tenth of a centimeter.

Read and Understand

1. What is the arc length of the first swing of the pendulum? _____

2. What is the ratio of each successive swing length to the one before it? _____

3. What are you asked to find? _____

Plan and Solve

4. Write the arc lengths of the first four swings. _____

5. Using $A(n) = a \cdot r^{n-1}$, write a formula for the arc length of the nth swing. _____

6. What does n equal for the first swing? The sixth swing? _____

7. Use the formula to find the arc length of the sixth swing, to the nearest 0.1 cm. _____

Look Back and Check

8. Make sure you are using the correct values of n by explaining how the formula for $A(n)$ matches up with the problem statement.

_____

_____

Solve Another Problem

9. A mechanism ticks as it winds down. The silence following the first tick lasts 0.2 seconds, and each silence is 10% longer than the silence before it. Find the length of the silence between the fourth and fifth ticks, to three decimal places. _____

Practice 8-7

Exponential Functions

Complete the table for each exercise.

1. Investment increases by 1.5 times every 5 yr.

Time	Value of Investment
Initial	$600
5 yr	$900
10 yr	$1350
15 yr	$2025
20 yr	■
25 yr	■

2. The number of animals doubles every 3 mo.

Time	Number of Animals
Initial	2
3 mo	4
6 mo	6
9 mo	■
12 mo	■
■	■

Evaluate each function for the domain {–2, 0, 2}.

3. $y = 2^x$

_____

4. $y = 10 \cdot 3^x$

_____

5. $y = 25 \cdot 5^x$

_____

Graph each function.

6. $y = 3^x$

7. $y = 6^x$

8. $y = 1.5^x$

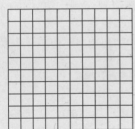

Evaluate each function rule for the given values.

9. $y = 5.5^x$ for $x = 1$ and 4

_____

10. $y = 3 \cdot 4^x$ for $x = 1$ and 5

_____

11. $y = 6^x$ for $x = 2$ and 4

_____

12. $y = 5^x$ for $x = -2$ and 4

_____

Solve each equation.

13. $4^x = \frac{1}{64}$

_____

14. $2 \cdot 4^x = 128$

_____

Name _____ Class _____ Date _____

8-7 • Guided Problem Solving

GPS Student Page 471, Exercise 34

Biology A certain species of bacteria in a laboratory culture begins with
75 cells and doubles in number every 20 min.

a. Extend the table to find when there will be more than 5000 bacteria
cells.

Time (min)	Number of 20-min Time Periods	Pattern	Number of Bacteria Cells
Initial	0	75	75
20	1	$75 \cdot 2$	$75 \cdot 2^\square =$
40		$75 \cdot 2 \cdot 2$	$75 \cdot 2^\square =$
60			$75 \cdot 2^\square =$

b. Write a function rule to model the situation.

Read and Understand

1. How many bacteria cells are in the culture to start with? _____

2. How long does it take for the number of cells to double? _____

3. What are you asked to do? _____

Plan and Solve

4. Complete the table above.

5. Add lines to the table until the number of bacteria cells
exceeds 5000. How many 20-minute periods does that take? _____

Look Back and Check

6. Write a function rule, and verify that $A(x) > 5000$ for the x found in Step 5. _____

Solve Another Problem

7. What would the formula be if the initial number of cells were 2? _____

Practice 8-8

Exponential Growth and Decay

Write an exponential function to model each situation. Find each amount after the specified time.

1. Suppose you have $1500 in a savings account paying 4.75% annual interest. Find the account balance after 25 yr with the interest compounded the following ways.

   a. annually

   b. monthly

   _____

   _____

2. The salary for a new employee is $25,000. Salaries increase by 8% per year. What is the salary after each of the following?

   a. 3 yr

   b. 15 yr

   _____

   _____

3. The tax revenue that a town receives increases by 3.5% per year. In 1990, the town received $250,000 in tax revenue. Determine the tax revenue in each of the following years.

   a. 1995

   b. 2006

   _____

   _____

4. Suppose the acreage of forest is decreasing by 2% per year because of development. If there are currently 4,500,000 acres of forest, determine the amount of forest land after each of the following.

   a. 5 yr

   b. 10 yr

   _____

   _____

5. A $25,000 car decreases 12% in value per year. Determine the value of the car after each of the following.

   a. 1 yr

   b. 5 yr

   _____

   _____

8-8 • Guided Problem Solving

Population Growth Since 1990, the population of Virginia has grown at an average annual rate of about 1%. In 1990, the population was about 6,284,000.

a. Write an equation to model the population growth in Virginia since 1990.

b. Suppose this rate of growth continues. Predict Virginia's population in 2010.

Read and Understand

1. What is the annual growth rate of Virginia's population? _____

2. What was the population in 1990? _____

3. What are you asked to find? _____

Plan and Solve

4. In the equation $y = a \cdot b^x$ modeling the situation, what is a, the starting amount? _____

5. What is b, the growth factor? (*Hint:* It is not 0.01.) _____

6. Write the equation that models the situation. What does x represent? _____

7. What is x in 2010? _____

8. Use the equation to predict the population of Virginia in 2010. _____

Look Back and Check

9. Does the population increase over 20 years seem reasonable? _____

Solve Another Problem

10. Since 1995, the population of Alaska has been growing at an average annual rate of about 1%. In 1995, the population was about 604,000.

    a. Write an equation to model the population growth in Alaska since 1995.

    _____

    b. Suppose this rate of growth continues. Predict Alaska's population in 2010.

    _____

8A: Graphic Organizer

For use before Lesson 8-1

Study Skill When taking notes, write down everything written on the chalkboard or overhead. What you write down may be a clue as to what might be on an exam or test.

Write your answers.

1. What is the chapter title? _____

2. Find the Table of Contents page for this chapter at the front of the book. Name four topics you will study in this chapter.

   _____   _____

   _____   _____

3. Complete the graphic organizer as you work through the chapter.
   1. Write the title of the chapter in the center oval.
   2. When you begin a lesson, write the name of the lesson in a rectangle.
   3. When you complete that lesson, write a skill or key concept from that lesson in the outer oval linked to that rectangle.
   Continue with steps 2 and 3 clockwise around the graphic organizer.

8B: Reading Comprehension

For use after Lesson 8-7

Study Skill You often need to follow written directions. Read carefully and slowly, and do not skip steps.

The following procedure can be used to measure the height of tall objects.

Step 1. Draw a vertical line to represent the tall object.

Step 2. Draw a horizontal line to represent the object's shadow.

Step 3. Draw a vertical line to represent the height of something you can measure, such as your height or the height of a mailbox.

Step 4. Draw a horizontal line to represent the shadow of the measurable object.

Step 5. Connect endpoints of the segments to make two similar triangles.

Step 6. Measure the second object and the two shadows, and label each corresponding part of the drawing. Make sure the measurements are in the same unit. Label the missing height x.

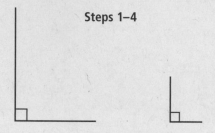

Steps 1–4

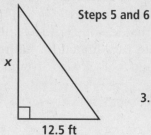

Steps 5 and 6

x

12.5 ft   3.5 ft   2.5 ft

Step 7 Write a proportion.

$$\frac{tall\ object's\ height}{tall\ object's\ shadow} = \frac{measurable\ object's\ height}{measurable\ object's\ shadow} \Rightarrow \frac{x}{12.5} = \frac{3.5}{2.5}$$

Step 8 Solve the proportion.

$2.5x = 43.75$ Write cross products.

$x = 17.5$ The unknown height is 17.5 feet.

Use the steps above to find the missing heights.

1. Mark needs to determine the height of a radio tower. He measured the shadow of the tower and found that it was 40 ft long. His own shadow was 3 ft long. If Mark is 6 ft tall, how tall is the radio tower?

2. Celia needed to find the height of a tree for her botany report. She measured the shadow of the tree and found it was 5 m long. Her own shadow was 0.8 m long. If Celia is 1.6 m tall, how tall is the tree?

3. A girl who is 172 cm tall wants to find the height of a flagpole. If her shadow is 120 cm and the shadow of the flagpole is 4.5 m, how tall is the flagpole? (*Hint:* Make sure all units are the same before calculating.)

4. **High-Use Academic Words** In Step 6, what does *measure* mean for you to do?
   a. use a tool to find the weight of an object
   b. use a tool to find the distance from one point to another

8C: Reading/Writing Math Symbols

For use after Lesson 8-2

Study Skill After completing your homework, take a break. Then come back and check your homework. You will sometimes discover mistakes that you missed before.

Write how you would read each of the following expressions. The first one has been done for you.

Expression   **Read as:**

1. $2x^3y^4$ _____2 times x cubed, y to the fourth power_____

2. 4^{-3} _____

3. x^2 _____

4. xy _____

5. $(x^2)^3$ _____

6. $\frac{x}{y}$ _____

7. $5x \cdot y^4$ _____

8. $x^5 + x^7$ _____

9. $\sqrt{x^2y}$ _____

10. $8x^2 - 3y$ _____

11. $\frac{x^2}{x^8}$ _____

12. $4x^{11}$ _____

8D: Visual Vocabulary Practice

For use after Lesson 8-6

Study Skill A rational number can be written as a decimal, a fraction, in factored form or in scientific notation. Use the context of the situation to choose the form.

Concept List

algebraic expression	base	common ratio
exponent	geometric sequence	integers
order of operations	scientific notation	power

Write the concept that best describes each exercise.
Choose from the concept list above.

1. The number 3 for the sequence $1, 3, 9, 27, \ldots$ because $\frac{3}{1} = \frac{9}{3} = \frac{27}{9} \cdots = 3$	**2.** $\begin{aligned} 3^{7-5} + 4 &= 3^2 + 4 \\ &= 9 + 4 \\ &= 13 \end{aligned}$	**3.** The number 4 in the expression 4^5
4. 7.36×10^8	**5.** $2, 4, 8, 16, \ldots$	**6.** $\ldots, -2, -1, 0, 1, 2, \ldots$
7. The number 2 in the expression 7^2	**8.** $3x - 5^x$	**9.** An expression like 5^x

Vocabulary and Study Skills

8E: Vocabulary Check

For use after Lesson 8-3

Study Skill Strengthen your vocabulary. Use these pages and add cues and summaries by applying the Cornell Notetaking style.

Write the definition for each word at the right. To check your work, fold the paper back along the dotted line to see the correct answers.

_____

_____

_____   Equivalent equations

_____

_____   Exponent

_____

_____   Base

_____

_____

_____   Power

_____

_____

_____   Scientific notation

_____

_____

8E: Vocabulary Check (continued)

For use after Lesson 8-3

Write the vocabulary word for each definition. To check your work, fold the paper forward along the dotted line to see the correct answers.

Equations that have the
same solution.

_____

A number that shows
repeated multiplication.

_____

A number that is
multiplied repeatedly.

_____

The base and the exponent
of an expression of the
form a^x.

_____

A number expressed in
the form $a \times 10^n$, where
n is an integer and
$1 \le a < 10$.

_____

Vocabulary and Study Skills

8F: Vocabulary Review

Study Skill Always read direction lines carefully before doing any exercises.

Circle the word that best completes the sentence.

1. A number in (*standard form*, *scientific notation*) is written as a product of two factors in the form $a \times 10^n$, where n is an integer and $1 \leq a < 10$.

2. Each number in a sequence is called a (*term*, *constant*).

3. In a(n) (*arithmetic*, *geometric*) sequence you multiply a term in the sequence by a fixed number.

4. The (*Substitution*, *Elimination*) method is a way of solving systems of equations by replacing one variable with an equivalent expression.

5. A system of linear equations has (*no solution*, *many solutions*) when the graphs of the equations are parallel lines.

6. In the function $f(x) = 5^x$, as the values of the domain increase, the values of the range (*increase*, *decrease*).

7. When a bank pays interest on both the principal and interest the account has already earned, the bank is paying (*simple*, *compound*) interest.

8. A(n) (*interest*, *growth*) period is the length of time over which interest is calculated.

9. Lines in the same plane that intersect to form a 90° angle are said to be (*perpendicular*, *parallel*).

10. The result of a single trial is called the (*outcome*, *probability*).

11. In the exponential function $y = a \cdot b^x$, $a > 0$ and $b > 1$, the base (b) is the (*decay*, *growth*) factor.

12. $-2, 4, \frac{1}{2}, \frac{3}{4}, -8, 6$ are examples of (*real numbers*, *integers*).

Practice 9-1

Write each polynomial in standard form. Then name each polynomial based on its degree and number of terms.

1. $4y^3 - 4y^2 + 3 - y$

2. $x^2 + x^4 - 6$

3. $x + 2$

_____

_____

_____

4. $n^2 - 5n$

5. $6 + 7x^2$

6. $3a^2 + a^3 - 4a + 3$

_____

_____

_____

7. $2 + 4x^2 - x^3$

8. $4x^3 - 2x^2$

9. $y^2 - 7 - 3y$

_____

_____

_____

Simplify. Write each answer in standard form.

10. $(3x^2 - 5x) - (x^2 + 4x + 3)$

11. $(2x^3 - 4x^2 + 3) + (x^3 - 3x^2 + 1)$

_____

_____

12. $(x^2 - 6) + (5x^2 + x - 3)$

13. $(5n^2 - 7) - (2n^2 + n - 3)$

_____

_____

14. $(3x + x^2 - x^3) - (x^3 + 2x^2 + 5x)$

15. $(d^2 + 8 - 5d) - (5d^2 + d - 2d^3 + 3)$

_____

_____

16. $(4x^2 + 13x + 9) + (12x^2 + x + 6)$

17. $(2x - 13x^2 + 3) - (2x^2 + 8x)$

_____

_____

18. $(3x^2 - 2x + 9) - (x^2 - x + 7)$

19. $(2x^2 - 6x + 3) - (2x + 4x^2 + 2)$

_____

_____

20. $(x^3 + 3x) - (x^2 + 6 - 4x)$

21. $(7s^2 + 4s + 2) + (3s + 2 - s^2)$

_____

_____

22. $(x^2 + 15x + 13) + (3x^2 - 15x + 7)$

23. $(7 - 8x^2) + (x^3 - x + 5)$

_____

_____

9-1 • Guided Problem Solving

GPS **Student Page 497, Exercise 39**

Find an expression for the perimeter of the figure.

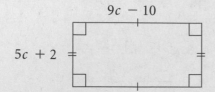

$9c - 10$

$5c + 2$

Read and Understand

1. Describe how to determine the perimeter of a rectangle. _____

_____

2. What do the single and double marks drawn on the sides of the figure mean? _____

_____

Plan and Solve

3. What additional information do you need to know before
   you can determine the perimeter of the rectangle above? _____

4. Label the lengths of the two missing sides of the rectangle above.

5. Write an expression for the perimeter of the rectangle. _____

Look Back and Check

6. Check the reasonableness of your answer by substituting a number for *c*.
   Substitute the number in the expressions for each side of the rectangle.
   Add the numbers and determine the perimeter. Substitute the same number
   in the expression you wrote for the perimeter and simplify. The answers should
   be the same.

Solve Another Problem

7. Find an expression for the perimeter of the rectangle above
   if the length is $7x - 2$ and the width is $5x + 1$.

_____

Practice 9-2

Multiplying and Factoring

Simplify each product.

1. $4(a - 3)$

_____

2. $-5(x - 2)$

_____

3. $-3x^2(x^2 + 3x)$

_____

4. $-x^2(-2x^2 + 3x - 2)$

_____

5. $4d^2(d^2 - 3d - 7)$

_____

6. $5m^3(m + 6)$

_____

Find the GCF of the terms of each polynomial.

7. $8x - 4$

_____

8. $15x + 45x^2$

_____

9. $x^2 + 3x$

_____

10. $14x^3 + 7x^2$

_____

11. $8x^3 - 12x$

_____

12. $9 - 27x^3$

_____

13. $8d^3 + 4d^2 + 12d$

_____

14. $6x^2 + 12x - 21$

_____

15. $8g^2 + 16g - 8$

_____

Factor each polynomial.

16. $8x + 10$

_____

17. $12n^3 - 8n$

_____

18. $14d - 2$

_____

19. $x^3 - 5x^2$

_____

20. $8x^3 - 12x^2 + 4x$

21. $7x^3 + 21x^4$

_____

22. $2w^3 + 6w^2 - 4w$

23. $12c^3 - 30c^2$

_____

24. $2x^2 + 8x - 14$

25. $18c^4 - 9c^2 + 7c$

_____

26. $6y^4 + 9y^3 - 27y^2$

27. $6c^2 - 3c$

_____

9-2 • Guided Problem Solving

GPS **Student Page 502, Exercise 33**

Building Models Suppose you are building a model of the square castle shown on the right. The moat of the model castle is made of blue paper.

a. Find the area of the moat using the diagram with the photo.
b. Write your answer in factored form.

Read and Understand

1. What shape is the moat? _____

2. What is the formula for finding the area of a circle? _____

3. What does the white square in the middle of the blue circle represent? _____

Plan and Solve

4. Suppose the entire circle were shaded blue. Write an expression for the area of the entire blue circle. _____

5. Write an expression that represents the area of the castle. _____

6. Write an expression that represents the area of the moat only. _____

7. Write your answer in factored form. _____

Look Back and Check

8. Of the three different areas determined above (complete circle, castle, moat), which should have the largest area? Check the reasonableness of your answer by determining each area if $x = 5$.

_____

_____

Solve Another Problem

9. Determine the area of the moat if the castle is rectangular, with a width of $2x$ and a length of $3x$.

_____

_____

Practice 9-3

Multiplying Binomials

Simplify each product. Write in standard form.

1. $(x + 3)(2x - 5)$

2. $(x^2 + x - 1)(x + 1)$

_____

_____

3. $(3w + 4)(2w - 1)$

4. $(x + 6)(x^2 - 4x + 3)$

_____

_____

5. $(5x - 3)(4x + 2)$

6. $(3y + 7)(4y + 5)$

_____

_____

7. $(x - 2)(x^2 + 4x + 4)$

8. $(2r + 1)(3r - 1)$

_____

_____

9. $(k + 4)(3k - 4)$

10. $(2x + 1)(4x + 3)$

_____

_____

11. $(3x + 4)(3x - 4)$

12. $(6x - 5)(3x + 1)$

_____

_____

13. $(n - 7)(n + 4)$

14. $(3x - 1)(2x + 1)$

_____

_____

15. $(d + 9)(d - 11)$

16. $(2x^2 + 5x - 4)(2x + 7)$

_____

_____

17. $(x^2 + 6x + 11)(3x + 5)$

18. $(5x + 7)(7x + 3)$

_____

_____

19. $(4x - 7)(2x - 5)$

20. $(x - 9)(3x + 5)$

_____

_____

9-3 • Guided Problem Solving

GPS **Student Page 508, Exercise 39**

Construction You are planning a rectangular garden. Its length is twice its width x. You want a walkway 2 ft wide around the garden.

a. Write an expression for the area of the garden and walk.
b. Write an expression for the area of the walk only.
c. You have enough gravel to cover 76 ft^2 and want to use it all on the walk. How big should you make the garden?

Read and Understand

1. Draw a picture of the garden and its walk. Shade in the walk only.

2. Label the dimensions of the garden.

3. Label the dimensions of the outside of the walkway.

Plan and Solve

4. Write an expression for the area of the garden and walk. _____

5. Write an expression for the area of the walk only. _____

6. You have enough gravel to cover 76 ft^2 and want to use it all on the walk. How big should you make the garden? _____

Look Back and Check

7. Check if your answer is reasonable by subtracting the area of the garden from the area of the garden and walk and verifying that this amount is less than or equal to 76 ft^2.

Solve Another Problem

8. How big should you make the garden if you now have 100 ft^2 of gravel?

_____

Practice 9-4

Multiplying Special Cases

Find each product.

1. $(w - 2)^2$

2. $(y + 4)^2$

3. $(4w + 2)^2$

4. $(w - 9)^2$

5. $(3x + 7)^2$

6. $(3x - 7)^2$

7. $(2x - 9)^2$

8. $(x - 12)^2$

9. $(6x + 1)^2$

10. $(4x - 7)^2$

11. $(x + 8)(x - 8)$

12. $(x - 11)(x + 11)$

13. $(x - 12)(x + 12)$

14. $(y + w)(y - w)$

15. $(2x + 1)(2x - 1)$

16. $(5x - 2)(5x + 2)$

17. $(6x + 1)(6x - 1)$

18. $(2x - 4)(2x + 4)$

19. 18^2

20. $(64)^2$

21. $(29)(31)$

22. $(19)(42)$

Find the area.

23.

$2x + 1$

$2x + 1$

24.

$3x - 2$

$3x + 2$

9-4 • Guided Problem Solving

GPS **Student Page 516, Exercise 40**

Biology The coat color of shorthorn cattle is determined by two genes, Red *R* and White *W*.

RR produces red, *WW* produces white, and *RW* produces a third type of coat color called roan.

a. Model the Punnett square with the square of a binomial.
b. If both parents have *RW*, what is the probability the offspring will also be *RW*?
c. Write an expression to model a situation where one parent is *RW* while the other is *RR*.
d. What is the probability that the offspring of the parents in step (c) will have a white coat?

	R	W
R	RR	RW
W	RW	WW

Read and Understand

1. Describe the information given in the Punnett square. _____
   _____

2. Explain how to determine the probability that an event will occur. _____
   _____

3. What does the notation *RW* mean? _____

Plan and Solve

4. Model the Punnett square with the square of a binomial. _____

5. If both parents have *RW*, what is the probability the offspring will also be *RW*? _____

6. Write an expression to model a situation where one parent is *RW* and the other is *RR*. _____

7. What is the probability that the offspring of the parents in Step 6 will have a white coat? _____

Look Back and Check

8. Check that the probability you found in Step 7 is a possible value for probability. That is, check that it is greater than or equal to 0 and less than or equal to 1.

Solve Another Problem

9. Write an expression to model a situation where one parent is *RW* and the other is *WW*.

_____

Practice 9-5

Factoring Trinomials of the Type $x^2 + bx + c$

Factor each expression.

1. $x^2 + 8x + 16$

2. $y^2 + 6y + 8$

3. $x^2 - 9x + 20$

4. $a^2 + 3a + 2$

5. $x^2 + 5x - 14$

6. $x^2 + 14x + 45$

7. $x^2 - 8x + 12$

8. $n^2 - 7n + 10$

9. $x^2 - 6x - 27$

10. $x^2 + 7x + 10$

11. $x^2 - 5x - 24$

12. $x^2 - 3x - 18$

13. $x^2 + 9x + 20$

14. $x^2 - 8x + 16$

15. $n^2 - n - 6$

16. $x^2 + 7x + 12$

17. $b^2 + 4b - 12$

18. $x^2 + x - 20$

19. $a^2 + 2a - 35$

20. $x^2 + 3x - 10$

21. $x^2 + 2x - 63$

22. $x^2 - 11x - 60$

23. $x^2 - 8x + 15$

24. $c^2 + 3c - 10$

25. $y^2 - 16y + 64$

26. $r^2 - 14r - 51$

27. $a^2 + 7a + 6$

28. $x^2 - 11x + 28$

9-5 • Guided Problem Solving

GPS **Student Page 522, Exercise 55**

Write the standard form for the polynomial modeled below. Then factor the expression.

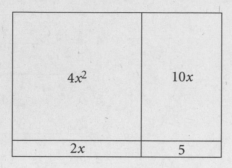

Read and Understand

1. Explain what the standard form of a polynomial is. _____

_____

2. Describe how you can write a polynomial from a rectangle model. _____

_____

Plan and Solve

3. Write the standard form of the polynomial by adding the area of each rectangle. _____

4. Factor the standard form of the polynomial you wrote in Step 3. _____

Look Back and Check

5. Check the reasonableness of your answer in Steps 3 and 4 by substituting a number in each expression. Why should the result be the same for each expression?

Solve Another Problem

6. Write the standard form for the polynomial modeled below. Then factor each expression.

$9x^2$	$3x$
$6x$	2

_____

Guided Problem Solving

Practice 9-6

Factoring Trinomials of the Type $ax^2 + bx + c$

Factor each expression.

1. $2x^2 + 3x + 1$

_____

2. $2n^2 + n - 6$

_____

3. $3x^2 - x - 4$

_____

4. $5x^2 - 2x - 7$

_____

5. $7n^2 + 9n + 2$

_____

6. $3x^2 + 8x + 4$

_____

7. $3y^2 - 16y - 12$

_____

8. $5x^2 + 2x - 3$

_____

9. $7x^2 - 10x + 3$

_____

10. $3x^2 + 8x + 5$

_____

11. $5x^2 - 7x + 2$

_____

12. $5x^2 - 22x + 8$

_____

13. $5x^2 - 33x - 14$

_____

14. $3x^2 - 2x - 8$

_____

15. $4y^2 - 11y - 3$

_____

16. $5y^2 - 3y - 2$

_____

17. $7y^2 + 19y + 10$

_____

18. $3x^2 + 17x + 10$

_____

19. $2x^2 + 5x - 3$

_____

20. $3x^2 + 10x + 3$

_____

21. $2x^2 - x - 21$

_____

22. $3x^2 - 7x - 6$

_____

23. $2x^2 - 5x - 12$

_____

24. $4x^2 + 7x + 3$

_____

Name_____ Class_____ Date_____

9-6 • Guided Problem Solving

GPS **Student Page 526, Exercise 31**

a. Write each area as a product of two binomials.

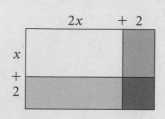
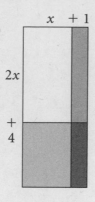

b. Are the products equal?

c. **Critical Thinking** Explain how the two products you found in part (a) can equal the same trinomial.

Read and Understand

1. What does the word *product* mean? _____

2. What are binomials? _____

Plan and Solve

3. Write each area as a product of two binomials. _____

4. Are the products equal? _____

5. Explain how the two products you found in Step 3 can equal the same trinomial.

_____

_____

Look Back and Check

6. Check the reasonableness of your answer by factoring each product completely to show that they are the same.

Solve Another Problem

7. Show that these two products are equal: $(3x - 1)(2x + 2)$ and $(6x - 2)(x + 1)$.

_____

Practice 9-7

Factor each expression.

1. $x^2 - 9$

_____

2. $a^2 + 2a + 1$

_____

3. $4x^2 + 12x + 9$

_____

4. $n^2 - 4$

_____

5. $9x^2 - 4$

_____

6. $9x^2 - 30x + 25$

_____

7. $3n^2 - 3$

_____

8. $9d^2 - 49$

_____

9. $3a^2 - 48$

_____

10. $b^2 + 4b + 4$

_____

11. $25x^2 - 64$

_____

12. $12w^2 - 27$

_____

13. $x^2 + 6x + 9$

_____

14. $a^2 - 25$

_____

15. $x^2 - 16x + 64$

_____

16. $d^2 - 49$

_____

17. $5n^3 - 20n$

_____

18. $9n^2 + 12n + 4$

_____

19. $4a^2 - 81$

_____

20. $9d^2 - 64$

_____

21. $y^2 + 8y + 16$

_____

22. $x^2 - 10x + 25$

_____

23. $y^2 - 81$

_____

24. $a^2 - 100$

_____

25. $2d^3 - 50d$

_____

26. $x^2 - 18x + 81$

_____

27. $b^2 - 64$

_____

28. $4r^2 - 25$

_____

29. $b^2 - 14b + 49$

_____

30. $b^2 + 20b + 100$

_____

9-7 • Guided Problem Solving

GPS Student Page 532, Exercise 54

a. Geometry Write an expression in terms of n and m
for the area of the top of the block that was drilled at
the right. Use 3.14 for π. Factor your expression.
b. Find the area of the top of the block if $n = 10$ in.
and $m = 3$ in.

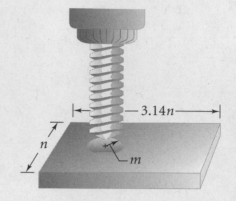

Read and Understand

1. Describe the information given to you in the picture. _____

_____

2. What is the formula used to find the area of a rectangle? _____

3. What is the formula used to find the area of a circle? _____

Plan and Solve

4. Write an expression for the area of the rectangular block. _____

5. Write an expression for the area of the circular hole drilled into the block. _____

6. Write an expression for the area of the top of the block that was drilled. _____

7. Factor your expression from Step 6. _____

8. Find the area of the top of the block if $n = 10$ and $m = 3$. _____

Look Back and Check

9. In Steps 6 and 7 you wrote two different expressions for the area of the block.
Check your answer in Step 8 by substituting the values into the expression that
you did not use.

Solve Another Problem

10. What is the area of the top of the block if $n = 15$ and $m = 6$?

Practice 9-8

Factoring by Grouping

Factor each expression.

1. $x(a + 2) - 2(a + 2)$

2. $m(x - 3) + k(x - 3)$

   _____

   _____

3. $a(y + 1) - b(y + 1)$

4. $y^2 - 5wy + 4y - 20w$

   _____

   _____

5. $xy + 4y - 2x - 8$

6. $ax + bx + ay + by$

   _____

   _____

7. $ax + bx - ay - by$

8. $3x^2 - 6xy + 2x - 4y$

   _____

   _____

9. $2ax + 6xc + ba + 3bc$

10. $6 + 2y + 3x^2 + x^2y$

    _____

    _____

11. $2x^2 - 3x + 1$

12. $6x^2 + 7x + 2$

    _____

    _____

13. $4x^2 + 8x + 3$

14. $4x^2 - 9x + 2$

    _____

    _____

15. $2x^2 - 3x - 2$

16. $6x^2 + 19x + 3$

    _____

    _____

17. $12y^2 - 5y - 2$

18. $5y^2 + 13y + 6$

    _____

    _____

19. $16y^2 + 10y + 1$

20. $16x^2 + 16x + 3$

    _____

    _____

21. $10x^2 - 3x - 1$

22. $14x^2 + 15x - 9$

    _____

    _____

23. $2x^3 + 8x^2 + x + 4$

24. $5x^3 - x^2 + 15x - 3$

    _____

    _____

25. $x^3 + 3x^2 + 4x + 12$

26. $3x^3 + 9x^2 + 2x + 6$

    _____

    _____

27. $9x^3 - 12x^2 + 3x - 4$

28. $4x^3 - 20x^2 + 3x - 15$

    _____

    _____

9-8 • Guided Problem Solving

GPS **Student Page 538, Exercise 39**

Geometry The polynomial shown at the right represents the volume of the rectangular prism. Factor the polynomial to find possible expressions for the length, width, and height of the prism.

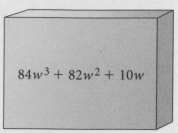

$84w^3 + 82w^2 + 10w$

Read and Understand

1. What is the formula for finding the volume of a rectangular prism? _____

   _____

2. What is the first type of factoring that you should look for? _____

   _____

Plan and Solve

3. What is the common factor for the expression $84w^3 + 82w^2 + 10w$? _____

4. What polynomial is left after factoring out the common factor? _____

5. Factor the polynomial you wrote in Step 4. _____

6. What are the three factors that represent the length, width, and height of the prism?

   _____

Look Back and Check

7. Multiply the three factors you wrote for Step 6. How can you tell if these are the correct factors?

   _____

   _____

Solve Another Problem

8. What are the possible expressions for the length, width, and height of a rectangular prism that has a volume of $18m^3 + 33m^2 + 9m$?

   _____

9A: Graphic Organizer

For use before Lesson 9-1

Study Skill To remember the math concepts, you can study with a friend. Quiz each other on the details of the algebra rules and procedures. Use your notes to help you determine possible test questions. Reviewing right before bedtime will help you retain the material you study.

Write your answers.

1. What is the chapter title? _____

2. Find the Table of Contents page for this chapter at the front of the book. Name four topics you will study in this chapter.

   _____   _____

   _____   _____

3. Complete the graphic organizer as you work through the chapter.
   1. Write the title of the chapter in the center oval.
   2. When you begin a lesson, write the name of the lesson in a rectangle.
   3. When you complete that lesson, write a skill or key concept from that lesson in the outer oval linked to that rectangle.

   Continue with steps 2 and 3 clockwise around the graphic organizer.

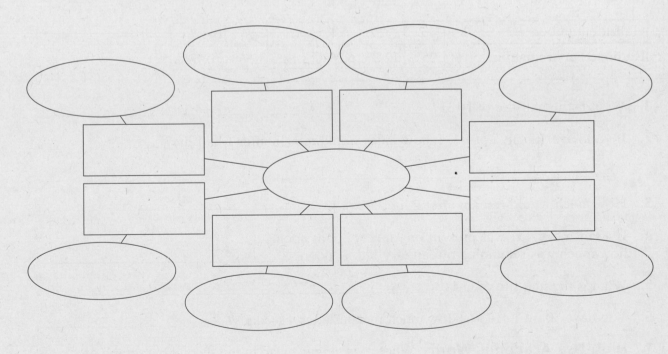

9B: Reading Comprehension

Study Skill Many reading passages contain a great amount of information. It is essential to recognize which information is necessary for a particular question. You can designate corresponding information by circling, underlining, or boxing that information.

Read the passage below and answer the following questions.

Radioactive material is here today and gone tomorrow. Radioisotopes disintegrate into stable isotopes of different elements at a decreasing rate, but never quite reach zero. Radioactive material is measured in curies (Ci) and 1 Ci = 3.7×10^{10} atoms. A mathematical formula known as the radioactive decay law can measure the rate of radioactive decay and the quantity of material present at any given time. From this formula we obtain a quantity known as half-life. Half-life is the amount of time required for a quantity of radioactive material to be reduced to one-half its original quantity.

Each radioisotope has a unique half-life. For example I-131 has a half-life of 8 days, C-11 has a half-life of 20 minutes, and H-6 has a half-life of 0.8 seconds.

Although this can sound quite difficult, it does not have to be. The following chart can help you calculate the amount of radioactive material that has decayed.

Half-life number	1	2	3	4	5	6	7
Radioactivity remaining	50%	25%	12.5%	6.25%	3.12%	1.56%	0.78%

1. What is the half-life of I-131? _____

2. If you have 100 mCi of I-131, how much would remain after 1 half-life?

   _____

3. How much would remain after 2 half-lives? _____

4. If 40 mCi of I-131 was present on January 3rd at noon, how much was remaining on January 19th at noon? _____

5. What is the half-life of C-11? _____

6. You have 50 mCi of H-6. How much remains after 4 seconds? _____

7. **High-Use Academic Words** What does *unique* mean in the second paragraph of the passage?

   a. unpredictable   **b.** its own

9C: Reading/Writing Math Symbols

For use after Lesson 9-7

Study Skill Make mental pictures from what you read. This will help you remember it.

In equations and inequalities, *x* and *y* represent coordinates of points, *b* represents the *y*-intercept, and *m* represents the slope. Inequality symbols mean to shade on one side of a boundary line. Match each equation or inequality to the graph that best represents it.

1. $y < b$

2. $x = k$

3. $y = mx + b; m < 0$

4. $y \geq mx + b$

5. $y < mx + b; b \neq 0$

6. $y = mx; m > 0$

A.

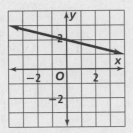

B.

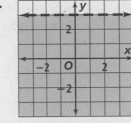

C.

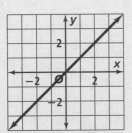

D.

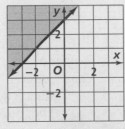

E.

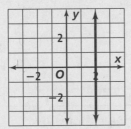

F.

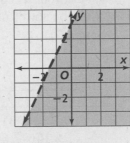

9D: Visual Vocabulary Practice
High-Use Academic Words

For use after Lesson 9-8

Study Skill Mathematics is like learning a foreign language. You have to know the vocabulary before you can speak the language correctly.

Concept List

apply	consecutive	formula
interpret	methods	notation
simplify	solve	test

Write the concept that best describes each exercise. Choose from the concept list above.

1. $f(x)$ for y _____	**2.** The slope of the linear graph is 3, which indicates the class charged \$3 per car. _____	**3.** n and $n + 1$ _____
4. $A(n) = a \cdot r^{n-1}$ _____	**5.** Expenses are \$.90 for printing and mailing a newsletter, plus \$600 for writing. The price is \$1.50 per copy. Find the number of copies that must be sold to break even. _____	**6.** $2(c + 4) - 5c = -3c + 8$ _____
7. 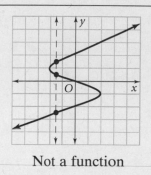 Not a function _____	**8.** $2(5x - 3) = 14$ $10x - 6 = 14$ $10x = 20$ $x = 2$ _____	**9.** Solving systems by • Graphing • Substitution • Elimination _____

Vocabulary and Study Skills

9E: Vocabulary Check

Study Skill Strengthen your vocabulary. Use these pages and add cues and summaries by applying the Cornell Notetaking style.

Write the definition for each word at the right. To check your work, fold the paper back along the dotted line to see the correct answers.

_____

_____

_____   Degree of a monomial

_____

_____   Polynomial

_____

_____

_____   Standard form of a
                                             polynomial

_____

_____

_____   Degree of a polynomial

_____

_____   Greatest common factor

_____

_____

Vocabulary and Study Skills

9E: Vocabulary Check (continued)

For use after Lesson 9-3

Write the vocabulary word for each definition. To check your work, fold the paper forward along the dotted line to see the correct answers.

The sum of the exponents of its variables.

_____

A monomial or the sum or difference of two or more monomials.

_____

The form of a polynomial in which the degree of the terms decreases from left to right.

_____

The degree of the term with the greatest exponent for a polynomial in one variable.

_____

The greatest factor that divides evenly into each term of the expression.

_____

9F: Vocabulary Review Puzzle

For use with Chapter Review

Study Skill When you complete a puzzle such as a word search, remember to read the list of words carefully and completely. As you identify each word in the word search, circle it and then cross off the word from the list. Pay special attention to the spelling of each word.

Complete the word search.

binomial	interest	translation
factor	common ratio	median
monomial	sequence	distributive
standard form	scatter plot	variable
polynomial	outlier	probability
trinomial	reciprocal	degree
systems	elimination	substitution

```
E  Y  R  N  P  O  L  Y  N  O  M  I  A  L  N
L  T  E  E  O  L  A  I  M  O  N  I  R  T  O
I  I  C  J  S  I  S  F  A  C  T  O  R  S  I
M  L  I  L  M  C  T  M  L  Q  H  M  T  E  T
I  I  P  A  R  O  A  U  E  A  P  O  V  Q  A
N  B  R  I  E  M  N  T  T  B  B  Y  U  L
A  A  O  M  I  E  D  O  T  I  S  T  H  E  S
T  B  C  O  L  D  A  L  M  E  T  Y  N  N
I  O  A  N  T  I  R  W  Q  I  R  S  S  C  A
O  R  L  I  U  A  D  W  M  U  A  P  B  E  R
N  P  V  B  O  N  F  I  Z  W  W  L  L  U  T
S  Q  C  O  M  M  O  N  R  A  T  I  O  O  S
Q  V  I  N  T  E  R  E  S  T  E  M  S  T  T
E  E  R  G  E  D  M  E  L  B  A  I  R  A  V
E  V  I  T  U  B  I  R  T  S  I  D  G  B  W
```

Practice 10-1

Exploring Quadratic Graphs

Identify the vertex of each graph. Tell whether it is a minimum or a maximum.

1.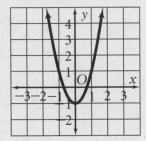

_____

2.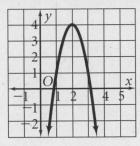

_____

3.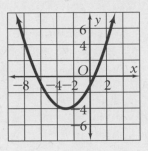

_____

Order each group of quadratic functions from widest to narrowest graph.

4. $y = x^2, y = 5x^2, y = 3x^2$

_____

5. $y = -8x^2, y = \frac{1}{2}x^2, y = -x^2$

_____

6. $y = 5x^2, y = -4x^2, y = 2x^2$

_____

7. $y = 6x^2, y = -7x^2, y = 4x^2$

_____

Graph each function.

8. $y = x^2$

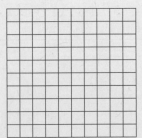

9. $y = 4x^2$

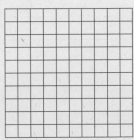

10. $y = -3x^2$

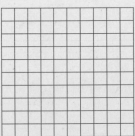

11. $y = -x^2 - 4$

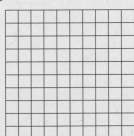

12. $y = 2x^2 - 2$

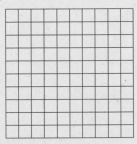

13. $y = 2x^2 + 3$

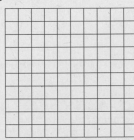

14. $y = 5x^2 + 8$

15. $y = 5x^2 - 8$

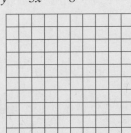

16. $y = -3.5x^2 - 4$

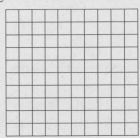

10-1 • Guided Problem Solving

GPS **Student Page 555, Exercise 39**

Suppose that a pizza must fit into a box with a base that is 12 in. long and 12 in. wide. You can use the quadratic function $A = \pi r^2$ to find the area of a pizza in terms of its radius.

a. What values of r make sense for the function?

b. What values of A make sense for the function?

c. Graph the function. Round values of A to the nearest tenth.

Read and Understand

1. What shape is the pizza? _____

2. What shape is the box? _____

3. What information is given to you in the problem? _____

Plan and Solve

4. What values of r make sense for the function? _____

5. What values of A make sense for the function? _____

6. Graph the function. Round values of A to the nearest tenth.

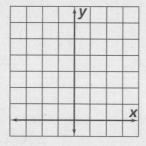

Look Back and Check

7. The equation $A = \pi r^2$ is a quadratic function. What shape is the graph of a quadratic function? Verify the reasonableness of your graph by verifying that it is the shape you would expect.

   _____

Solve Another Problem

8. If the size of the box is changed so the base is now 10 in. long and 10 in. wide, what values of r and A would make sense? _____

Practice 10-2

Quadratic Functions

Find the equation of the axis of symmetry and the coordinates of the vertex of the graph of each function.

1. $y = x^2 - 10x + 2$

_____

2. $y = x^2 + 12x - 9$

_____

3. $y = -x^2 + 2x + 1$

_____

4. $y = 3x^2 + 18x + 9$

_____

5. $y = 3x^2 + 3$

_____

6. $y = 16x - 4x^2$

_____

Graph each function. Label the axis of symmetry and the vertex.

7. $y = x^2 - 6x + 4$

8. $y = x^2 + 4x - 1$

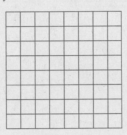

9. $y = x^2 + 2x + 1$

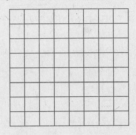

10. $y = -2x^2 - 8x + 5$

11. $y = 4x^2 + 8x$

12. $y = -3x^2 + 6$

Graph each quadratic inequality.

13. $y > x^2 + 1$

14. $y \geq x^2 - 4$

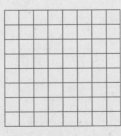

15. $y > x^2 + 6x + 3$

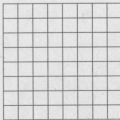

16. $y < x^2 - 4x + 4$

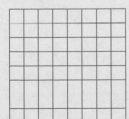

17. $y \geq -2x^2 - 8x - 5$

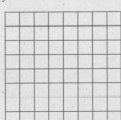

18. $y \leq -3x^2 + 6x + 1$

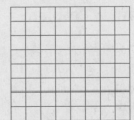

Name _____ Class _____ Date _____

10-2 • Guided Problem Solving

Road Construction An archway over a road is cut out of rock. Its shape is modeled by the quadratic function $y = -0.1x^2 + 12$ for $y \geq 0$.

   a. Write an inequality that describes the opening of the archway.
   b. Graph the inequality.
   c. Critical Thinking Can a camper 6 ft wide and 7 ft high fit under the arch without crossing the median line? Explain.

Read and Understand

1. Make a rough sketch of what the archway should look like.

2. What information do you know about the archway? _____

Plan and Solve

3. Write an inequality that describes the opening of the archway. _____

4. Graph the inequality.

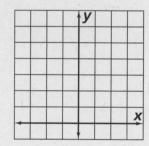

5. On your graph above, show where the camper would be located.

6. Can a camper 6 ft wide and 7 ft high fit under the arch without crossing the median line? Explain. _____

_____

Look Back and Check

7. Check the reasonableness of your inequality graph. Pick a point in the shaded region and check to see that it makes the inequality true.

Solve Another Problem

8. The road passing through the archway is being converted to a one-way road so a trailer with an extra-wide load can pass through it. If the trailer's load is 12 feet wide and 10 feet high, can the trailer fit under the arch?

Guided Problem Solving

Practice 10-3

Solving Quadratic Equations

Solve each equation by finding square roots. If the equation has no real solution, write *no solution*. If necessary, round to the nearest tenth.

1. $x^2 = 16$

2. $x^2 - 144 = 0$

3. $3x^2 - 27 = 0$

_____

_____

_____

4. $x^2 + 16 = 0$

5. $x^2 = 12$

6. $x^2 = 49$

_____

_____

_____

7. $x^2 + 8 = -10$

8. $3x^2 = 300$

9. $2x^2 - 6 = 26$

_____

_____

_____

10. $x^2 = 80$

11. $81x^2 - 10 = 15$

12. $2x^2 = 90$

_____

_____

_____

13. $x^2 = 300$

14. $4x^2 + 9 = 41$

15. $2x^2 + 8 = 4$

_____

_____

_____

16. $x^2 + 8 = 72$

17. $4x^2 + 6 = 7$

18. $x^2 = 121$

_____

_____

_____

19. $5x^2 + 20 = 30$

20. $x^2 + 6 = 17$

21. $3x^2 + 1 = 54$

_____

_____

_____

22. $2x^2 - 7 = 74$

23. $x^2 + 1 = 0$

24. $4x^2 - 8 = -20$

_____

_____

_____

25. $9x^2 = 1$

26. $x^2 + 4 = 4$

27. $3x^2 = 1875$

_____

_____

_____

28. $x^2 = 9$

29. $x^2 - 10 = 100$

30. $4x^2 - 2 = 1$

_____

_____

_____

10-3 • Guided Problem Solving

GPS **Student Page 568, Exercise 26**

Framing Find dimensions for the square picture at the right that would make the area of the picture equal to 75% of the total area enclosed by the square frame. Round to the nearest tenth of an inch.

x 12 in.

Read and Understand

1. What information is given to you in the problem? _____

2. What additional information is given to you in the picture? _____

_____

Plan and Solve

3. Write an expression for the area of the picture only. _____

4. Write an expression for the total area enclosed by the frame. _____

5. What is 75% of the total area enclosed by the frame? _____

6. Write and solve an equation to find the dimensions of the square picture that would make the area of the picture equal to 75% of the total area enclosed by the square frame. _____

Look Back and Check

7. Use the dimensions you found in Step 6 to check if the area of the picture is 75% of the total area enclosed by the square frame. Explain why it is not exactly 75%.

_____

Solve Another Problem

8. What would the dimensions of the square picture be that would make the area of the picture equal to 60% of the total area enclosed by the square frame?

_____

Practice 10-4

Use the Zero-Product Property to solve each equation.

1. $(x + 5)(x - 3) = 0$

2. $(x - 2)(x + 9) = 0$

3. $(b - 12)(b + 12) = 0$

4. $(2n + 3)(n - 4) = 0$

5. $(x + 7)(4x - 5) = 0$

6. $(2x + 7)(2x - 7) = 0$

7. $(3x - 7)(2x + 1) = 0$

8. $(8y - 3)(4y + 1) = 0$

9. $(5x + 6)(4x + 5) = 0$

Solve by factoring.

10. $x^2 + 5x + 6 = 0$

11. $b^2 - 7b - 18 = 0$

12. $r^2 - 4 = 0$

13. $x^2 + 8x - 20 = 0$

14. $y^2 + 14y + 13 = 0$

15. $s^2 - 3s - 10 = 0$

16. $x^2 + 7x = 8$

17. $x^2 = 25$

18. $h^2 + 10h = -21$

19. $2t^2 + 8t - 64 = 0$

20. $3a^2 - 36a + 81 = 0$

21. $5x^2 - 45 = 0$

22. $2a^2 - a - 21 = 0$

23. $3n^2 - 11n + 10 = 0$

24. $2x^2 - 7x - 9 = 0$

25. $2n^2 - 5n = 12$

26. $3m^2 - 5m = -2$

27. $5s^2 - 17s = -6$

28. $6m^2 = 13m + 28$

29. $4a^2 - 4a = 15$

30. $4r^2 = r + 3$

10-4 • Guided Problem Solving

GPS **Student Page 574, Exercise 33**

Baseball Suppose you throw a baseball into the air with an initial upward velocity of 29 ft/s and an initial height of 6 ft. The formula $h = -16t^2 + 29t + 6$ gives the ball's height h in feet at time t in seconds.

a. The ball's height h is 0 when it is on the ground. Find the number of seconds that pass before the ball lands by solving $0 = -16t^2 + 29t + 6$.

b. **Graphing Calculator** Graph the related function for the equation in part (a). Use your graph to estimate the maximum height of the ball.

Read and Understand

1. What information about the baseball is given to you in the problem? _____
   _____

2. Explain what each variable in the formula represents. _____
   _____

Plan and Solve

3. What method will you use to solve the quadratic equation $0 = -16t^2 + 29t + 6$? _____
   _____

4. Solve the equation $0 = -16t^2 + 29t + 6$ to find the number of seconds that pass before the ball lands. _____

5. What is the related function for the equation $0 = -16t^2 + 29t + 6$? _____

6. On your graphing calculator graph the related function from Step 5 and use your graph to estimate the maximum height of the ball.

Look Back and Check

7. Using your graphing calculator, what is the time when the ball reaches the maximum height? Substitute that value for t in the equation to see if your height estimate is reasonable.

   _____

Solve Another Problem

8. The formula $h = -16t^2 + 45t + 9$ also gives the ball's height h in feet at time t in seconds. How many seconds pass before the ball lands on the ground?

   _____

Practice 10-5

Completing the Square

Find the value of *n* such that each expression is a perfect square trinomial.

1. $x^2 - 14x + n$

_____

2. $x^2 + 6x + n$

_____

3. $x^2 + 2x + n$

_____

4. $x^2 - 10x + n$

_____

Solve each equation by completing the square. If necessary, round to the nearest hundredth.

5. $x^2 - 4x = 5$

_____

6. $x^2 - x - 2 = 0$

_____

7. $x^2 - 6x = 10$

_____

8. $x^2 + 4x + 4 = 0$

_____

9. $x^2 - 3x = 18$

_____

10. $x^2 - 8x - 4 = 0$

_____

11. $x^2 - 6x = 0$

_____

12. $x^2 - 6x = 8$

_____

13. $x^2 - 7x = 0$

_____

14. $x^2 + 4x - 12 = 0$

_____

15. $x^2 + 11x + 10 = 0$

_____

16. $x^2 + 2x = 15$

_____

17. $x^2 - 8x = 9$

_____

18. $x^2 + 5x = -6$

_____

19. $x^2 - 2x = 120$

_____

20. $x^2 - 22x = -105$

_____

21. $2x^2 = 3x + 9$

_____

22. $2x^2 + 8x - 10 = 0$

_____

23. $2x^2 - 3x - 2 = 0$

_____

24. $2x^2 + 12x - 32 = 0$

_____

10-5 • Guided Problem Solving

Gardening Suppose you want to enclose a rectangular garden plot against a house using fencing on three sides, as shown. Assume you have 50 ft of fencing material and want to create a garden with an area of 150 ft².

a. Let w = the width. Write an expression for the length of the plot.
b. Write and solve an equation for the area of the plot. Round to the nearest tenth of a foot.
c. What dimensions should the garden have?
d. **Critical Thinking** Find the area of the garden by using the dimensions you found in part (b). Does the area equal 150 ft²? Explain.

150 ft² ℓ

w

Read and Understand

1. What information is given to you in the problem? _____

_____

2. How many sides of the garden must be fenced in? _____

Plan and Solve

3. Write an expression for the length of the plot. _____

4. Write and solve an equation for the area of the plot. Round to the nearest foot.

_____

_____

5. What dimensions should the garden have? _____

Look Back and Check

6. Find the area of the garden by using the dimensions you found in part (b). Does the area equal 150 ft²? Explain. _____

_____

Solve Another Problem

7. Suppose you decide to move your garden away from the house, so you now have to use 50 ft of fencing for four sides. The length of the garden must be twice as long as the width. If the area is now 139 ft², what dimensions should the garden have?

_____

Practice 10-6

Use the quadratic formula to solve each equation. If the equation has no real solutions, write *no real solutions*. If necessary, round to the nearest hundredth.

1. $x^2 + 8x + 5 = 0$

2. $x^2 - 36 = 0$

3. $d^2 - 4d - 96 = 0$

_____

_____

_____

4. $x^2 + 12x - 40 = 0$

5. $4n^2 - 81 = 0$

6. $x^2 + 13x + 30 = 0$

_____

_____

_____

7. $6w^2 - 23w + 7 = 0$

8. $4x^2 + 33x = 27$

9. $7s^2 - 7 = 0$

_____

_____

_____

10. $x^2 + 5x - 90 = 0$

11. $5b^2 - 20 = 0$

12. $4x^2 - 3x + 6 = 0$

_____

_____

_____

13. $5y^2 = 17y + 12$

14. $g^2 - 15g = 54$

15. $27f^2 = 12$

_____

_____

_____

16. $x^2 + 36x + 60 = 0$

17. $x^2 + 10x + 40 = 0$

18. $t^2 - 10t = 39$

_____

_____

_____

19. $4x^2 + 7x - 9 = 0$

20. $8x^2 + 25x + 19 = 0$

21. $36w^2 - 289 = 0$

_____

_____

_____

22. $3x^2 - 19x + 40 = 0$

23. $14x^2 = 56$

24. $32x^2 - 18 = 0$

_____

_____

_____

25. $5a^2 - 9a + 5 = 0$

26. $x^2 = 9x + 120$

27. $8h^2 - 38h + 9 = 0$

_____

_____

_____

28. $x^2 + 3x + 8 = 0$

29. $6m^2 - 13m = 19$

30. $9x^2 - 81 = 0$

_____

_____

_____

10-6 • Guided Problem Solving

GPS **Student Page 589, Exercise 36**

Geometry Find the base and height of the triangle below.
If necessary, round to the nearest hundredth.

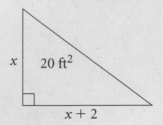

Read and Understand

1. What is the formula for finding the area of a triangle? _____

2. What information can be found from the figure? _____

Plan and Solve

3. Write an equation for the area of the triangle. _____

4. If the area is 20 ft^2, write your equation in Step 3 in standard form. _____

5. Solve your equation in Step 4. _____

6. What are the base and height of the triangle? _____

Look Back and Check

7. Use the base and height you found in Step 6 to find the area of the triangle. What should it be? Explain.

   _____

   _____

Solve Another Problem

8. Find the length and width of the rectangle below.

   _____

   15 ft^2 x

   $x + 3$

Guided Problem Solving

Practice 10-7

Using the Discriminant

Find the number of real solutions of each equation.

1. $x^2 + 6x + 10 = 0$

2. $x^2 - 4x - 1 = 0$

3. $x^2 + 6x + 9 = 0$

_____

_____

_____

4. $x^2 - 8x + 15 = 0$

5. $x^2 - 5x + 7 = 0$

6. $x^2 - 4x + 5 = 0$

_____

_____

_____

7. $3x^2 - 18x + 27 = 0$

8. $4x^2 - 8 = 0$

9. $-5x^2 - 10x = 0$

_____

_____

_____

10. $-x^2 = 4x + 6$

11. $4x^2 = 9x - 3$

12. $8x^2 + 2 = 8x$

_____

_____

_____

13. $7x^2 + 16x + 11 = 0$

14. $12x^2 - 11x - 2 = 0$

15. $-9x^2 - 25x + 20 = 0$

_____

_____

_____

16. $16x^2 + 8x = -1$

17. $-16x^2 + 11x = 11$

18. $12x^2 - 12x = -3$

_____

_____

_____

Find the number of x-intercepts of the related function of each equation.

19. $-16 = x^2 + 10x$

20. $-5 = x^2 + 3x$

21. $7 = x^2 - 2x$

_____

_____

_____

22. $0 = 3x^2 - 3$

23. $0 = 2x^2 + x$

24. $-1 = 3x^2 + 2x$

_____

_____

_____

Algebra 1 Lesson 10-7

10-7 • Guided Problem Solving

GPS **Student Page 594, Exercise 25**

Business A software company is producing a new computer application. The equation $S = p(54 - 0.75p)$ relates price p in dollars to total sales S in thousands of dollars.

a. Write the equation in standard form.
b. Use the discriminant to determine if it is possible for the company to earn $1,000,000 in sales.
c. According to the model, what price would generate the greatest sales?
d. **Critical Thinking** Total sales S decrease as p increases beyond the value in part (c). Why does this make sense in the given situation? Explain.

Read and Understand

1. Explain what the equation describes. _____

_____

2. What do the variables S and p represent? _____

Plan and Solve

3. Write the equation in standard form. _____

4. Use the discriminant to determine if it is
   possible for the company to earn $1,000,000 in sales. _____

5. According to the model, what price would generate the greatest sales? _____

6. Total sales S decrease as p increases beyond the value in
   part (c). Why does this make sense in the given situation? Explain. _____

_____

Look Back and Check

7. On your graphing calculator, graph the equation. Use your graph to check the reasonableness of the price that would generate the greatest sales.

Solve Another Problem

8. The height of a firework can be modeled by the equation $h = t(256 - 16t)$, which relates the time t in seconds since the firework was released to height h in feet.

   a. Write the equation in standard form. _____

   b. Use the discriminant to determine if it is possible for the firework to reach 1000 ft. _____

   c. According to the model, at what time would the firework be at its highest? _____

Name_____ Class_____ Date_____

Practice 10-8   Choosing a Linear, Quadratic, or Exponential Model

Which kind of function best models the data? Write an equation to model the data.

1. $(-1, 3), (1, 3), (3, 27), (5, 75), (7, 147)$

2. $(-2, 4), (-1, 2), (0, 0), (1, -2), (2, -4)$

3. $(-6, -1), (-3, 0), (0, 1), (3, 2), (6, 3)$

4. $(-4, -32), (-2, -8), (0, 0), (2, -8), (4, -32)$

5.

x	y
−3	$\frac{9}{2}$
−2	2
−1	$\frac{1}{2}$
0	0

6.

x	y
−1	−2
0	−4
1	−6
2	−8

7.

x	y
−4	−4
−2	−1
0	0
2	−1

8.

x	y
0	−2
1	−8
2	−32
3	−128

9.

x	y
−7	−245
−5	−125
−3	−45
−1	−5

10.

x	y
−2	$\frac{3}{2}$
0	$\frac{1}{2}$
2	$-\frac{1}{2}$
4	$-\frac{3}{2}$

11. The cost of shipping computers from a warehouse is given in the table below.

Number of Computers	50	75	100	125
Cost (dollars)	1700	2500	3300	4100

a. Determine which kind of function best models the data.

b. Write an equation to model the data.

c. On the basis of your equation, what is the cost of shipping 27 computers?

d. On the basis of your equation, how many computers could be shipped for $5500?

10-8 • Guided Problem Solving

GPS Student Page 602, Exercise 17

Population The table at the right shows the world population in millions from 1980 to 2000. The year $t = 0$ corresponds to 1980.

a. What is the difference in years?

b. Find the differences of consecutive terms. Divide by the differences in years to find possible common differences.

c. Find the average of the common differences you found in part (b).

d. Write a linear equation to model the data based on your answer to part (c).

e. Use your equation to predict the world population in 2010.

Year	Population (millions)
0	4457
5	4855
10	5284
15	5691
20	6080

Sources: U. S. Census Bureau.
Go to **www.PHSchool.com**
for a data update.

Read and Understand

1. Describe the information given in the table. _____

_____

2. What are the three types of models that could be used? _____

_____

Plan and Solve

3. What is the difference in years? _____

4. Find the differences of consecutive terms. Divide by
the differences in years to find possible common differences. _____

5. Find the average of the common differences you found in Step 4. _____

6. Write a linear equation to model the data based on your answer in Step 5. _____

7. Use your equation to predict the world population in 2010. _____

Look Back and Check

8. Test the accuracy of your equation by checking to see if it gives a reasonable population for year 5 and year 15 in your table.

Solve Another Problem

9. Write an exponential equation to model the data in the table. _____

10A: Graphic Organizer

For use before Lesson 10-1

Study Skill To help remember formulas and other important information, use a mnemonic. A mnemonic is a memory device to help us associate new information with something familiar. For example, to remember a formula or equation, change it into something meaningful. To remember the metric terms kilo, hecto, deka, deci, centi, and milli in order, use the first letter of each metric term to represent a word, such as *k*angaroo *h*ops *d*own, *d*rinking *c*hocolate *m*ilk. The key is to create your own; then you won't forget them.

Write your answers.

1. What is the chapter title? _____

2. Find the Table of Contents page for this chapter at the front of the book. Name four topics you will study in this chapter.

_____   _____

_____   _____

3. Complete the graphic organizer as you work through the chapter.
   1. Write the title of the chapter in the center oval.
   2. When you begin a lesson, write the name of the lesson in a rectangle.
   3. When you complete that lesson, write a skill or key concept from that lesson in the outer oval linked to that rectangle.
   Continue with steps 2 and 3 clockwise around the graphic organizer.

Name_____ Class_____ Date_____

10B: Reading Comprehension
For use after Lesson 10-4

Study Skill Many mathematical applications are related to graphs. Many times you are required to interpret information given in graphs. Being able to identify the specific parts of a graph will help you to answer questions regarding the graph.

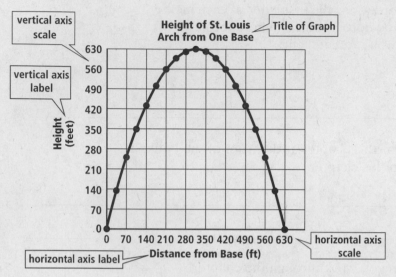

In Exercises 1–6, refer to the graph shown below.

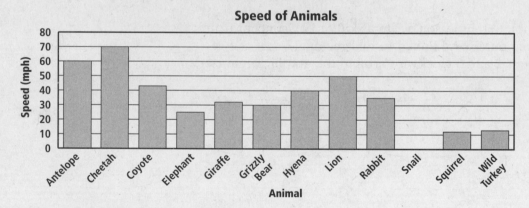

1. What is the title of the graph? _____

2. What is the title of the vertical axis? _____

3. What is the range of the vertical scale? _____

4. What type of graph is this? _____

5. Which animal is the fastest? _____

6. Which animal is the slowest? _____

7. **High-Use Academic Words** What does it mean to *interpret* as mentioned in the study skill?

   a. understand   **b.** verify

Vocabulary and Study Skills

10C: Reading/Writing Math Symbols   For use after Lesson 10-6

Study Skill When interpreting mathematical statements, be sure you use the correct words or symbols. Check your written or numerical expressions to make sure you wrote the correct symbols or words.

The graphs below represent the solutions of different linear systems. Some are equations and some are inequalities. The graphs intersect, are parallel, or coincide. Match the graphs with the appropriate system, without actually graphing the systems, by looking for symbols and other indicators (such as slopes and *y*-intercepts).

1. $\begin{cases} x + y = 4 \\ 2x - y = 2 \end{cases}$

A.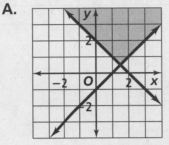

2. $\begin{cases} 3x - 2y = -2 \\ 3x - 2y = 6 \end{cases}$

B.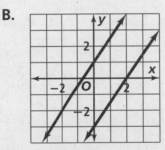

3. $\begin{cases} 2x - 4y \geq 4 \\ x + y < 0 \end{cases}$

C.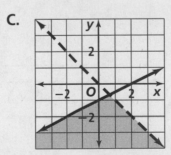

4. $\begin{cases} x + y \geq 2 \\ x - y \leq 1 \end{cases}$

D.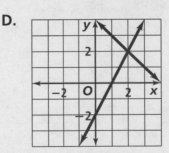

10D: Visual Vocabulary Practice

For use after Lesson 10-8

Study Skill Math symbols give us a way to express complex ideas in a small space.

Concept List

completing the square	discriminant	exponential function
factor	linear function	parabola
perfect square trinomial	quadratic formula	Zero-Product Property

Write the concept that best describes each exercise. Choose from the concept list above.

1. $x = \dfrac{-b \pm \sqrt{b^2 - 4ac}}{2a}$ _____	**2.** $\quad y = mx + b$ _____	**3.** $\quad x^2 - 5x - 14$ $\quad (x - 7)(x + 2)$ _____
4. $\quad y = a \cdot b^x$ _____	**5.** 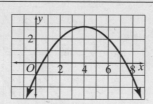 _____	**6.** $\quad x^2 - 12x + n$ $\quad x^2 - 12x + 36$ $\quad (x - 6)^2$ _____
7. For every real number a and b, if $ab = 0$ then $a = 0$ or $b = 0$. _____	**8.** $\quad 4x^2 - 4x + 1$ _____	**9.** $\quad b^2 - 4ac$ _____

10E: Vocabulary Check

Study Skill Strengthen your vocabulary. Use these pages and add cues and summaries by applying the Cornell Notetaking style.

Write the definition for each word at the right. To check your work, fold the paper back along the dotted line to see the correct answers.

_____

_____

_____   Quadratic function

_____

_____   Axis of Symmetry

_____

_____   Vertex

_____

_____   Standard form of a
                                                     quadratic equation

_____

_____   Zeros of a quadratic
                                                     function

_____

10E: Vocabulary Check (continued)

Write the vocabulary word for each definition. To check your work, fold the paper forward along the dotted line to see the correct answers.

A function that can be written in the form $y = ax^2 + bx + c$.

_____

The fold or line that divides a curve into two matching halves.

_____

The highest or lowest point of a parabola.

_____

A quadratic equation written in the form $ax^2 + bx + c = 0$.

_____

The solutions of the quadratic equation.

_____

10F: Vocabulary Review

Study Skill When taking notes, make your original notes as easy to read as possible. The amount of time needed to interpret messy notes would be better spent rereading and thinking about them.

Fill in the blanks with the word(s) that best completes the sentence.

1. The function $y = ax^2 + bx + c$ is a _____ function.

2. The function $Ax + By = C$ is written in _____ form.

3. The _____ of a monomial is the sum of the exponents of its variables.

4. When solving a system of linear equations by graphing, any point where all the lines intersect is the _____.

5. A term that has no variable is known as a _____.

6. The "fold" or line that divides a curve into two matching halves is called the _____.

7. The expression $b^2 - 4ac$ is known as the _____.

8. The _____ of a line is its rate of vertical change over horizontal change.

9. The equation $4(5 - 2 + 3) = 4(5) - 4(2) + 4(3)$ represents the _____ property.

10. A relation that assigns exactly one value in the range to each value in the domain is called a _____.

11. Two or more linear equations together form a _____.

12. When a parabola opens upward, the y-coordinate of the vertex is a _____ value of the function.

13. The point at which a parabola intersects the axis of symmetry is called the _____.

Practice 11-1

Simplify each radical expression.

1. $\sqrt{32}$

2. $\sqrt{22} \cdot \sqrt{8}$

3. $\sqrt{147}$

4. $\sqrt{\dfrac{17}{144}}$

5. $\dfrac{2}{\sqrt{6}}$

6. $\sqrt{80}$

7. $\sqrt{27}$

8. $\dfrac{8}{\sqrt{7}}$

9. $\sqrt{12x^4}$

10. $\sqrt{200}$

11. $\sqrt{15} \cdot \sqrt{6}$

12. $\sqrt{120}$

13. $\dfrac{4}{\sqrt{2a}}$

14. $\sqrt{250}$

15. $\dfrac{\sqrt{65}}{\sqrt{13}}$

16. $\sqrt{48s^3}$

17. $3\sqrt{24}$

18. $\sqrt{160}$

19. $\dfrac{6}{\sqrt{3}}$

20. $\dfrac{\sqrt{180}}{\sqrt{9}}$

21. $\sqrt{18} \cdot \sqrt{8}$

22. $\sqrt{\dfrac{17}{64}}$

23. $\sqrt{50}$

24. $\sqrt{48}$

25. $\sqrt{20}$

26. $\sqrt{8}$

27. $\sqrt{25x^2}$

28. $\sqrt{\dfrac{13}{81}}$

29. $\dfrac{\sqrt{48}}{\sqrt{8}}$

30. $\dfrac{\sqrt{120}}{\sqrt{10}}$

31. $\dfrac{5}{\sqrt{2}}$

32. $\sqrt{75}$

33. $\sqrt{300}$

34. $\sqrt{125}$

35. $\sqrt{28x^4}$

36. $\dfrac{7}{\sqrt{3}}$

37. $\sqrt{\dfrac{15}{49}}$

38. $\dfrac{\sqrt{60}}{\sqrt{12}}$

39. $\dfrac{3}{\sqrt{3}}$

40. $\left(2\sqrt{3}\right)^2$

41. $\sqrt{12} \cdot \sqrt{27}$

42. $\left(7\sqrt{5}\right)^2$

43. $\sqrt{14} \cdot \sqrt{8}$

44. $\left(5\sqrt{5}\right)^2$

45. $\sqrt{8} \cdot \sqrt{7}$

46. $\sqrt{3x} \cdot \sqrt{5x}$

47. $2\sqrt{5} \cdot 2\sqrt{5}$

48. $4\sqrt{3} \cdot 2\sqrt{2}$

11-1 • Guided Problem Solving

GPS **Student Page 620, Exercise 74**

A square picture on the front page of a newspaper occupies an area of 24 in.^{2}.

a. Find the length of each side in simplest radical form.

b. Calculate the length of each side to the nearest hundredth of an inch.

Read and Understand

1. What formula will you use to find the area of a square? _____

2. What is simplest radical form? _____

Plan and Solve

3. Draw a picture to illustrate this situation.

4. Label the picture with the given information and identify the unknown.

5. Write and solve an equation that relates the side length and area.

6. Find the length of each side in simplest radical form. _____

7. Calculate the length of each side to the nearest hundredth of an inch. _____

Look Back and Check

8. Verify the reasonableness of your answers in Steps 6 and 7 by
   squaring each answer to see if the area is 24 in.^{2}. Explain why
   the square of your decimal answer in Step 7 is not exactly 24 in.^{2}.

   _____

   _____

Solve Another Problem

9. The area of a square puzzle is 120 cm^2. What is the length of a side? _____

Name_____ Class_____ Date_____

Practice 11-2

Operations With Radical Expressions

Simplify each expression.

1. $3\sqrt{7} + 5\sqrt{7}$

2. $10\sqrt{4} - \sqrt{4}$

3. $4\sqrt{2}(2 + 2\sqrt{3})$

4. $\sqrt{45} + 2\sqrt{5}$

5. $12\sqrt{11} + 7\sqrt{11}$

6. $\sqrt{2}(2\sqrt{3} - 4\sqrt{2})$

7. $\sqrt{28} + \sqrt{63}$

8. $3\sqrt{6} - 8\sqrt{6}$

9. $\sqrt{3}(\sqrt{6} - \sqrt{12})$

10. $\sqrt{18} - \sqrt{50}$

11. $4\sqrt{2} + 2\sqrt{8}$

12. $13\sqrt{15} - 11\sqrt{15}$

13. $3(8\sqrt{3} - 7)$

14. $8(2\sqrt{5} + 5\sqrt{2})$

15. $17\sqrt{21} - 12\sqrt{21}$

16. $\sqrt{6}(7 + 3\sqrt{3})$

17. $8(4 - 3\sqrt{2})$

18. $2\sqrt{12} + 6\sqrt{27}$

19. $19\sqrt{3} + \sqrt{12}$

20. $8\sqrt{26} + 10\sqrt{26}$

21. $\sqrt{10}(3 - 2\sqrt{6})$

22. $9\sqrt{2} - \sqrt{50}$

23. $10\sqrt{13} - 7\sqrt{13}$

24. $12\sqrt{6} - 4\sqrt{24}$

25. $5\sqrt{7} + \sqrt{28}$

26. $8\sqrt{13} - 12\sqrt{13}$

27. $13\sqrt{40} + 6\sqrt{10}$

28. $-3\sqrt{3}(\sqrt{6} + \sqrt{3})$

29. $12\sqrt{29} - 15\sqrt{29}$

30. $10\sqrt{6} - 2\sqrt{6}$

31. $8\sqrt{3} - \sqrt{75}$

32. $17\sqrt{35} + 2\sqrt{35}$

33. $\sqrt{19} + 4\sqrt{19}$

34. $12\sqrt{9} - 4\sqrt{9}$

35. $\sqrt{8}(\sqrt{2} - 7)$

36. $\dfrac{1}{\sqrt{2} - \sqrt{3}}$

37. $\dfrac{3}{\sqrt{5} + 5}$

38. $(\sqrt{6} - 3)^2$

39. $(3\sqrt{5} + \sqrt{5})^2$

40. $\dfrac{-12}{\sqrt{6} - 3}$

11-2 • Guided Problem Solving

GPS **Student Page 626, Exercise 54**

You can make a box kite like the one at the right in the shape of a rectangular solid. The opening at each end of the kite is a square.

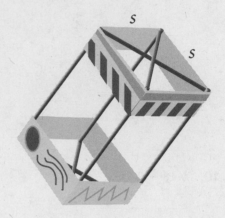

a. Suppose the sides of the square are 2 ft long. How long are the diagonal struts used for bracing?

b. Suppose each side of the square has length s. Find the length of the diagonal struts in terms of s. Write your answer in simplest form.

Read and Understand

1. What information are you given in the problem? _____

2. What relationship is there between the side lengths and the diagonal? _____

Plan and Solve

3. Write and solve an equation that relates the side lengths of the square and the diagonal.

   _____

4. How long are the diagonal struts used for bracing? _____

5. If each side of the square has length s, find the length of the diagonal struts in terms of s^2. _____

6. Write your answer from Step 5 in simplest form. _____

Look Back and Check

7. Substitute the answer you found for the length of the diagonal struts into the equation you used in step 3 to check the reasonableness of your answer.

   _____

Solve Another Problem

8. A diagonal board is used to brace a wall that measures 8 ft by 8 ft. How long must the board be?

   _____

Class _____ Date _____

Practice 11-3

Solving Radical Equations

Solve each radical equation. Check your solutions. If there is no solution, write *no solution*.

1. $\sqrt{x} + 3 = 11$

2. $\sqrt{x + 2} = \sqrt{3x - 6}$

3. $x = \sqrt{24 - 10x}$

4. $\sqrt{4x} - 7 = 1$

5. $\sqrt{x} = \sqrt{4x - 12}$

6. $x = \sqrt{11x - 28}$

7. $\sqrt{x} = 12$

8. $x = \sqrt{12x - 32}$

9. $x = \sqrt{13x - 40}$

10. $\sqrt{3x + 5} = \sqrt{x + 1}$

11. $\sqrt{x + 3} = 5$

12. $\sqrt{6x - 4} = \sqrt{4x + 6}$

13. $2 = \sqrt{x + 6}$

14. $x = \sqrt{2 - x}$

15. $\sqrt{4x + 2} = \sqrt{x + 14}$

16. $\sqrt{x} + 8 = 9$

17. $x = \sqrt{7x + 8}$

18. $\sqrt{3x + 8} = \sqrt{2x + 12}$

19. $\sqrt{2x + 3} = 5$

20. $\sqrt{3x + 13} = \sqrt{7x - 3}$

21. $x = \sqrt{6 + 5x}$

22. $\sqrt{3x} - 5 = 4$

23. $\sqrt{3x + 4} = \sqrt{5x}$

24. $x = \sqrt{x - 12}$

25. $\sqrt{x - 4} + 3 = 9$

26. $x = \sqrt{8x + 20}$

27. $12 = \sqrt{6x}$

28. $x = \sqrt{60 - 7x}$

29. $\sqrt{x + 14} = \sqrt{6x - 1}$

30. $\sqrt{5x - 7} = \sqrt{6x + 11}$

11-3 • Guided Problem Solving

The equation $v = 8\sqrt{h - 2r}$ gives the velocity v in feet per second of a car at the top of the loop of a roller coaster.

a. Find the radius of the loop when the hill is 150 ft high and the velocity of the car is 30 ft/sec.

b. Find the approximate speed in mi/h for 30 ft/sec. (*Hint:* 1 mi = 5280 ft)

c. Critical Thinking Would you expect the velocity of the car to increase or decrease as the radius of the loop increases? As the height of the hill decreases?

d. Explain your reasoning for your answer in part (c).

Read and Understand

1. What information is given to you in the problem? _____

2. What do the variables v, h, and r represent? _____

Plan and Solve

3. Which variable will you be solving for initially? _____

4. Write the formula with numbers substituted for the two variables. _____

5. Solve your equation for r. _____

6. Find the approximate speed in mi/h for 30 ft/sec. _____

7. Would you expect the velocity of the car to increase
   or decrease as the radius of the loop increases? _____

8. Would you expect the velocity of the car to increase
   or decrease as the height of the hill decreases? _____

9. Explain your reasoning in your answer for Step 7 and Step 8. _____

   _____

Look Back and Check

10. Does your speed in mi/h in Step 6 seem reasonable? Explain. _____

    _____

Solve Another Problem

11. What is the height if the velocity of the car is 40 ft/s and the radius is 90 ft? ____

Guided Problem Solving

Practice 11-4

Graphing Square Root Functions

Find the domain of each function.

1. $f(x) = \sqrt{x - 7}$

2. $y = \sqrt{x - 12}$

3. $f(x) = \sqrt{x + 14}$

_____

_____

_____

4. $y = \sqrt{x + 8}$

5. $y = \sqrt{2x}$

6. $y = \sqrt{6x}$

_____

_____

_____

Make a table of values and graph each function.

7. $y = \sqrt{x} - 12$

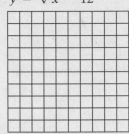

8. $y = 3\sqrt{x}$

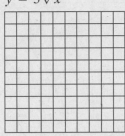

9. $y = \sqrt{x + 8}$

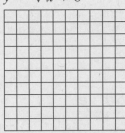

10. $y = \sqrt{x + 7} - 6$

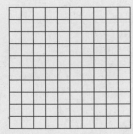

11. $y = \sqrt{x - 6} - 8$

12. $y = \sqrt{x - 10}$

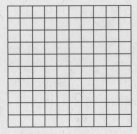

Describe how to translate the graph of $y = \sqrt{x}$ to obtain the graph of each function.

13. $y = \sqrt{x} - 9$

14. $y = \sqrt{x} - 8$

15. $y = \sqrt{x + 20}$

_____

_____

_____

16. $y = \sqrt{x + 18}$

17. $y = \sqrt{x - 32}$

18. $y = \sqrt{x - 4} - 7$

_____

_____

_____

11-4 • Guided Problem Solving

Business Last year a store had an advertising campaign. The graph shows the sales for single-use cameras. The function $n = 27\sqrt{5t} + 53$ models the sales volume n for the cameras as a function of time t, the number of months after the start of the advertising campaign.

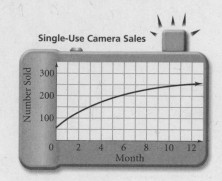

Single-Use Camera Sales

a. Evaluate the function to find how many disposable cameras the store sold in the seventh month.

b. Solve an equation to find the month in which the number of single-use cameras sold was about 175.

Read and Understand

1. Describe the information in the graph. _____

2. Explain what the formula describes. _____

_____

Plan and Solve

3. Write the equation you will use to determine how many disposable cameras the store sold in the seventh month.

_____

4. Simplify your function from Step 3 to determine the number of cameras. _____

5. Write the equation you will solve to determine the month in which the number of single-use cameras sold was about 175.

_____

6. Solve your equation in Step 5. _____

Look Back and Check

7. Check the reasonableness of your answers in Steps 4 and 6 by estimating the answers to both questions by reading the graph.

_____

Solve Another Problem

8. The advertising campaign was so successful it was extended an extra six months. Evaluate the function to see how many cameras were sold after 18 months. _____

Practice 11-5

Trigonometric Ratios

Use △*ABC* at the right. Find the value of each expression.

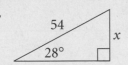

1. sin *A*

_____

2. cos *A*

_____

3. tan *A*

_____

4. sin *B*

_____

5. cos *B*

_____

6. tan *B*

_____

Find the value of each expression. Round to the nearest ten-thousandth.

7. tan 59°

_____

8. sin 75°

_____

9. sin 8°

_____

10. cos 13°

_____

11. sin 32°

_____

12. tan 67°

_____

Find the value of *x* to the nearest tenth.

13.

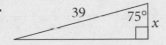

_____

14.

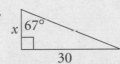

_____

15.

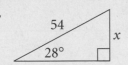

_____

16.

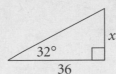

_____

17.

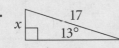

_____

18.

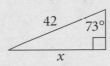

_____

19. A 12-ft-long guy wire is attached to a telephone pole 10.5 ft from the top of the pole. If the wire forms a 52° angle with the ground, how high is the telephone pole?

_____

11-5 • Guided Problem Solving

GPS **Student Page 649, Exercise 30**

Find the value of the variable in the figure below to the nearest tenth.

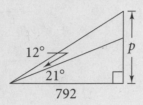

Read and Understand

1. What information is given to you in the picture? _____

_____

2. What are the trigonometric ratios that can be used in a right triangle? _____

Plan and Solve

3. Write an equation you will use to solve for p. _____

4. Solve your equation for p. _____

Look Back and Check

5. Explain why the tangent ratio is used for this problem.

_____

_____

Solve Another Problem

6. In right triangle ABC, the hypotenuse measures 29 cm, $m\angle A = 15°$. How long are the other two sides of the triangle?

_____

Practice 11-6

1. A tree casts a shadow that is 20 ft long. The angle of elevation of the sun is 29°. How tall is the tree?

_____

2. Suppose your angle of elevation to the top of a water tower is 78°. If the water tower is 145 ft tall, how far are you standing from the water tower?

_____

3. The angle of elevation from the control tower to an airplane is 49°. The airplane is flying at 5000 ft. How far away from the control tower is the plane?

_____

4. A boy scout on top of a 1700-ft-tall mountain spots a campsite. If he measures the angle of depression at 35°, how far is the campsite from the foot of the mountain?

_____

5. A 100-foot kite string makes a 35° angle of elevation to the ground. How high is the kite?

_____

11-6 • Guided Problem Solving

GPS **Student Page 652, Exercise 8**

Hobbies Suppose you are flying a kite. The kite string is 60 m long, and the angle of elevation of the string is 65° from your hand. Your hand is 1 m above the ground. How high above the ground is the kite?

Read and Understand

1. Draw and label a picture that illustrates this situation.

2. In your picture use a variable to label the distance the kite is above the ground.

Plan and Solve

3. What trigonometric function can be used to solve this problem? _____

4. Write and solve an equation to determine the side of your right triangle. _____

5. How high above the ground is the kite? _____

Look Back and Check

6. Explain why the side of your right triangle is not the distance the kite is above the ground.

_____

_____

Solve Another Problem

7. A tree casts a shadow that is 50 ft long. At this time of day, the angle of elevation to the sun is 20°. How tall is the tree?

_____

11A: Graphic Organizer

For use before Lesson 11-1

Study Skill After reading a section, recall the information. Ask yourself questions about the section. If you cannot recall enough information reread portions you had trouble remembering. The more time you spend studying the more you can recall.

Write your answers.

1. What is the chapter title? _____

2. Find the Table of Contents page for this chapter at the front of the book. Name four topics you will study in this chapter.

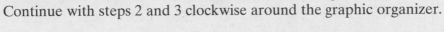

_____   _____

_____   _____

3. Complete the graphic organizer as you work through the chapter.
1. Write the title of the chapter in the center oval.
2. When you begin a lesson, write the name of the lesson in a rectangle.
3. When you complete that lesson, write a skill or key concept from that lesson in the outer oval linked to that rectangle.
Continue with steps 2 and 3 clockwise around the graphic organizer.

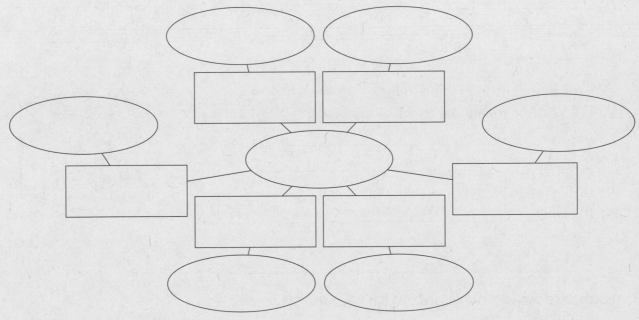

11B: Reading Comprehension

For use after Lesson 11-3

Study Skill Diagrams of three-dimensional objects have solid lines and dashed lines. The dashed lines are the ones that would be hidden from view if you were to look at the object from the perspective that has been drawn.

Answer the question about each figure to practice extracting and deducing information from diagrams.

1. **a.** What is the shape of the base of the figure?

    _____

    b. If you make a slice through the figure from the top of the figure through the center of the base, what is the shape of the slice?

    _____

    c. What figure is formed by the height of the cone, the radius of the base, and the "slant height" of the cone (the distance PQ)?

    _____

    d. How is the slant height of the cone related to the height of the cone and the radius of its base?

    _____

    _____

    _____

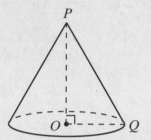

2. Assume that the length of the side of the cube is known.

    a. Is it possible to find the length of diagonal k? _____
    Explain. _____

    _____

    b. Is it possible to find the length of diagonal d? _____
    Explain. _____

    _____

    _____

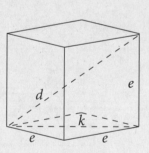

3. **High-Use Academic Words** What does *deducing* mean in the direction line?

    a. observe what is given
    b. figure out by using the given information with other knowledge

11C: Reading/Writing Math Symbols

For use after Lesson 11-5

Study Skill When you take notes in any subject, it helps if you learn to use abbreviations and symbols such as @ (at); #, #s (number, numbers); w/ (with); w/o (without); s/b (should be).

Match each written expression or statement in Column A with its symbolic form in Column B by drawing a line between them.

Column A

1. eight times x equals 40
2. the square root of xy
3. x divided by y
4. the square root of the quantity x plus 4 equals 3
5. 5 is less than or equal to 8
6. x squared y to the fourth power
7. w divided into 6 equal parts

Column B

A. $w \div 6$
B. $8x = 40$
C. $x^2 y^4$
D. $5 \leq 8$
E. $\frac{x}{y}$
F. $\sqrt{xy}$
G. $\sqrt{x + 4} = 3$

Match each written expression or statement in Column C with its symbolic form in Column D by drawing a line between them.

Column C

8. the quantity x plus four, cubed
9. 2 less than 4 times a number
10. one-third of a number x
11. three plus x
12. eight is greater than 5
13. two times x squared minus three times y
14. the quantity x plus four, squared

Column D

A. $\frac{1}{3}x$
B. $8 > 5$
C. $4x - 2$
D. $(x + 4)^2$
E. $2x^2 - 3y$
F. $3 + x$
G. $(x + 4)^3$

11D: Visual Vocabulary Practice

For use after Lesson 11-6

Study Skill As you master more vocabulary, more concepts are within your reach.

Concept List

angle of elevation	cosine	Division Property of Square Roots
like radicals	radical equation	sine
square root function	tangent	trigonometric ratios

Write the concept that best describes each exercise. Choose from the concept list above.

1. $3\sqrt{2}$ and $5\sqrt{2}$	**2.** $\dfrac{\text{opposite leg}}{\text{hypotenuse}}$	**3.** sine, cosine, tangent
4. $\dfrac{\text{adjacent}}{\text{hypotenuse}}$	**5.** $y = \sqrt{2x + 5}$	**6.** $\sqrt{x + 7} = 5$
7. For every number $a \geq 0$ and $b > 0$, $\sqrt{\dfrac{a}{b}} = \dfrac{\sqrt{a}}{\sqrt{b}}$.	**8.** an angle from the horizontal up to a line of sight	**9.** $\dfrac{\text{opposite leg}}{\text{adjacent leg}}$

11E: Vocabulary Check

Study Skill Strengthen your vocabulary. Use these pages and add cues and summaries by applying the Cornell Notetaking style.

Write the definition for each word at the right. To check your work, fold the paper back along the dotted line to see the correct answers.

_____

_____

_____
              Radical expression

_____

_____
              Rationalize

_____

_____
              Unlike radicals

_____

_____
              Conjugates

_____

_____
              Extraneous solution

_____

Vocabulary and Study Skills

11E: Vocabulary Check (continued)

Write the vocabulary word for each definition. To check your work, fold the paper forward along the dotted line to see the correct answers.

An expression that contains a radical.

_____

Rewrite as a rational number. It may be necessary to obtain the simplest radical form.

_____

Expressions that do not have the same radicand.

_____

The sum and difference of the same two terms.

_____

A solution that does not satisfy the original equations.

_____

11F: Vocabulary Review Puzzle

For use with Chapter Review

Study Skill When you read, your eyes make small stops along a line of words. Good readers make fewer stops when they read. The more stops you make when you read, the harder it is for you to comprehend what you've read. Try to concentrate and free yourself of distractions as you read.

Complete the crossword puzzle.

Choose a word from the list below for each of the clues.

binomial	converse	cosine	discriminant
extraneous	hypotenuse	leg	midpoint
parabola	polynomial	radical equation	radicand
rationalize	sine	tangent	vertex

ACROSS	DOWN
1. the sum or difference of two or more monomials	**1.** the graph of a quadratic function
4. the expression under the radical sign	**2.** reversing the *if and then* parts of a statement
8. a polynomial with two terms	**3.** multiplying the numerator and denominator by the same radical expression to simplify the denominator
11. a type of equation with a variable in the radicand	**5.** the highest or lowest point of a parabola
13. the expression under the radical sign in the quadratic formula	**6.** divides a segment into two equal segments
14. opposite side over hypotenuse	**7.** a solution that does not satisfy the original equation
15. side opposite the right angle in a right triangle	**9.** each of the sides forming the right angle of a triangle
	10. adjacent side over hypotenuse
	12. opposite side over adjacent side

Name _____ Class _____ Date _____

Practice 12-1

Graphing Rational Functions

Describe the graph of each function.

1. $f(x) = x^2 - 4$

2. $y = \frac{5}{x} - 1$

_____

_____

3. $g(x) = \sqrt{x + 2} - 1$

4. $y = -8x + 2$

_____

_____

5. $h(x) = |2x + 7|$

6. $y = 0.2^x$

_____

_____

What value of x makes the denominator of each function equal to zero?

7. $y = \frac{12}{x}$

8. $y = \frac{5}{x + 7}$

_____

_____

9. $y = \frac{7x}{x + 3}$

10. $y = \frac{3}{x - 8}$

_____

_____

Identify the vertical asymptote of each function. Then graph the function.

11. $y = \frac{2}{x}$

12. $y = \frac{2}{x - 1}$

13. $y = \frac{1}{x + 4}$

14. $y = \frac{2}{x} + 3$

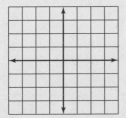
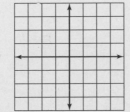
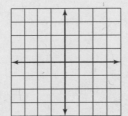
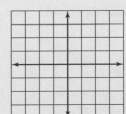

12-1 • Guided Problem Solving

GPS **Student Page 669, Exercise 53**

Light In the formula $I = \frac{445}{x^2}$, I is the intensity of light in lumens at a distance x feet from a light bulb with 445 watts. What is the intensity of light 5 ft from the light bulb? 15 ft from the light bulb?

Read and Understand

1. Explain what each variable in the equation represents. _____

2. What information in the problem will not be used? _____

Plan and Solve

3. Write the equation that you will use to find the intensity of light 5 ft away from the light bulb.

   _____

4. Solve your equation in Step 3. _____

5. Write the equation that you will use to find the intensity of light 15 ft away from the light bulb.

   _____

6. Solve your equation in Step 5. _____

Look Back and Check

7. Should the intensity of the light increase or decrease as the distance from the light bulb increases? Check the reasonableness of your answer by seeing if this is true. _____

Solve Another Problem

8. How far away from the light bulb are you if the intensity is 10 lumens? _____

Practice 12-2

Simplifying Rational Expressions

• •

Simplify each expression.

1. $\dfrac{6x^4}{18x^2}$

2. $\dfrac{15a^2}{25a^4}$

3. $\dfrac{32h^3}{48h^2}$

4. $\dfrac{12n^4}{21n^6}$

_____

5. $\dfrac{3x - 6}{6}$

6. $\dfrac{x^2 - 2x}{x}$

7. $\dfrac{4t^2 - 2t}{2t}$

8. $\dfrac{a^3 - 2a^2}{2a^2 - 4a}$

_____

9. $\dfrac{21x^2y}{14xy^2}$

10. $\dfrac{32x^3y^2}{24xy^4}$

11. $\dfrac{x^2 + 3x}{3x + 9}$

_____

12. $\dfrac{x^2 - 5x}{5x - 25}$

13. $\dfrac{x^2 + 13x + 12}{x^2 - 144}$

14. $\dfrac{x^2 - 9}{x^3 - 3x^2}$

_____

15. $\dfrac{x^3 + x^2}{x + 1}$

16. $\dfrac{3x - 2y}{2y - 3x}$

17. $\dfrac{x^2 + x - 6}{x^2 - x - 2}$

_____

18. $\dfrac{x^2 + 3x + 2}{x^3 + x^2}$

19. $\dfrac{2x^2 - 8}{x^2 - 3x + 2}$

20. $\dfrac{2x^2 - 5x + 3}{x^2 - 1}$

_____

21. $\dfrac{3x + 3y}{x^2 + xy}$

22. $\dfrac{10 + 3x - x^2}{x^2 - 4x - 5}$

23. $\dfrac{9 - x^2}{x^2 + x - 12}$

_____

24. $\dfrac{x^2 + 2x - 15}{x^2 - 7x + 12}$

25. $\dfrac{x^2 + 7x - 8}{x^2 + 6x - 7}$

26. $\dfrac{x^2 + 3x - 10}{25 - x^2}$

_____

• •

Name_____ Class_____ Date_____

12-2 • Guided Problem Solving

a. Construction To keep heating costs down for a structure, architects want the ratio of surface area to volume as small as possible. Find an expression for the ratio of the surface area to volume for each shape.
i. square prism   **ii.** cylinder

b. Find the ratio for each figure when $b = 12$ ft, $h = 18$ ft, and $r = 6$ ft.

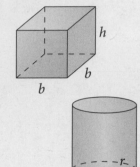

Read and Understand

1. What is the formula for finding the surface area of a prism?

_____

2. What is the formula for finding the volume of a prism? _____

3. What is the formula for finding the surface area of a cylinder? _____

4. What is the formula for finding the volume of a cylinder? _____

Plan and Solve

5. Write an expression for the surface area of the square prism. _____

6. Write an expression for the volume of the square prism. _____

7. Write an expression for the ratio of surface area to volume for the square prism. _____

8. Write an expression for the surface area of the cylinder. _____

9. Write an expression for the volume of the cylinder. _____

10. Write an expression for the ratio of the surface area to volume for the cylinder. _____

11. Find the ratio for each figure when $b = 12$ ft, $h = 18$ ft, and $r = 6$ ft.

     square prism: _____   cylinder: _____

Look Back and Check

12. Explain why keeping the ratio of surface area to volume
    as small as possible will help keep heating costs down.

_____

Solve Another Problem

13. Write an expression for the ratio of surface area to volume
    for a square prism that has a length and width of 4 and a height of h. _____

Practice 12-3

Multiplying and Dividing Rational Expressions

Multiply or divide.

1. $\frac{5}{9} \cdot \frac{6}{15}$

2. $\frac{8}{3} \div \frac{16}{27}$

3. $\left(-\frac{3}{4}\right) \div \frac{16}{21}$

4. $\frac{2}{9} \div \left(-\frac{10}{3}\right)$

5. $\frac{18m}{4m^2} \div \frac{9m}{8}$

6. $\frac{8x}{12} \cdot \frac{4x}{6}$

7. $\frac{9}{15x} \cdot \frac{25x}{27}$

8. $\frac{12x^3}{25} \div \frac{16x}{5}$

9. $\frac{6x^3}{18x} \div \frac{9x^2}{10x^4}$

10. $\frac{4r^3}{10} \cdot \frac{25}{16r^2}$

11. $\frac{8n^2}{3} \div \frac{20n}{9}$

12. $\frac{4n^3}{11} \cdot \frac{33n}{36n^2}$

13. $\frac{24r^3}{35r^2} \div \frac{12r}{14r^3}$

14. $\frac{a^2-4}{3} \cdot \frac{9}{a+2}$

15. $\frac{4b-12}{5b^2} \cdot \frac{6b}{b-3}$

16. $\frac{2b}{5} \cdot \frac{10}{b^2}$

17. $\frac{2b}{b+3} \div \frac{b}{b+3}$

18. $\frac{5y^3}{7} \cdot \frac{14y}{30y^2}$

19. $\frac{4p+16}{5p} \div \frac{p+4}{15p^3}$

20. $\frac{3(h+2)}{h+3} \div \frac{h+2}{h+3}$

21. $\frac{h^2+6h}{h+3} \cdot \frac{4h+12}{h+6}$

22. $\frac{n^2-1}{n+2} \cdot \frac{n^2-4}{n+1}$

23. $\frac{x^2-x}{x} \cdot \frac{3x-6}{3x-3}$

24. $\frac{5x-10}{x+2} \cdot \frac{3}{3x-6}$

25. $\frac{x^2-16}{x-4} \div \frac{3x+12}{x}$

26. $\frac{x^2-1}{3x-3} \div \frac{x+1}{3}$

27. $\frac{x^2-2x-24}{x^2-5x-6} \cdot \frac{x^2+5x+6}{x^2+6x+8}$

12-3 • Guided Problem Solving

Geometry Find the volume of the rectangular solid.

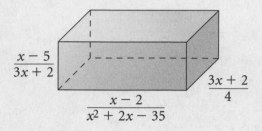

Read and Understand

1. What information is given to you in the picture? _____

2. How do you find the volume of a rectangular solid? _____

Plan and Solve

3. Write an expression for the volume of the rectangular solid. _____

4. Explain how you can simplify your expression before multiplying. _____

   _____

5. What is the final product? _____

Look Back and Check

6. Check the reasonableness of your answer by evaluating your original expression for $x = 2$ and then evaluating your final product for $x = 2$ also.

Solve Another Problem

7. Find the volume of a cube if each edge measures $\dfrac{3x}{6x^2 + 9x}$. _____

Practice 12-4

Divide.

1. $\dfrac{10x - 25}{5}$

2. $\dfrac{4x^3 - 3x}{x}$

_____

3. $(3x^2 - 6x) \div 3x$

4. $(10x^2 - 6x) \div 2x$

_____

5. $(-8x^5 + 16x^4 - 24x^3 + 32x^2) \div 8x^2$

6. $(15x^2 - 30x) \div 5x$

_____

7. $(x^2 - 14x + 49) \div (x - 7)$

8. $(2x^2 - 13x + 21) \div (x - 3)$

_____

9. $(4x^2 - 16) \div (2x + 4)$

10. $(x^2 + 4x - 12) \div (x - 2)$

_____

11. $(x^2 + 10x + 16) \div (x + 2)$

12. $(12x^2 - 5x - 2) \div (3x - 2)$

_____

13. $(x^2 + 5x + 10) \div (x + 2)$

14. $(x^2 - 8x - 9) \div (x - 3)$

_____

15. $(3x^2 - 2x - 13) \div (x - 2)$

16. $(x^3 + 3x^2 + 5x + 3) \div (x + 1)$

_____

17. $(2x^2 + 11x - 5) \div (x + 6)$

18. $(x^2 + 5x - 10) \div (x + 2)$

_____

19. $(8x + 3 + 4x^2) \div (2x - 1)$

20. $(3x^2 + 11x - 4) \div (3x - 1)$

_____

12-4 • Guided Problem Solving

GPS **Student Page 685, Exercise 42**

Use the function rule $y = \dfrac{2x + 5}{x + 3}$.

  a. Rewrite the function rule as a quotient plus a remainder.
  b. Make a table of values and graph the function.
  c. What are the vertical and horizontal asymptotes?

Read and Understand

  1. What type of function is $y = \dfrac{2x + 5}{x + 3}$? _____

  2. Explain how you determine the vertical and horizontal asymptotes.

      _____

      _____

Plan and Solve

  3. Use long division to rewrite the function rule as a quotient plus a remainder. _____

  4. Make a table of values and graph the function.

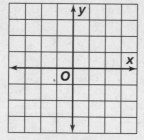

  5. What is the vertical asymptote? _____

  6. What is the horizontal asymptote? _____

Look Back and Check

  7. Check the reasonableness of your graph by choosing another point for your table and verifying that it is on your graph.

Solve Another Problem

  8. Rewrite the function $y = \dfrac{3x + 4}{x + 1}$ as a quotient plus a remainder. _____

Practice 12-5

Adding and Subtracting Rational Expressions

Add or subtract.

1. $\dfrac{3x}{4} - \dfrac{x}{4}$

2. $\dfrac{3}{x} + \dfrac{5}{x}$

3. $\dfrac{5x}{6} - \dfrac{2x}{3}$

_____

4. $\dfrac{x}{3} + \dfrac{x}{5}$

5. $\dfrac{3m}{4} + \dfrac{5m}{12}$

6. $\dfrac{4x}{7} - \dfrac{3x}{14}$

_____

7. $\dfrac{6}{7t} - \dfrac{3}{7t}$

8. $\dfrac{d}{3} + \dfrac{4d}{3}$

9. $\dfrac{7}{2d} - \dfrac{3}{2d}$

_____

10. $\dfrac{3}{2d^2} + \dfrac{4}{3d}$

11. $\dfrac{9}{m+1} - \dfrac{6}{m-1}$

12. $\dfrac{3}{x} - \dfrac{7}{x}$

_____

13. $\dfrac{7a}{6} + \dfrac{a}{6}$

14. $\dfrac{4}{k+3} - \dfrac{8}{k+3}$

15. $\dfrac{3}{4z^2} + \dfrac{7}{4z^2}$

_____

16. $\dfrac{6}{x^2-1} + \dfrac{7}{x-1}$

17. $\dfrac{2x}{x^2-1} - \dfrac{3}{x+1}$

18. $\dfrac{3t}{8} + \dfrac{3t}{8}$

_____

19. $\dfrac{4}{3a^2} - \dfrac{1}{2a^3}$

20. $\dfrac{4}{a+4} + \dfrac{6}{a+4}$

21. $\dfrac{4}{x+3} + \dfrac{6}{x-2}$

_____

22. $\dfrac{6}{7t^3} - \dfrac{8}{3t}$

23. $\dfrac{3}{2x+6} + \dfrac{4}{6x+18}$

24. $\dfrac{5}{8a} - \dfrac{3}{8a}$

_____

25. $\dfrac{5}{r^2-4} + \dfrac{7}{r+2}$

26. $\dfrac{6}{a^2-2} + \dfrac{9}{a^2-2}$

27. $\dfrac{5x}{4} - \dfrac{x}{4}$

_____

Name_____ Class_____ Date_____

12-5 • Guided Problem Solving

GPS **Student Page 690, Exercise 42**

Rowing A rowing team practices rowing 2 mi upstream and 2 mi downstream. The team can row downstream 25% faster than they can row upstream.

a. Let r represent their rate upstream. Write and simplify an expression for the amount of time they spend rowing.

b. Let d represent their rate downstream. Write and simplify an expression for the amount of time they spend rowing.

c. **Critical Thinking** Do the expressions you wrote in parts (a) and (b) represent the same time? Explain.

Read and Understand

1. Explain why the team rows faster going downstream than upstream. _____

_____

2. What is the relationship between rate, time, and distance that you will need to use? _____

Plan and Solve

3. Let r represent their rate upstream. Write and simplify an expression for the amount of time they spend rowing. _____

4. Let d represent their rate downstream. Write and simplify an expression for the amount of time they spend rowing. _____

5. Do the expressions you wrote in Steps 3 and 4 represent the same time? Explain.

_____

_____

Look Back and Check

6. Check the accuracy of your expressions by verifying that they are equal when $r = 4$ and $d = 5$.

Solve Another Problem

7. Write new expressions for times rates upstream and downstream if they can only row downstream 10% faster than they can row upstream. _____

Practice 12-6

Solving Rational Equations

Solve each equation. Check your solution. If there is no solution, write *no solution*.

1. $\frac{1}{x} + \frac{1}{2x} = \frac{1}{6}$

2. $\frac{x}{x + 2} + \frac{4}{x - 2} = 1$

3. $\frac{1}{3s} = \frac{s}{2} - \frac{1}{6s}$

_____

4. $\frac{x + 2}{x + 8} = \frac{x - 2}{x + 4}$

5. $1 - \frac{3}{x} = \frac{4}{x^2}$

6. $\frac{7}{3(a - 2)} - \frac{1}{a - 2} = \frac{2}{3}$

_____

7. $\frac{n}{n - 4} = \frac{2n}{n + 4}$

8. $x + \frac{6}{x} = -7$

9. $\frac{2}{r^2 - r} - 1 = \frac{2}{r - 1}$

_____

10. $\frac{y}{y + 3} = \frac{6}{y + 9}$

11. $\frac{d}{3} + \frac{1}{2} = \frac{1}{3d}$

12. $\frac{2m}{m - 5} = \frac{2m + 16}{m + 3}$

_____

13. $\frac{1}{m - 4} + \frac{1}{m + 4} = \frac{8}{m^2 - 16}$

14. $\frac{5}{x - 2} = \frac{5x + 10}{x^2}$

15. $\frac{k^2}{k + 3} = \frac{9}{k + 3}$

_____

16. $\frac{h - 3}{h + 6} = \frac{2h + 3}{h + 6}$

17. $\frac{h}{6} - \frac{3}{2h} = \frac{8}{3h}$

18. $4 - \frac{3}{y} = \frac{5}{y}$

_____

19. $\frac{1}{b - 3} = \frac{b}{4}$

20. $\frac{1}{t^2} - \frac{2}{t} = \frac{3}{t^2}$

21. $\frac{2}{3n} + \frac{3}{4} = \frac{2}{3}$

_____

12-6 • Guided Problem Solving

GPS **Student Page 696, Exercise 38**

Electricity Lamps can be connected to a battery in a circuit in series or in parallel. You can calculate the total resistance R_T in a circuit if you know the resistance in each lamp. Resistance is measured in ohms (Ω).

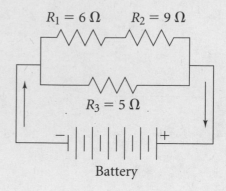

Read and Understand

1. How do you calculate the total resistance in a circuit connected in series with two resistors R_1 and R_2? _____

2. How do you find the total resistance in a circuit with two resistors R_1 and R_2 connected in parallel? _____

Plan and Solve

3. Calculate the total resistance for lamps R_1 and R_2. _____

4. Calculate the total resistance for the lamps connected in parallel. Use your answer in Step 3 as your first resistance. _____

Look Back and Check

5. Verify that you solved the equation in Step 4 correctly by checking that you get a true statement when you substitute the values into the equation.

Solve Another Problem

6. Find R_T.

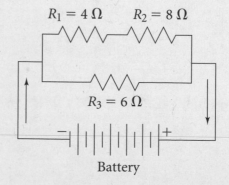

Guided Problem Solving

Practice 12-7

Counting Methods and Permutations

Simplify each expression.

1. $_7P_2$

2. $_{12}P_6$

3. $_{11}P_3$

_____

_____

_____

4. $_{10}P_3$

5. $_9P_8$

6. $_{12}P_7$

_____

_____

_____

7. Suppose a license plate consists of five different letters.

a. How many five-letter license plates are possible?

_____

b. In how many ways can a five-letter license plate be made with the letters from APRIL if none of the letters are repeated?

_____

c. Suppose a license plate is assigned randomly. What is the probability that it will contain the letters from APRIL?

_____

8. In how many ways can nine mopeds be parked in a row?

_____

9. Suppose there are three different ways in which you could go from your house to a friend's house. From your friend's house, there are four different ways in which you could go to the library. In how many different ways can you go from your house to the library after meeting your friend?

_____

10. A sports card collection contains 20 baseball players, 15 basketball players, and 25 football players. In how many ways can you select one of each?

_____

11. Suppose you are electing student council officers. The student council contains 24 students. In how many ways can a president, a vice-president, and a secretary be elected?

_____

12-7 • Guided Problem Solving

GPS **Student Page 703, Exercise 27**

License Plate In Indiana, a regular license plate has two numbers that are fixed by county, then one letter, and then four numbers.

   a. How many different license plates are possible in each county?
   b. There are 92 counties in Indiana. How many license plates are possible in the entire state?

Read and Understand

1. Explain how to use the Fundamental Counting Principle. _____

_____

2. Give an example of one possible license plate. _____

Plan and Solve

3. Which information is not needed in order to determine how many license plates are possible in one county? _____

4. How many different license plates are possible in each county? _____

5. There are 92 counties in Indiana. How many license plates are possible in the entire state?

_____

Look Back and Check

6. Which number should be greater, your answer in Step 4 or your answer in Step 5? Explain.

_____

_____

Solve Another Problem

7. How many license plates are possible in one county if the letter is replaced by another number?

_____

Guided Problem Solving

Practice 12-8

Combinations

Simplify each expression.

1. $_9C_4$

_____

2. $_{12}C_8$

_____

3. $_9C_6$

_____

4. $_{15}C_9$

_____

5. $_{10}C_8$

_____

6. $_{13}C_6$

_____

7. A group of six tourists arrive at the airport 15 min before flight time. At the gate, they learn that only three seats are left on the airplane. How many different groups of three could get on the airplane?

_____

8. In how many ways can you select 5 greeting cards from a choice of 12 cards at a store?

_____

9. A committee of 4 students is to be formed from members of the student council. The student council contains 13 girls and 12 boys.

   a. How many different committees of four students are possible?

   _____

   b. How many committees will contain only boys?

   _____

   c. What is the probability that the committee will contain only boys?

   _____

10. Suppose your math class consists of 24 students. In how many ways can a group of 5 students be selected to form a math team?

_____

11. A jar of marbles contains 6 yellow and 8 red marbles. Three marbles are selected at random.

   a. How many different groups of three marbles are possible?

   _____

   b. How many groups of three marbles will contain only red ones?

   _____

   c. What is the probability that the group of marbles will contain only red ones?

   _____

Algebra 1 Lesson 12-8   **439**

12-8 • Guided Problem Solving

GPS **Student Page 710, Exercise 24**

Locks A lock like the one at the right is called a combination lock. However, mathematically speaking, it should be called a permutation lock! This is because the order of the numbers *is* important. Suppose a three-number sequence opens the lock and no numbers are repeated.

a. How many different sequences are possible?
b. How many sequences use 32 as the first number?
c. What is the probability that the sequence of numbers that opens this lock uses 32 as the first number?
d. Explain why the lock is unlikely to be opened by someone who does not know the correct sequence.

Read and Understand

1. Explain why the combination to a lock like the one described is a permutation. _____

_____

2. What information do you need from the picture? _____

Plan and Solve

3. How many different sequences are possible? _____

4. How many sequences use 32 as the first number? _____

5. What is the probability that the sequence of numbers that opens this lock uses 32 as the first number? _____

6. Explain why the lock is unlikely to be opened by someone who does not know the correct sequence. _____

_____

Look Back and Check

7. Check the reasonableness of your answer in Step 4 by multiplying it by 40. Your result should be the total number of different sequences possible.

Solve Another Problem

8. Another type of lock has a set of different rings that must be turned in order to get the correct numbers lined up. If there are 5 rings and each ring has 10 digits, how many combinations are possible? _____

12A: Graphic Organizer

For use before Lesson 12-1

Study Skill What do the pages before the first page of Chapter 2 tell you? Keep notes as you work through each chapter to help you organize your thinking and to make it easier to review the material when you complete the chapter.

Write your answers.

1. What is the chapter title? _____

2. Find the Table of Contents page for this chapter at the front of the book. Name four topics you will study in this chapter.

    _____   _____

    _____   _____

3. Complete the graphic organizer as you work through the chapter.
    1. Write the title of the chapter in the center oval.
    2. When you begin a lesson, write the name of the lesson in a rectangle.
    3. When you complete that lesson, write a skill or key concept from that lesson in the outer oval linked to that rectangle.
    Continue with steps 2 and 3 clockwise around the graphic organizer.

12B: Reading Comprehension

Study Skill Some word problems contain so much information it is difficult to know how to deal with it all. Sometimes it helps to organize information in a table.

Jessica Hernandez bakes and sells gourmet cookies. She bakes two types of cookies: oatmeal and white chocolate macadamia nut. Each batch of oatmeal cookies requires 2 cups of flour and 2 cups of sugar. Each batch of white chocolate macadamia nut cookies requires 3 cups of flour and 1 cup of sugar. Jessica makes a $3 profit on each batch of oatmeal cookies and a $2 profit on each batch of white chocolate macadamia nut cookies. She has 18 cups of flour and 10 cups of sugar on hand. How many batches of each type of cookie should she bake to maximize her profits?

Organize the information you are given into the following table.

	Batches of Cookies	Cups of Flour	Cups of Sugar	Total Profit ($)
Oatmeal	x			
White Chocolate Macadamia Nut	y			
Totals				P

1. What are you asked to find? _____

2. Write a function for the quantity to be maximized. In this case, that is the total profit. _____

3. Write the constraints as inequalities.

   a. The total number of cups of flour to be used is no more than 18. _____

   b. The total number of cups of sugar to be used is no more than 10. _____

   c. The number of batches of oatmeal cookies to be made is greater than or equal to zero. _____

   d. The total number of batches of white chocolate macadamia nut cookies to be made is greater than or equal to zero. _____

4. On a separate sheet of paper, graph the constraints written in Exercise 3.

5. The maximum profit occurs at a vertex of the feasible region. Evaluate the profit function at each vertex. _____

   _____

6. How many batches of each type of cookie need to be made to maximize profit? _____

7. **High-Use Academic Words** What does it mean to *organize* as mentioned in the direction line?

   a. write an equation   **b.** categorize

12C: Reading/Writing Math Symbols

For use after Lesson 12-3

Study Skill It is important to read directions carefully before doing any exercises. Sometimes the directions are asking for more than one answer, or something entirely different than what you think at first glance.

Given the formulas below, write out what the formula means in words, and write a brief description of what the formula is used for or what it represents. The first one is done for you.

1. $a^2 + b^2 = c^2$ leg squared plus leg squared equals hypotenuse squared; Pythagorean Theorem—used to find a side of a right triangle

2. $I = prt$

3. $ax^2 + bx + c = 0$

4. $b^2 - 4ac$

5. $\tan A = \dfrac{\text{opp}}{\text{adj}}$

6. $\cos A = \dfrac{\text{adj}}{\text{hyp}}$

7. $\sin A = \dfrac{\text{opp}}{\text{hyp}}$

8. $\left(\dfrac{x_1 + x_2}{2}, \dfrac{y_1 + y_2}{2} \right)$

9. $x = \dfrac{-b \pm \sqrt{b^2 - 4ac}}{2a}$

10. $d = \sqrt{(x_2 - x_1)^2 + (y_2 - y_1)^2}$

12D: Visual Vocabulary Practice

For use after Lesson 12-6

Study Skill When interpreting a graph, identify the most specific concept represented.

Concept List

absolute value function	asymptotes	exponential function
linear function	quadratic function	rational expression
rational function	rational proportion	square root function

Write the concept that best describes each exercise.
Choose from the concept list above.

1. 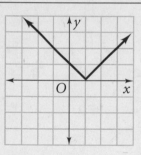	**2.** The dashed lines in the graph	**3.** 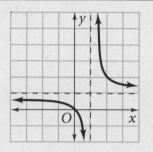
4. 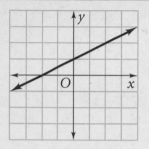	**5.** $\dfrac{x^2 - 3}{x^2 - 6x + 9}$	**6.** 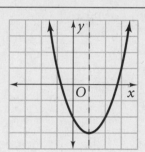
7. 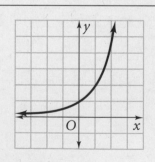	**8.** $\dfrac{5}{x} = \dfrac{1}{x - 2}$	**9.** 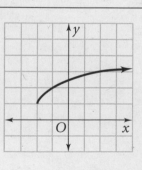

12E: Vocabulary Check

Study Skill Strengthen your vocabulary. Use these pages and add cues and summaries by applying the Cornell Notetaking style.

Write the definition for each word at the right. To check your work, fold the paper back along the dotted line to see the correct answers.

_____

_____

_____

Rational function

_____

_____

Asymptote

_____

_____

Rational expression

_____

_____

_____

Multiplication Counting Principle

_____

_____

Permutation

_____

_____

_____

12E: Vocabulary Check (continued)

For use after Lesson 12-8

Write the vocabulary word for each definition. To check your work,
fold the paper forward along the dotted line to see the correct answers.

A function that can be
written in the form.
$f(x) = \dfrac{\text{polynomial}}{\text{polynomial}}$.

_____

A line which the graph
of a function gets closer
to x or y gets larger in
absolute value.

_____

An expression which can
be written in the form
$\dfrac{\text{polynomial}}{\text{polynomial}}$.

_____

If there are m ways to
make a first selection and
n ways to make a second
selection, there are $m \times n$
ways to make the two
selections.

_____

An arrangement of some
or all of a set of objects
in a specific order.

_____

12F: Vocabulary Review Puzzle

For use with Chapter Review

Study Skill Read aloud or recite the new terms as you read them. This will help you remember and recall rules, definitions, and formulas for future use.

Unscramble the UPPERCASE letters to form a math word or phrase that completes each sentence.

1. An METPYSTOA is a line that the graph of a function gets closer and closer to, but does not intersect.

2. A OCMINNOIBAT uses the notation $_nC_r$.

3. An SEVNIER ITVIANARO can be written in the form $xy = k$ or $y = \frac{k}{x}$.

4. A RUTTEAPONMI uses the notation $_nP_r$.

5. A TAIRNLOA OFINUTCN can be written in the form $f(x) = \frac{\text{polynomial}}{\text{polynomial}}$.

6. The graph of a quadratic function is a BAAPARLO.

7. The quantity $b^2 - 4ac$ is the RIDNMCITSINA of $ax^2 + bx + c = 0$

8. The highest or lowest point on a parabola is its XTERVE.

9. In a right triangle, the NTNATEG ratio compares the length of the side opposite an acute angle to the length of the side adjacent to the same acute angle.

10. You may TAEZIONILRA the denominator of a radical expression when simplifying the expression.